The Mystery of Time

Understanding the Time and Season You Are In

DONNELL DUNCAN

DEDICATION

I dedicate this book to my father, Apostle Emanuel Vivian Duncan. I know it would be a bit much to dedicate every book I ever write to you but if I could, I would. Thank you for inspiring me to be a writer. Your discipline and passion for expressing thoughts through literature are unmatched. I also dedicate this book to my mother, Apostle Jemma Patricia Duncan. You taught me the art and science of writing. You were understanding and considerate as you reinforced my analytical strengths as a child while bolstering my creative weaknesses.

TABLE OF CONTENTS

ACKNOWLEDGMENTS

To my wife Angel, thank you for your patience as I stayed up late nights and spent long weekends with my head down writing this book. There's always a cost for producing something of great value. Because we are one, we must pay the price together. Thank you for doing so with a tender heart.

THE MYSTERY OF TIME

INTRODUCTION

I, the Teacher, was king of Israel, and I lived in Jerusalem. I devoted myself to search for understanding and to explore by wisdom everything being done under heaven. I soon discovered that God has dealt a tragic existence to the human race. I observed everything going on under the sun, and really, it is all meaningless—like chasing the wind. What is wrong cannot be made right. What is missing cannot be recovered. - **Ecclesiastes 1:12-15 (NLT)**

While growing up in church I heard The Word of God through sermons, songs, prayers, conversations, and every other available form of communication. What I heard made sense to me in the context of my Christian faith, so I believed it all. God answers prayer. Faith moves mountains. You reap what you sow. Givers prosper. Good things happen to those who do what is right in God's sight. Every Christian is blessed and favored by God. The righteous never have to beg or be put to shame. God rewards the faithful. Wait on the Lord and He will renew your strength. I could go on and on.

I admit that, in some ways, I was idealistic, to say the least, perhaps even naïve. In my adolescent mind, life was supposed to work a certain way and very rarely did things happen that shouldn't. However, with adulthood came a bitterly cold dose of reality. I had to learn relatively quickly that life is full of contradictions. Good things happen to bad people while bad things happen to good people. You don't always reap what you sow when you sow or even during your lifetime. Some people live right and struggle through life while others live wrong and have it easy. Promotion is rarely merit-based. Your success in life is not necessarily a direct reflection of your level of effort, qualifications or even talent. You see, strange things happen in life and sometimes, we have no easy way to explain them.

Thankfully, King Solomon had the same epiphany during the later years of his life and that's one reason why we have the Book of Ecclesiastes. With more supernatural wisdom than any other man to walk the earth outside of Jesus Christ, Solomon still could not understand why reality didn't always fit the universal principles of ethics, morality and overall fairness. It seems like life just happens and we can't control it. We live in a fallen world and because of that, everything is supposed to be messed up. Yet, despite it all, we're not hopeless and neither should we be. Our confidence is in God's Kingdom which operates by His principles. So, even though we live in this confusing world, we live within His Kingdom which is not of this world. That's really all we need to keep moving forward.

> *This wisdom I have also seen under the sun, and it seemed great to me: There was a little city with few men in it; and a great king came against it, besieged it, and built great snares around it. Now there was found in it a poor wise man, and he by his wisdom delivered the city. Yet no one remembered that same poor man. Then I said: "Wisdom is better than strength. Nevertheless, the poor man's wisdom is despised, And his words are not heard.* - **Ecclesiastes 9:13-16 (NKJV)**

Apostle Paul was on to something in 1 Corinthians 13:9 when he said we know in part and prophesy in part. Typically, when I preached from Ecclesiastes 9:13-16, my focus was on the fact that people without money don't have a voice. It was true in Solomon's time and remains true now. The poor wise man delivered the city with his wisdom and then faded into the background for no other reason than his poverty. From all indications, the city's leadership took his advice because they were desperate. Still, as soon as they received their deliverance they were done with the poor man. Does that sound familiar to you? It does to me.

Outside of elections, lawsuits, protests, criminal activity, and charity, the voice of the poor tends to be ignored. People in poor neighborhoods can complain for years about unsatisfactory working conditions, substandard schools, inefficient Government services, unfair law enforcement practices or general neighborhood blight and get no response. While at the same time, let something happen in a rich neighborhood and see how quickly the authorities respond with solutions. It's not right and it's not fair but it's reality. In fact, it's human nature and it won't change until human nature changes. Yet, God showed me that my perspective on Ecclesiastes 9:13-16 was quite narrow. He has much more to say out of that scripture and it starts with a few pointed questions.

How could the wise man be wise enough to deliver the city from dire straits but not wise enough to deliver himself out of poverty? Why did his wisdom work when the stakes were so high for everyone else, but he had no answer for his own financial situation? I once heard a preacher say that he had the answer to everyone's problems. It's simple; switch problems with someone else. Of course, he was being sarcastic, but he did have a point.

We always seem to know what's best for someone else but don't exhibit the same level of expertise for ourselves. We like telling other people what they should do to solve their problems, but we don't know what to do to solve our own. That's ironic, isn't it? That same level of irony extends to the premise for this book and is again expressed by King Solomon through another passage of scripture in the Book of Ecclesiastes.

> *I returned and saw under the sun that— The race is not to the swift, Nor the battle to the strong, Nor bread to the wise, Nor riches to men of understanding, Nor favor to men of skill; But time and chance happen to them all.* - **Ecclesiastes 9:11(NKJV)**

If this is not the most misquoted or misinterpreted scripture in The Bible, it's near the top of the list. It's on the same level as making up the word helpmeet by combining two distinct words in Genesis 2:18 (KJV). It's as bad as assuming the word gift in Proverbs 18:16 means special ability or my personal favorite, separating the timing of the return of Jesus from the Resurrection after reading 1 Thessalonians 4:13-18. I can't find a scriptural misinterpretation more egregious. Instead of reading the scripture for themselves, I have heard intelligent, well-meaning Christians say the following: *"The race is not for the swift, nor the battle to the strong… but for those who endure to the end."*

I'm sure there's a good reason why someone made that up and then spread it like wildfire throughout the world instead of sticking to the scripture. Like many other made-up Christian sayings, it sounds good and it contains a positive principle that can be substantiated by a combination of actual scriptures if needs be. For instance, in Matthew 10:22 and 24:13 as well as Mark 13:13, Jesus said, in the context of the Great Tribulation, that those who endure to the end will be saved. You can then perhaps connect that with victory coming not by might, nor by power but by God's Spirit according to Zechariah 4:6. Then maybe, just maybe, you could believe the race is not for the swift but for those who endure to the end. However, that is not what Ecclesiastes 9:11 is saying and it is not even closely related to what that scripture is even about. Look at it again in another translation.

I have observed something else under the sun. The fastest runner doesn't always win the race, and the strongest warrior doesn't always win the battle. The wise sometimes go hungry, and the skillful are not necessarily wealthy. And those who are educated don't always lead successful lives. It is all decided by chance, by being in the right place at the right time. - **Ecclesiastes 9:11(NLT)**

Do you want to know the secret to success according to Ecclesiastes 9:11? Be in the right place at the right time. After all the wisdom of the Proverbs, life happened to King Solomon and he reflected on the irony of his observations in Ecclesiastes. One such observation was the importance of timing. Good things happen when people are in the right place at the right time. In other words, you can do everything else right and still fail if your timing is off or you can do everything else wrong but get your timing right and still succeed. Like I said earlier about how poor people are treated, it's not right and it's not fair but it's reality. You can waste energy complaining about it, trying to change it or being a victim of it. On the other hand, you can choose to accept it and make it work in your favor.

I have chosen the latter option and that's what this book is about. Natural ability, physical strength, wisdom, intelligence, and skill alone don't make you a winner. You must be in the right place at the right time to take advantage of opportunities. It's time (pun intended) for a mindset change. Don't just think about what you need to do or how you need to do it to be successful. Think about when. Windows of opportunity open for limited periods of time and the people who jump through them reap all the benefits. God is no respecter of persons according to Acts 10:34 and though He doesn't give us equal resources, talents or even time, He does present us all with opportunities. Our failure or success is based on what we do when these opportunities are presented to us.

1 WHAT IS TIME?

Daniel answered and said: "Blessed be the name of God forever and ever, For wisdom and might are His. And He changes the times and the seasons; He removes kings and raises up kings; He gives wisdom to the wise And knowledge to those who have understanding. He reveals deep and secret things; He knows what is in the darkness, And light dwells with Him. "I thank You and praise You, O God of my fathers; You have given me wisdom and might, And have now made known to me what we asked of You, For You have made known to us the king's demand." - **Daniel 2:20-23(NKJV)**

The ability to clearly discern the wisdom and might of God is one of the most valuable gifts you could ever receive from God. With so many voices speaking contradicting versions of the truth, it's difficult to know who or what to believe. Fortunately, Daniel was gifted by God with the insight he needed right on time. God chose to reveal deep and secret things to him, and it opened the door for him to provide value to kings for the rest of his life. I believe that God wants to do the same thing for you. What you have in your hand is the result of God opening the scriptures and shining His light on some dark areas of our understanding. As you read these words, expect The Lord to illuminate your mind with deep truths that will leave an indelible mark on your psyche.

Yet, before this book could have been released, the COVID-19 pandemic gripped the world and changed everything. While the health impacts became increasingly evident, people across the globe were introduced to the concept of social (physical) distancing by the Centers for Disease Control and Prevention (CDC) and the World Health Organization (WHO). With a plethora of stay-at-home orders by local jurisdictions, many of us were forced to rethink how we spend our time. We could not go to our work-places. We had to close the doors of our churches. We canceled our vacations. We canceled all social events. We had one option; stay home. It's like God changed the times and seasons we were living in and we walked into a dimension of our existence we had never experienced before.

What started as one of the busiest and potentially most productive years of our generation suddenly ground to a halt. People who never had any free time to do anything, but sleep, eat and work had gaping holes in their calendars. It's like the earth stopped moving and even though the clock kept ticking, it sure didn't feel like it. People struggled to reconcile the experience of their new reality. So much so, that many lamented on social media that they did not know what to do with their time. It's like COVID-19 exposed the truth about how our society operates. We do so many activities daily that we barely have time to hear our own thoughts. Then, when all that we do is stripped away and we get the time back, we lose our sense of identity. For some reason, what we do with our time is intricately related to who we are. Hopefully, that experience reshaped how people see their time. I know it did for me.

So teach us to number our days, That we may gain a heart of wisdom. - **Psalm 90:12(NKJV)**

Time is a gift from God to each person. One of my favorite college professors described time as one of the earth's non-renewable resources. Once time is spent, you can never get it back. You also can't make up for lost time which makes wasting time such an indictment against those who do. Time must be treasured like the precious, limited, resource it truly is. You get one chance at life and a limited time to live it so you must make the most of the time you have. It is like the package on the popular movie, Mission Impossible, which self-destructs after its contents are delivered. Time essentially begins running down the moment it begins.

Regardless of how smart or creative you are, you cannot create time. What's even worse is that you have no idea how much time you have available. You only know that it is limited. You cannot even truly manage time. You can manage what you do with the time you have and that's about it. Essentially, time as an entity progresses regardless of what you do. If you accomplish something important over the next six months or you do absolutely nothing of consequence, six months will still be gone. Time doesn't depend on you and there's nothing you can do to affect it. As a result, if you don't do something of consequence with your time you will lose it. So, what are you doing with your time? Are you living like time is running out or are you letting precious time go to waste?

THE MYSTERY OF TIME

In the beginning God created the heaven and the earth. - **Genesis 1:1(KJV)**

God is everlasting, He has no beginning nor end. He exists outside the realm of time and space in a dimension called eternity. The word "beginning" is defined as the point in time or space at which something starts. Based on Genesis 1:1, in the beginning, God created everything we know in human existence including the fundamental building blocks of time and space. While time fits into eternity because God created it, we cannot use time as our frame of reference to define eternity. For instance, eternity is not an endless period nor is it a very, very long time. It has nothing to do with time because the very concept of time has built-in limits that do not apply to eternity. Time as an entity has a beginning and an end while eternity does not have any such constraints.

Keeping all of that in mind, what is time? It's a word we use frequently in the English language to mean many different things. While we may default to the most common use of the word, there are more dimensions of time than we typically imagine. Here's a quick exercise to demonstrate that point. What's the first thing that comes to your mind when you think of time? For me, it's the time on the clock. I hate being late to anything because I believe that time is something valuable. It must be honored and respected. Consequently, when I first think of time I think of the question; *"What's the time?"* What about you?

My times are in Your hand; Deliver me from the hand of my enemies, And from those who persecute me. - **Psalm 31:15(NKJV)**

God holds my times in His hand; not my time (singular), but my times (plural). I know this train of thought may not have been the intention of the psalmist, but it still has me thinking. What if time is multidimensional and my typical linear interpretation of time in the context of the numbers on a clock represents just one dimension? Here is what triggered those thoughts. I attended the ministry school graduation of my wife, Angel, in 2018 as she received her master's degree in Ministry. In the opening remarks, one of the school's founders, Tim Scott, talked about four dimensions of time. What he said fascinated me and propelled me on this journey of discovering the mystery of time. So, I ask the question again; *"What is time?"*

Believe it or not, prior to commencing this book I spent several months studying time from a Biblical perspective, and not once did I open the dictionary for a scholarly definition of the word. Once I finally researched the definition in the dictionary, I was quite fascinated by the variety of meanings available in the English language for just that one word. On top of that, here's an interesting anecdote that bears mentioning. The word "time" is one of the 100 most used words in English. (Fry, 2000)

Ironically, in the summer of 2000, as an Applied Physics student at Morehouse College in Atlanta, I had the opportunity to travel to California to study the Cosmic Microwave Background at the Lawrence Berkeley National Laboratory in Berkeley, California under Dr. George Smoot, a distinguished professor from the University of California, Berkeley. His research focused on evidence of The Big Bang, which is considered by many scientists as the most feasible theory for the origin of time, space, and matter as we know it. He would later win the Nobel Prize in Physics in 2004. Though the Big Bang does not define time, it provides a premise for where it started.

The Merriam Webster Dictionary provides the following comprehensive 14-part definition of time. (Merriam-Webster, Incorporated)

1. a: the measured or measurable period during which an action, process, or condition exists or continues: DURATION
   b: a nonspatial continuum that is measured in terms of events which succeed one another from past through present to future
   c: LEISURE
   eg. time for reading

2. the point or period when something occurs: OCCASION

3. a: an appointed, fixed, or customary moment or hour for something to happen, begin, or end
   eg. arrived ahead of time
   b: an opportune or suitable moment
   eg. decided it was time to retire
   —often used in the phrase about time
   eg. about time for a change

4. a: a historical period: AGE
   b: a division of geologic chronology
   c: conditions at present or at some specified period —usually used in plural
   eg. times are hard
   eg. move with the times
   d: the present time
   eg. issues of the time

5. a: LIFETIME
    b: a period of apprenticeship
    c: a term of military service
    d: a prison sentence

6. SEASON
    eg. very hot for this time of year

7. a: rate of speed: TEMPO
    b: the grouping of the beats of music: RHYTHM

8. a: a moment, hour, day, or year as indicated by a clock or calendar
    eg. what time is it
    b: any of various systems (such as a sidereal or solar system) of reckoning time

9. a: one of a series of recurring instances or repeated actions
    eg. you've been told many times
    b: times (plural)
        (1): added or accumulated quantities or instances
        eg. five times greater
        (2): equal fractional parts of which an indicated number equal a comparatively greater quantity
        eg. seven times smaller
        eg. three times closer
    c: TURN
    eg. three times at bat

10. finite as contrasted with infinite duration

11. a person's experience during a specified period or on a particular occasion
    eg. a good time
    eg. a hard time

12. a: the hours or days required to be occupied by one's work
    eg. make up time
    eg. on company time
    b: an hourly pay rate
    eg. straight time
    c: wages paid at discharge or resignation
    eg. pick up your time and get out

13. a: the playing time of a game
    b: TIME-OUT

14. a period during which something is used or available for use
    eg. computer time

As I sit here contemplating the meaning of time, I'm fascinated by the 14 different definitions or perspectives provided by the dictionary. Let's start with the first one which starts with the period it takes for something to happen. That's not too hard to understand but the second part really got my attention. Time is a nonspatial continuum measured in terms of successive events. I guess that's why during the COVID-19 global shutdown it felt like time stopped. Without our typical succession of daily events, we lost our sense of time. For some, minutes turned to hours and hours turned to days with nothing much to do which gave time little meaning. The second definition of time as the moment an event takes place is directly related. Without events, we lose our sense of time. What's the point of paying attention to time if nothing's happening? That's some good food for thought.

The third definition is all about appointments on the calendar as a measure of time. When my calendar is full of appointments I feel like I don't have any time even though that's not true. I still have 24 hours each day. I just can't do whatever I feel with those hours. An opportune moment is an interesting way of looking at the time. The phrase: *"it's about time"* is a favorite of mine because to me, it has prophetic significance. When God gives me a promise and it finally happens, that's the phrase that comes to mind. It's about time! The fourth definition of time is loaded. It views time from the perspective of the age we live in. It's much broader than the first three definitions and is commonly used particularly when referring to conditions during defined periods. For instance, what comes to my mind are phrases like the *"the end times"* or *"the good old days"*.

Have you ever heard the term, *"doing time"* in relation to someone's jail sentence? That's what the fifth definition is all about. Some people also consider completing a term of military service as putting in time. Most importantly, your time on earth, otherwise known as your lifetime, is the period between your birth and death. I like the sixth definition of time as a season. I get emotional every time I hear the song, "Seasons" by Donald Lawrence & The Tri-City Singers. Here's a sample of the lyrics to help you understand why.

"...I know that you've invested alot

The return
Has been slow
You throw up your hands
And say I give up
I just can't take it anymore
But I hear the Spirit say that
It's your time
The waiting is over
Walk into your season

You survived
The worst of times
God was always on your side
State your claim, write your name
Walk into this wealthy place…"

Excerpt from "Seasons" by Donald Lawrence & The Tri-City Singers

I consider myself an amateur musician with a very rudimentary understanding of the art and science of music. At the core of my understanding is the role of tempo or keeping time. Beyond this, is the concept of rhythm which broadly means an orderly sequence. In that way, art imitates life because there is a rhythm to life as we know it, one that reflects God's Will. When we discover it, we become more efficient and effective with our output of energy. That's the seventh definition of time. That's followed by the eighth definition of time as what's indicated by the clock or calendar which is perhaps the most common definition.

In the ninth definition, the plural tense of the word "time" opens the door to an entirely different range of meanings. A series of repeated actions or occurrences can be described as something being done multiple times. Also, when something is multiplied by a certain number it's described as being times that number. It can be used in a sentence like this, *"Last year I made five times the amount of money I made just a few years before."* In that way, it's used as a mathematical term. The tenth definition addresses the finite nature of time which has a prescribed beginning and end. These limits don't exist when one considers eternity.

The eleventh definition is an expression of how someone feels and is also a common way that time is used in the English language. For example, I am having a great time writing this book. That's not a measure of anything tangible. It describes my feelings. I hope you're having a great time reading this book also. The twelfth definition of time is right up my alley. At the time that I'm writing this, I work as a consulting engineer which means the time I spend working on any project is charged to the client. In my line of work, that's called billable time. The more billable my time, the more value I bring to the company. The only exception is when I'm doing something else like business development or marketing that indirectly leads to more billable time for others.

The last two definitions of time are less used. One is the time set aside in a game for a break from the action and the other is the time set aside for a particular purpose. For example, I have quiet time built into my daily schedule for me to gather my thoughts and hear from The Lord. That's usually when I'm driving my car to work during the weekdays and when I'm preparing my message to preach on the weekends. That time is reserved. I also have my workout time set on my calendar during the week. It's the first thing I do when I leave the house in the morning. My day starts in the gym, then I get dressed for work. What time do you have reserved each week?

While the dictionary definitions are fascinating, my main interest in this book is the use of time within a Biblical context. There are powerful, life-changing revelations in the scriptures that are just waiting to be revealed. Whatever God makes available to me is going into this book for your benefit. Together, we will delve into the following seven dimensions of time outlined in the scriptures.

1. Age (Generational)
2. Everlasting (Perpetual)
3. Chrónos (Chronological)
4. Set (Appointed)
5. Experiences (Fortunes)
6. Cyclical (Repeated)
7. Kairos (Due)

May your journey through time, in all its dimensions, begin anew today.

2 AGE

"You shall not make for yourself a carved image—any likeness of anything that is in heaven above, or that is in the earth beneath, or that is in the water under the earth; you shall not bow down to them nor serve them. For I, the Lord your God, am a jealous God, visiting the iniquity of the fathers upon the children to the third and fourth generations of those who hate Me, but showing mercy to thousands, to those who love Me and keep My commandments. - **Exodus 20:4-6(NKJV)**

When God considers the appropriate duration of blessings and curses, He measures in generations. Based on Exodus 20:4-6, curses extend to three or four generations while blessings extend to thousands of generations. That's why even though we exist many thousands of years after the death of Abraham, through Christ, we can still enjoy the same blessing according to Galatians 3:29. This is just one example of how generations are used as an effective measure of time in the Bible. Here are a few others.

In Genesis 15, God made a covenant with Abraham which included a promise that after four generations his descendants would return to the land where he was at that time. In Numbers 32:13, God promised that the Children of Israel would wander in the wilderness for one generation until most of them died. In 2 Kings 10:30, God promised Jehu that four generations of his descendants would occupy the throne of Israel. The scripture states in Job 42:16, that after God restored Job, he lived one hundred and forty years allowing him to see four generations of his children and grandchildren.

"For David, after he had served his own generation by the will of God, fell asleep, was buried with his fathers, and saw corruption; - **Acts 13:36 (NKJV)**

The first definition of time we will consider in this book comes from the Greek word *"genea"* (pronounced ghen-eh-ah') which means *"an age (i.e. the time ordinarily occupied by each successive generation), a space of 30 - 33 years."* (Strong, The New Strong's Exhaustive Concordance of the Bible, 2003)

According to the scriptures, David served his own generation during his lifetime and that was God's expectation of him. Once David completed his assignment, he died and was buried like the generations who came before him. God's perspective on David's life is described as follows in Acts 13:22(NKJV); *"And when He had removed him, He raised up for them David as king, to whom also He gave testimony and said, 'I have found David the son of Jesse, a man after My own heart, who will do all My will.'"*

In the space of one generation, David completed God's Will for his life which in turn, was to serve his generation. Likewise, it is the Will of God for each of us to serve our own generation. That's why we were born during this time and not another. Whatever we are called by God to do with our lives should be relevant to the age or generation we live in. We cannot simply mimic the actions of heroes from past generations. We can only follow their examples or be inspired by them. What they accomplished had to fit within the time and season they lived in while what we must accomplish has to fit within our own.

For instance, I have always admired the legendary US Civil Rights leader, Dr. Martin Luther King, Jr. His speeches are timeless and when I truly listen to his words, I can't help but be brought to tears. Though the struggle for racial equality and equity is far from over, our generation does not need someone to be a Civil Rights copy-cat of Dr. King. Unfortunately, that is evident when we hear some Civil Rights activists give speeches today. Without question, they remain inspirational, but the real question is *"Are they relevant?"* It's difficult to span several generations with the same message without finding creative ways to communicate and connect it with the current generation. It's not impossible, it's just difficult. We already do it with the timeless principles of scripture, so we can do it with anything else.

Another example is my grandfather, Dr. Levi Duncan, whose healing, and deliverance ministry was a standard-setter in Trinidad and Tobago as well as the Caribbean. I still run into people that I do not know who remember witnessing the awesome power of God operating through him during that season. They tell stories of miraculous healings from major illnesses and people receiving dramatic deliverance from demonic possession. They saw things in his ministry they never saw before and never saw anywhere again.

Is that even possible? As Christians, we understand that it's the same Holy Spirit who lives in each of us which means the same gifts and abilities are available in each successive generation. So why don't we see the same things happening over and over wherever and whenever Christians gather?

> *There are different kinds of spiritual gifts, but the same Spirit is the source of them all. There are different kinds of service, but we serve the same Lord. God works in different ways, but it is the same God who does the work in all of us. A spiritual gift is given to each of us so we can help each other. To one person the Spirit gives the ability to give wise advice; to another the same Spirit gives a message of special knowledge. The same Spirit gives great faith to another, and to someone else the one Spirit gives the gift of healing. He gives one person the power to perform miracles, and another the ability to prophesy. He gives someone else the ability to discern whether a message is from the Spirit of God or from another spirit. Still another person is given the ability to speak in unknown languages, while another is given the ability to interpret what is being said. It is the one and only Spirit who distributes all these gifts. He alone decides which gift each person should have.* - **1 Corinthians 12:4-11(NLT)**

The Holy Spirit alone decides who receives a spiritual gift and only He knows why He distributes them the way He does. Per the scripture, He does so based on the needs of His people because the purpose of these gifts is for us to help one another. If people need a gift, The Holy Ghost chooses someone among the people or at least, accessible to them, to operate in it, so that the need would be met. On top of that, He also chooses when He wants the gift to be manifested in a prominent and public fashion. I also believe that manifestation is determined by the prophetic season. Perhaps, all spiritual gifts are always operating in some fashion. Yet, we only see certain gifts demonstrated publicly on a consistent basis in each season.

My father, Apostle Emanuel Vivian Duncan, has a powerful anointing on his life and followed his father's footsteps into the ministry. Yet, he admits that he can't do things exactly like his father. What God called him to do is relevant to his generation. While my father also operates in the gifts of healing and deliverance like his father, his most powerful and prominent gift is prophecy. I don't know anyone who can prophesy like my father. God has given him the power to declare words that have changed Governments and shifted the trajectory of nations. The source of his power is the same as his father, but they play different roles in different generations. My grandfather walked with Prime Ministers, my father prophesies to them and up until the writing of this book, I do neither. My calling, up to this point, has mostly been to the marketplace but I do have a role in the church.

God has called me to teach. The scripture describes that as a gift of special knowledge. If God wanted me to do what my grandfather did, He would have given me the same gifts of healing and deliverance. Also, if God wants me to do what my father does, He would have given me the same gifts of teaching, prophecy, healing, and deliverance all in one. Maybe He did, but at this point, He has called me to teach first, then the gift of prophecy. Every other gift only manifests according to the needs of people. When someone needs healing or deliverance the Holy Spirit will stir up my spirit to connect with His so that His will can be done to meet the need. Some gifts remain dormant until the time that they are needed so I'm open to the fact that all three of us could have been given the same gifts and anointings by God. Nevertheless, even if all three of us walked in the same gifts and anointings at the same time, they would not be expressed in the same way because we belong to three different generations. That's the bottom line.

How Apostle Paul Served his Generation

> *When I think of all this, I, Paul, a prisoner of Christ Jesus for the benefit of you Gentiles . . . assuming, by the way, that you know God gave me the special responsibility of extending his grace to you Gentiles. As I briefly wrote earlier, God himself revealed his mysterious plan to me. As you read what I have written, you will understand my insight into this plan regarding Christ. God did not reveal it to previous generations, but now by his Spirit he has revealed it to his holy apostles and prophets. And this is God's plan: Both Gentiles and Jews who believe the Good News share equally in the riches inherited by God's children. Both are part of the same body, and both enjoy the promise of blessings because they belong to Christ Jesus. By God's grace and mighty power, I have been given the privilege of serving him by spreading this Good News. -* **Ephesians 3:1-7(NLT)**

Both Gentiles and Jews who believe in Jesus equally share in the inheritance of God's Children. While that's common knowledge to us in The Body of Christ today, that was a radical departure from what was traditionally taught in Jewish circles. When Apostle Paul took this message "to the streets", it was revolutionary. Until then, only Apostle Peter's interaction with the Roman centurion Cornelius and his family in response to an open vision from God in Acts 10, hinted at what was coming for the Gentiles.

The Jews were historically considered to be God's chosen people and all foreigners were destined for second-class citizenship, if any at all, in the Kingdom of God. Then came Jesus, who opened the door to the rest of the world through His death on the cross and subsequent resurrection. While Jesus opened the door for all to enter God's family, it was the Apostle Paul who spread the good news to the world that the door was recently opened. In that way, he served his generation. Had others tried to preach that same message prior to the death and resurrection of Jesus, they would have been irrelevant or at best, ahead of their time.

Apostle Paul rightly stated that God did not reveal His plan for equality and equity for Jews and Gentiles through faith in Jesus to previous generations. A few years or so, after personally meeting the resurrected Jesus on the road to Damascus, Apostle Paul received the special responsibility to take that message of hope specifically to the Gentiles. It's also important to note that He was not alone. The Holy Spirit revealed it to several apostles and prophets at the time. Yet, it was the Apostle Paul whose writings established the baseline for our understanding of the message. For instance, here's an example of how his teachings bring clarity to the issue.

We received the following question in the "Ask Donnell" section of TheCrackedDoor.com; *"Some people believe that The Church is spiritual Israel. Has the Church replaced Israel in God's plan? If so, what's God's plan for The Nation of Israel?"*

I was able to respond based on scriptures written by Apostle Paul. Is The Church spiritual Israel? That is a fascinating question. I've heard the concept before and understand why someone would believe that to be the case. This idea has been referred to as *"Replacement Theology"*, *"supersessionism"* or some version of it by its critics. It purports that The Church replaced Israel in God's plans, prophecies, etc. especially when it comes to Eschatology or End Time Prophecies. (Charry, 2011) It also purports that God's New Covenant with The Church replaced His Old Covenant with Israel. Circumcision of the heart replaced physical circumcision, etc., etc. Therefore, after The Book of Acts, anywhere we see the future of Israel in the Bible we can put The Church in there. Here are two scriptures that could cause some to start thinking along those lines.

> *The Jewish ceremony of circumcision has value only if you obey God's law. But if you don't obey God's law, you are no better off than an uncircumcised Gentile. And if the Gentiles obey God's law, won't God declare them to be his own people? In fact, uncircumcised Gentiles who keep God's law will condemn you Jews who are circumcised and possess God's law but don't obey it. For you are not a true Jew just because you were born of Jewish parents or because you have gone through the ceremony of circumcision. No, a true Jew is one whose heart is right with God. And true circumcision is not merely obeying the letter of the law; rather, it is a change of heart produced by God's Spirit. And a person with a changed heart seeks praise from God, not from people.... 3:1 Then*

13

what's the advantage of being a Jew? Is there any value in the ceremony of circumcision? Yes, there are great benefits! First of all, the Jews were entrusted with the whole revelation of God... 9 Well then, should we conclude that we Jews are better than others? No, not at all, for we have already shown that all people, whether Jews or Gentiles, are under the power of sin. As the Scriptures say, "No one is righteous— "No one is righteous— not even one.... 29 After all, is God the God of the Jews only? Isn't he also the God of the Gentiles? Of course he is. There is only one God, and he makes people right with himself only by faith, whether they are Jews or Gentiles. Well then, if we emphasize faith, does this mean that we can forget about the law? Of course not! In fact, only when we have faith do we truly fulfill the law. - **Romans 2:25-29, 3:1-2, 9-10, 29-31(NLT)**

For you are all children of God through faith in Christ Jesus. And all who have been united with Christ in baptism have put on the character of Christ, like putting on new clothes. There is no longer Jew or Gentile, slave or free, male and female. For you are all one in Christ Jesus. And now that you belong to Christ, you are the true children of Abraham. You are his heirs, and God's promise to Abraham belongs to you. - **Galatians 3:26-29(NLT)**

What do you see in those two scriptures? Has The Church replaced the Jews as God's Children? It may appear so to the untrained eye. However, what we're really seeing here is a bit more nuanced. The believers in Christ who are Gentiles combined with the believers in Christ out of Israel make up the Church. Together, we are God's Children. All who are in Christ are one and God doesn't distinguish between us when it comes to His promise of blessings. We, The Church of Jesus Christ don't replace Israel, we join the believers in Christ from Israel. Hence, those who accept Christ of Jewish or Gentile heritage are treated the same in God's eyes.

In contrast, those who reject Jesus, both Jewish and Gentile will see the same fate for eternity. It's no longer good enough just to be born a Jew. Everyone, including Jews, must get saved through faith in Jesus. Let me say it another way to drive the point home. Jews who reject Jesus go to hell. Gentiles who reject Jesus go to hell. Jews who accept Jesus are in God's family and spend eternity with Him. Gentiles who accept Jesus join the Jewish believers in God's family. However, that doesn't mean Jews aren't special in God's sight. Jesus said in John 4:22(KJV) - *"Ye worship ye know not what: we know what we worship: for salvation is of the Jews."*

God's plan of redemption was fulfilled in Jesus who was a Jew and continued with The Apostles who were also Jews. They preached the gospel in Jerusalem to Jews who were the first to get saved and establish The

Church. It was all about Jews getting saved until God directed several Apostles to take the show on the road and preach the gospel to the Gentiles. Therefore, the Gentiles who received Jesus joined The Jews who believed in Jesus in the Church. So, the concept of The Church replacing Jews won't make sense because the Church is full of Jews. Nonetheless, ethnic, and religious Jews still exist. What's God's plan for them?

But the Lord will save the people of Israel with eternal salvation. Throughout everlasting ages, they will never again be humiliated and disgraced. - **Isaiah 45:17(NLT)**

God plans to save the people of Israel also. However, let's not get carried away and think this means they don't need Jesus to get saved. Fast forward to The New Testament for more clarity concerning God's plan to save His people Israel and Judah.

In the same way, even though God has the right to show his anger and his power, he is very patient with those on whom his anger falls, who were made for destruction. He does this to make the riches of his glory shine even brighter on those to whom he shows mercy, who were prepared in advance for glory. And we are among those whom he selected, both from the Jews and from the Gentiles. Concerning the Gentiles, God says in the prophecy of Hosea, "Those who were not my people, I will now call my people. And I will love those whom I did not love before." And, "Then, at the place where they were told, 'You are not my people,' there they will be called 'children of the living God.'" And concerning Israel, Isaiah the prophet cried out, "Though the people of Israel are as numerous as the sand of the seashore, only a remnant will be saved. For the Lord will carry out his sentence upon the earth quickly and with finality." And Isaiah said the same thing in another place: "If the Lord of Heaven's Armies had not spared a few of our children, we would have been wiped out like Sodom, destroyed like Gomorrah." - **Romans 9:22-29(NLT)**

Let's start with the good news. God has a plan for the Gentiles and a plan for the Jews. His plan for The Gentiles is Jesus. His plan for the Jews is Jesus. Are the Jews saved just because they are Jewish or from The Nation of Israel? No! Is Jewish salvation automatic? No! They need Jesus just like we need Jesus which explains why Jesus came to them first. Let's dig in some more into God's plan for Israel.

Dear brothers and sisters, the longing of my heart and my prayer to God is for the people of Israel to be saved. I know what enthusiasm they have for God, but it is misdirected zeal. For they don't understand God's way of making people right with himself. Refusing to accept God's way, they cling to their own way of getting right with God by trying to keep the law. For Christ has already accomplished the purpose for which the law was given. As a result, all who believe in him are made right with God. For Moses writes that the law's way of making a person right with God requires obedience to all of its commands. But faith's way of getting right with God says, "Don't say in your heart, 'Who will go up to heaven' (to bring Christ down to earth). And don't say, 'Who will go down to the place of the dead' (to bring Christ back to life again)." In fact, it says, "The message is very close at hand; it is on your lips and in your heart." And that message is the very message about faith that we preach: If you confess with your mouth that Jesus is Lord and believe in your heart that God raised him from the dead, you will be saved. For it is by believing in your heart that you are made right with God, and it is by confessing with your mouth that you are saved. - **Romans 10:1-11(NLT)**

Apostle Paul's prayer was for Israel's salvation. The only way they could receive that salvation was through confessing with their mouths that Jesus is Lord and believing in their hearts that God raised Him from the dead. It's a simple plan and it works for everyone. It was also the Apostle Paul's prayer that the remnant who would we saved would go ahead and accept the path to their salvation by grace through faith in Jesus. Let's now bring this discussion to a close with a powerful scripture.

So this is the situation: Most of the people of Israel have not found the favor of God they are looking for so earnestly. A few have—the ones God has chosen—but the hearts of the rest were hardened. As the Scriptures say, "God has put them into a deep sleep. To this day he has shut their eyes so they do not see, and closed their ears so they do not hear." Likewise, David said, "Let their bountiful table become a snare, a trap that makes them think all is well. Let their blessings cause them to stumble, and let them get what they deserve. Let their eyes go blind so they cannot see, and let their backs be bent forever." Did God's people stumble and fall beyond recovery? Of course not! They were disobedient, so God made salvation available to the Gentiles. But he wanted his own people to become jealous and claim it for themselves. Now if the Gentiles were enriched because the people of Israel turned down God's offer of salvation, think how much greater a blessing the world will share when they finally accept it.

I am saying all this especially for you Gentiles. God has appointed me as the apostle to the Gentiles. I stress this, for I want somehow to make the people of Israel jealous of what you Gentiles have, so I might save some of them. For since their rejection meant that God offered salvation to the rest of the world, their acceptance will be even more wonderful. It will be life for those who were dead! And since Abraham and the other patriarchs were holy, their descendants will also be holy—just as the entire batch of dough is holy because the portion given as an offering is holy. For if the roots of the tree are holy, the branches will be, too. But some of these branches from Abraham's tree—some of the people of Israel—have been broken off. And you Gentiles, who were branches from a wild olive tree, have been grafted in. So now you also receive the blessing God has promised Abraham and his children, sharing in the rich nourishment from the root of God's special olive tree. But you must not brag about being grafted in to replace the branches that were broken off. You are just a branch, not the root. "Well," you may say, "those branches were broken off to make room for me."

Yes, but remember—those branches were broken off because they didn't believe in Christ, and you are there because you do believe. So don't think highly of yourself, but fear what could happen. For if God did not spare the original branches, he won't spare you either. Notice how God is both kind and severe. He is severe toward those who disobeyed, but kind to you if you continue to trust in his kindness. But if you stop trusting, you also will be cut off. And if the people of Israel turn from their unbelief, they will be grafted in again, for God has the power to graft them back into the tree. You, by nature, were a branch cut from a wild olive tree. So if God was willing to do something contrary to nature by grafting you into his cultivated tree, he will be far more eager to graft the original branches back into the tree where they belong.

I want you to understand this mystery, dear brothers and sisters, so that you will not feel proud about yourselves. Some of the people of Israel have hard hearts, but this will last only until the full number of Gentiles comes to Christ. And so all Israel will be saved. As the Scriptures say, "The one who rescues will come from Jerusalem, and he will turn Israel away from ungodliness. And this is my covenant with them, that I will take away their sins." Many of the people of Israel are now enemies of the Good News, and this benefits you Gentiles. Yet they are still the people he loves because he chose their ancestors Abraham, Isaac, and Jacob. For God's gifts and his call can never be withdrawn. Once, you Gentiles were rebels against God, but when the people of Israel rebelled against him, God was merciful to you instead. Now they are the rebels, and God's mercy has come to you so that they, too, will share in God's mercy. - Romans 11:7-31 (NLT)

The Apostle Paul settled the issue in this passage of scripture. Israel is the root and we; the Gentiles were grafted into the tree because Israel rejected Jesus and made room for us. Those who were grafted in, have not replaced the original branches so we must stop saying that. The people of Israel will be grafted in again to join us when they accept Jesus. God added to His family those who would believe and will add the people of Israel again when they choose to believe in Jesus. Israel will be saved. In fact, the time is coming when they will open their hearts to hear the gospel and every one of them will accept Jesus.

WAIT? Did he also say what I thought he said? All Israel will be saved? How is that possible? I thought God would only save a remnant. Well, let's make sense of this. First, this scripture is referring to the end of time because it clearly states that a time is coming when the full number of Gentiles will come to Christ. Consequently, after that time, no more Gentiles will be saved. There will be a mass revival in Israel during which many will receive Jesus. They will finally understand that He was sent as their Savior to Jerusalem to turn them away from ungodliness. Obviously, those who are ALIVE at the time of the end will be able to accept the truth of the gospel. Those who are dead won't be in Jerusalem anymore, so I don't see how this scripture refers to them. If it does, I still don't see it. I would love to believe that every one of Jewish heritage, alive or dead will be saved but I can't support that with multiple scriptures.

When this scripture is compared with the others that say only a remnant of Israel will be saved there is one way to look at it that makes it easier to understand. All of Israel at that time will be saved. Everyone alive will recognize Jesus for who He truly is, and they will be welcomed into the Body of Christ. They will accept the Good News which is the gospel of Jesus Christ. So, in the end, only those who accept Jesus will be saved. Fortunately, the time is coming when the gospel will be preached in Israel in such a mighty way that all who hear it will believe. Perhaps, this explains why God never gives up on Israel. He knows that the day is coming when a generation of Jews, referred to as the remnant in the last days, will get it right and accept Jesus.

Know Your Age

> *For if you remain completely silent at this time, relief and deliverance will arise for the Jews from another place, but you and your father's house will perish. Yet who knows whether you have come to the kingdom for such a time as this?"*
> **- Esther 4:14(NKJV)**

It's important to understand the age you are living in and the generation you are called to serve. That understanding will help shape how you accomplish God's Will for your life. During a time of great personal struggle, Mordecai had to remind Esther of her age. He didn't have to remind her of how old she was but of the generation or age she was living in. God put her in a position of influence at that time for one purpose only, to save His people from certain death. Like any of us, she had cold feet when her window of opportunity opened but thank God she was not alone. What about you?

Do you know your age? What does your generation need that God has called you to do? Why are you alive during this season and what are you doing about it? One of my favorite books is called *"Well Done"*. I wrote it at a time when God was intensely working on my heart about my purpose. He led me through the scriptures in order to better understand how He chooses to work through certain key individuals during pivotal periods of human history. He also bridged the gap between His gifts and calling in Romans 11:29. Simply put; God won't call you to do something He didn't gift you to do and He won't give you any gifts without calling you to use them for His purpose.

Even though the broad definition of a generation is between 30 and 40 years, God's purpose in your life is broken down into much smaller segments. Hence, you don't just need to know your age or generation from a big picture, life-time perspective. You need to know the specific season you are in right now even if it's one year or one month long. As I write this book, I am in a completely different season of my life than I was merely 2 years ago. Only recently, has God slammed the door open for me to do something of significance with my engineering career. Like Esther, I must move quickly to accomplish His Will in this area of my life.

I recently sat down with two young engineers from my office who asked me to have lunch with them and share my "success" story. I told them about God's grace and favor in my life. I let them know about the obstacles I faced and how God showed me the way out. I encouraged them to make the most of their youth and to never let someone else define the limits of their success. They sought me out, not because I was a pastor but because I was an engineer operating successfully within that sphere of influence. That is part of serving my generation, it's a small part, but it's part, nonetheless. What about you? What are you doing to serve your generation? How are you making use of this dimension of your time? Remember, know your age!

AGE

3 EVERLASTING

And I will establish my covenant between me and thee and thy seed after thee in their generations for an everlasting covenant, to be a God unto thee, and to thy seed after thee. - **Genesis 17:7(KJV)**

In this chapter, the definition of time under consideration comes from the Hebrew word *"owlam"* which means, *"long duration, antiquity, futurity, for ever, ever, everlasting, evermore, perpetual, old, ancient, world"*. (Strong, The New Strong's Exhaustive Concordance of the Bible, 2003) It's most significantly used in scripture when referring to God's covenant with Abraham, which is everlasting. Based on Galatians 3:16 and 29, it goes on and on and on, extending to Christ, then to us, our children and the generations that will follow. It never ends.

What else is everlasting?

1. God's Reign– Exodus 15:18
2. His Mercy- Psalm 100:5
3. His Love- Jeremiah 31:3
4. His Name- Psalm 72:17
5. His Kingdom- Matthew 6:13

God's Reign is Everlasting

"The Lord shall reign forever and ever." - **Exodus 15:18(NKJV)**

I'm from the democratic republic of Trinidad and Tobago where the most powerful position is the Prime Minister. We also have a President who, though ranked higher, does not run the day-to-day operations of the country but plays a mostly ceremonial role in leadership. The term for each Prime Minister is five years without term limits. Hence, the same person can be elected over and over.

On election night in 2015, the early results pointed to a victory for the incumbent political party, United National Congress. Then, as more votes were counted, it swung in the direction of their main rival, People's National Movement, who were ultimately victorious. What was a major victory for one group of people turned out to be a devastating defeat for another. Nevertheless, even in defeat, those on the losing end could pick up the pieces and prepare for the next election in 2020. Why? Every five years, the people of Trinidad and Tobago get to choose who they want in political leadership.

There are many similarities to the political process in the United States, but things are done a bit differently. I will never forget the night in November 2016 when Mr. Donald Trump, the businessman, and reality television star became President Trump, the most powerful political figure in the world. My wife, Angel and I stayed up until the wee hours of the morning watching the results roll in from each state.

Even though the numbers looked all night like President Trump would win, it was so unlikely that we just thought somehow the results would suddenly flip. Alas, it never happened. Eventually, the election results were called by the major television networks. In an instant, the United States was destined for the leadership of President Donald Trump for the next four years. Again, one group of Americans was totally elated by the results while another group was completely devastated. Fortunately, four years later in the November 2020 election, they would have the opportunity to confirm the decision of 2016 or correct it.

That's how things work in this world. Nobody reigns forever. In democracies, any leader can be replaced during an election. In dictatorships and monarchies, while people don't get to choose their leaders, in the end, the dictator, king or queen eventually dies. We can confidently say that nobody reigns forever because nobody lives forever. Well, that's not entirely true. While that statement may be true about earthly rulers, it's not true about the everlasting reign of our immortal God. Throughout human history, many dictators or monarchs dreamed of remaining in power forever, but they had to die one day. So, the longest they can possibly reign is their lifetime. That's why God's eternal reign is so special. He outlasts every Pharaoh, Caesar, Hitler, Mussolini, Stalin, or anyone else whose power seems unchecked for a very long time.

Amid life's biggest challenges, you must remind yourself that God still sits on the throne. While it may seem at the time like the enemy is winning or his evil human agents have the upper hand, nothing can change God's position as the King of kings and Lord of lords. This should reassure you that The Lord, whose authority has no limit, is fully aware of what you're going through and can intervene when He sees fit.

If you keep that in mind, you will be able to make it through anything. I know that's much easier said than done but what's important to remember is that you don't have a choice. It must be done if you want to survive and even thrive during the storms of life. I have personally used this approach in my own life, and it has helped me through my own challenging experiences. Your problems might loom large for a season but remember that the same eternal God who lives inside of you will outlast them so you should too. His reign is everlasting.

God's Mercy is Everlasting

> *For the Lord is good; His mercy is everlasting, And His truth endures to all generations.* - **Psalm 100:5(NKJV)**

The mercy of God is the reason why we are alive. Due to our sinful nature, we deserve death. It's the only just compensation for sin. Yet, what seems quite simple in theory is a bit more complex in practice. While God's mercy is everlasting, there's a method to God's mercy and that's what we'll focus on now. In January 2013, The Lord spoke to me about this and I shared His thoughts on my blog at TheCrackedDoor.Com. Now, I'll share it with you.

> *And he said, I will make all my goodness pass before thee, and I will proclaim the name of the Lord before thee; and will be gracious to whom I will be gracious, and will shew mercy on whom I will shew mercy.* - **Exodus 33:19(KJV)**

> *As it is written, "Jacob I have loved, but Esau I have hated." What shall we say then? Is there unrighteousness with God? Certainly not! For He says to Moses, "I will have mercy on whomever I will have mercy, and I will have compassion on whomever I will have compassion."* - **Romans 9:13-15(NKJV)**

Wow! That's intense. God said He hated Esau but loved Jacob. Read Malachi 1:1-3 for the direct quotation from God. That's exactly what He said. Wow! Why did Jacob get God's mercy and not Esau? That makes me think and should make you think also. To whom does God show His mercy? That's a simple question with a simple answer. God shows mercy to whomever He chooses. He makes the rules and we just live by them.

For several days I wrestled with this question in my heart. Why is it that certain people get more chances after they slip up than others? Some people live in sin for decades without facing the judgment of God while others slip up once and are instantly judged. God is no respecter of persons according to Acts 10:34 so there must be some method to His mercy. Maybe it's beyond our human understanding but since He wants us to study it, let's try to understand what He shows us. Everyone reaps what they sow but how soon or how much depends on God's mercy.

Let's start by defining the word *"mercy"* as it's used in the Bible. It appears in many places in the Old Testament as the word *"chanan"* which means *"to show favor, be gracious or pity."* (Strong, The New Strong's Exhaustive Concordance of the Bible, 2003) Again, why is it that after people disobey God's directions, some are shown great favor or pity while others are not shown as much? Is it completely random or does God have a method to His mercy?

Before I go any further, let me clarify something that may trigger confusion. This topic is not about salvation or your eternal destiny. That's covered by The Blood of Jesus if you're saved according to Romans 10:9&10. However, after salvation, there are certain principles that still govern life on earth before the return of Jesus Christ. According to Apostle Paul's letter to The Church in Galatians 6:7-8, whatever you sow you shall reap. The Galatian Church contained Christians so if this principle applied to them, it also applies to us.

A Method to God's Mercy

1. **God only accepts true repentance. He looks at people's hearts and knows if their outward repentance is real or not.**

He that covereth his sins shall not prosper: but whoso confesseth and forsaketh them shall have mercy. - **Proverbs 28:13(KJV)**

God bless America, the land of the free, the home of the brave. It's also a country where so many public figures lie, deny and hide any wrongdoing until the evidence against them is so overwhelming that they have no option but to confess. After initially denying any involvement in any discretion whatsoever they end up with their backs against the wall. At that point, they suddenly claim to be sorry for what they've done, the people they've hurt and

24

the trust they've abused.

Sometimes, after years of denial, they suddenly strike a tone of true penitence as they are forced to face the consequences of their actions. Still, as many of us may have already figured out, some of them are not repentant at all, they're just sorry for getting caught. Why? Before their sins were exposed to the world, they had no desire to stop what they were doing. That's exactly what God sees and that's the criterion He uses to choose whether to show mercy.

> *"Now, therefore,"* says the Lord, *"Turn to Me with all your heart, With fasting, with weeping, and with mourning."* So rend your heart, and not your garments; Return to the Lord your God, For He is gracious and merciful, Slow to anger, and of great kindness; And He relents from doing harm. Who knows if He will turn and relent, And leave a blessing behind Him— A grain offering and a drink offering For the Lord your God? - **Joel 2:12-14(NKJV)**

Why did God tell His people not to rend their garments anymore? In those days people would tear their clothes as an outward display of repentance. Apparently, many were doing it as a mindless, religious exercise and God was having none of it. If His people were truly sorry for what they had done, He needed to see it in their hearts. They needed to be saddened by their sins. Their hearts needed to be broken for breaking His heart. They needed to be real.

God had enough of the acting, so He said; *"I'm not impressed. Quit ripping your clothes and repent for real this time."*

What's true repentance anyway? In The Bible, the word *"repentance"* is the English translation of the Greek word *"metanoia"* which means *"change of mind"* and *"to repent"* is *"to change one's mind for the better, heartily to amend with abhorrence of one's past sins"*. (Strong, The New Strong's Exhaustive Concordance of the Bible, 2003) Repentance is also a translation of the Hebrew word *"nocham"* which means *"sorrow."* Therefore, when someone truly repents there is an admission of guilt, complete disdain for what was done, Godly sorrow and a brand-new mindset concerning the issue. If one of those is missing, it is not true repentance and God will not accept it. Read about King Saul in 1 Samuel 15&16 to learn what true repentance is not then read about King David in 2 Samuel 12 for an illustration of what it is.

2. **God judges people based on what they know. Everyone is not treated equally.**

And the Lord said, "Who then is that faithful and wise steward, whom his master will make ruler over his household, to give them their portion of food in due season? Blessed is that servant whom his master will find so doing when he comes. Truly, I say to you that he will make him ruler over all that he has. But if that servant says in his heart, 'My master is delaying his coming,' and begins to beat the male and female servants, and to eat and drink and be drunk, the master of that servant will come on a day when he is not looking for him, and at an hour when he is not aware, and will cut him in two and appoint him his portion with the unbelievers. And that servant who knew his master's will, and did not prepare himself or do according to his will, shall be beaten with many stripes. But he who did not know, yet committed things deserving of stripes, shall be beaten with few. For everyone to whom much is given, from him much will be required; and to whom much has been committed, of him they will ask the more. - **Luke 12:42-48(NLT)**

God loves everyone equally but can judge everyone differently. Our ultimate standard is the Word of God but how much of it we know directly affects the level of mercy we receive. According to The Parable of The Servants in Luke 12:42-48, any servant who does not do the will of the master receives stripes. Nonetheless, the number of stripes is determined by the servant's knowledge base. Additionally, the servants to whom the master gives more, a higher return is expected on his investment. Usually, in parables like these, the master represents God and we are His servants. Therefore, we should be able to easily figure out how this applies to our lives.

Let me make this very practical. Two men can commit the same sin and God will judge both. Let's assume the first man knows exactly what he is doing while the second man acts out of ignorance. Based on the scripture, the second man will escape with lighter punishment than the first. Is that fair? In God's eyes, it sure is. Since He is the judge and jury that's all that matters. Now let's go even deeper.

For it is impossible [to restore and bring again to repentance] those who have been once for all enlightened, who have consciously tasted the heavenly gift and have become sharers of the Holy Spirit, And have felt how good the Word of God is and the mighty powers of the age and world to come, If they then deviate from the faith and turn away from their allegiance—[it is impossible] to bring them back to repentance, for (because, while, as long as) they nail upon the cross the Son of God afresh [as far as they are concerned] and are holding [Him] up to contempt and shame and public disgrace. - **Hebrews 6:4-6(AMP)**

Have you ever met someone who walked away from God and all hell broke loose? Better yet, have you ever been so offended that you considered walking away from The Lord? OK, maybe not forever but just for a little while? Have a little fun? Play around a little? Maybe you're all "churched out" so you need to take a break, worship an idol or two for a few years then maybe give this "Jesus" thing another try in the future? OK, let's fantasize together for a moment about backsliding.

We can see it already. We're going to have the time of our lives out there then come back with awesome testimonies and the church will treat us like heroes. The young people will think we're cool and we'll have *"church street cred."* Who knows? Maybe, we will write books about our experiences in the world and end up on TBN someday to tell our story?

It worked for the Prodigal Son so it should work for us too, right? I'm sure you have seen other people do it for years and walk right back into the fold almost unscathed haven't you? Well, depending on who you are that might not be your story. The Prodigal Son was young and naïve. I know of people who walked out on God and never made it back. They walked out the door and BAM! It was over! FLAMES!

When you get to a certain level in your Christianity you can't just walk away. When the Holy Spirit starts to move in your life, and you begin to receive deep revelation from The Word of God you can't just walk away. When you start hearing God's Voice on a regular basis and begin manifesting the gifts of the Spirit you can't just walk away. You have received much, so much is required of you.

3. **Those who have shown mercy to others will receive mercy from God. His Kingdom is based on seed, time, and harvest.**

Therefore let him who thinks he stands take heed lest he fall. - **1 Corinthians 10:12(NKJV)**

"If your neighbor's house is on fire, throw water on your own." - **Unknown**

That's some priceless advice. Never celebrate someone else's demise because you might be next. Be slow to point a critical index finger because at least three others will be pointing right back at you. It's not always easy and it rarely comes naturally but it pays to be merciful. I have learned over the years to take advantage of opportunities to show mercy to others because one day I may be the one looking for it.

There will be no mercy for those who have not shown mercy to others. But if you have been merciful, God will be merciful when he judges you. - **James 2:13(NLT)**

Wounded, hurting Christians are slow-moving, easy targets. Don't give in to the temptation to pick on them. Have you ever had mercy on someone who clearly did something wrong and thanked God later when someone did the same for you? Those who show mercy are figuratively sowing seeds of mercy into the lives of others which they will harvest as fruit later in their own lives. However, the direct opposite is also true.

People who don't show mercy end up needing some later in their lives and don't always find it. Why is it that some of the most critical, judgmental people end up getting caught in indiscretion of their own? They sentence people to hell with their words while their secrets are safe until God exposes their sins for the world to see. Everyone is then completely shocked when the tables are turned, and they must beg others for mercy. Ouch!

*"Therefore, the Kingdom of Heaven can be compared to a king who decided to bring his accounts up to date with servants who had borrowed money from him. In the process, one of his debtors was brought in who owed him millions of dollars. He couldn't pay, so his master ordered that he be sold—along with his wife, his children, and everything he owned—to pay the debt. "But the man fell down before his master and begged him, 'Please, be patient with me, and I will pay it all.' Then his master was filled with pity for him, and he released him and forgave his debt. "But when the man left the king, he went to a fellow servant who owed him a few thousand dollars. He grabbed him by the throat and demanded instant payment. "His fellow servant fell down before him and begged for a little more time. 'Be patient with me, and I will pay it,' he pleaded. But his creditor wouldn't wait. He had the man arrested and put in prison until the debt could be paid in full. "When some of the other servants saw this, they were very upset. They went to the king and told him everything that had happened. Then the king called in the man he had forgiven and said, 'You evil servant! I forgave you that tremendous debt because you pleaded with me. Shouldn't you have mercy on your fellow servant, just as I had mercy on you?' Then the angry king sent the man to prison to be tortured until he had paid his entire debt. "That's what my heavenly Father will do to you if you refuse to forgive your brothers and sisters from your heart." - **Matthew 18:23-35(NLT)**

If you give mercy you will get mercy. If you don't give mercy you won't get it when you really need it. That's a Kingdom principle that God established. Why do some people get more mercy than others? Some people give more mercy than others. One of the master principles of The Kingdom of God is the principle of seed, time, and harvest. In short, it means, whatever you sow you will reap.

The servant who showed no mercy for the debt of a few thousand dollars had a right to demand payment. He was justified to put his fellow servant in jail until he got his money. If this was based purely on a man's rights, this man had the right to do what he did. Yet, exercising your rights is not the only or best option in every situation. That's what mercy is all about.

Mercy is demonstrated when a man has a right to punish or execute judgment on another but gives up that right and liberates the person who does not deserve it. Like the unforgiving servant, you don't have to show mercy if you don't want to. However, if you have been shown mercy or will need some in the future you probably should.

You have a right to sue that brother in The Lord who owes you money but should you? You have a right to expose that person's past to other people, but should you? If someone cheated on you, shouldn't you be free to cheat too? After what he did, you have a right to walk away when he needs you the most but should you? She hit you first so you have a right to beat her like she stole something, but should you? Mercy is a choice, choose it.

Blessed are the merciful: for they shall obtain mercy. - **Matthew 5:7(KJV)**

Life is strange. You never know what's around the corner or what the future holds for you. That's why you should always play it safe. Create your future by sowing the right types of seeds today. Be quick to forgive. Be quick to give people the benefit of the doubt. Be quick to accept other people's flaws. Be quick to show mercy. By doing so, you store up mercy for your future.

4. People who judge themselves before receiving God's judgment get special access to God's mercy.

For God speaks again and again, though people do not recognize it. He speaks in dreams, in visions of the night, when deep sleep falls on people as they lie in their beds. He whispers in their ears and terrifies them with warnings. He makes them turn from doing wrong; he keeps them from pride. He protects them from the grave, from crossing over the river of death. - **Job 33:14-18(NLT)**

When God's judgment is closing in on someone, He sends out clear warning signals. First, The Holy Spirit convicts the person's heart (John 16:7-8). He also reaches out by speaking to the person directly through dreams or visions. That's the most common and effective way to communicate a warning. It's private, simple and undeniable. If private communication doesn't work, God employs the help of others through prophetic words, pointed sermons, books, blogs or other forms of written or verbal communication (Ezekiel 33:1-11). These messengers from God are only responsible for delivering the message. Once the delivery is complete, they are free to move on with their lives.

Nonetheless, when a person consistently ignores the voice of The Holy Spirit, the person's sensitivity to God decreases (Romans 1:18-28). In that case, drastic times call for drastic measures. God may then choose to use external signs including unusual natural phenomena to get the person's attention. At the same time, God may also employ the services of angels, His heavenly messengers (Numbers 22:21-31). When the angels get involved, things go to a whole new level.

These are all part of God's plan to save a person from impending judgment.

For if we would judge ourselves, we would not be judged. But when we are judged, we are chastened by the Lord, that we may not be condemned with the world. - **1 Corinthians 11:31-32(NKJV)**

God warns people so they can impose self-judgment before receiving His judgment. Even though His judgment is fair and merciful it's better to judge yourself first before He gets involved. His judgment is designed to cause repentance so if repentance comes first it won't be necessary. How many times have you seen someone receive stiff judgment from God and wondered why it had to go that far? Judgment was the last resort. Before God chastened the person, He probably sent conviction by The Holy Spirit, warnings in dreams and visions, warnings through people, along with even natural and supernatural signs.

Over and over, God tries to get people's attention before He does something drastic. He loves His children so much that He won't leave us to suffer the consequences of our sins without first giving us an opportunity to repent. He even gives us a chance to escape His judgment which is much more lenient than the harvest of sin. His judgment is an expression of His love because it is designed to save us from disaster. His warnings are an even greater expression of His love because they are designed to save us from His judgment. Warnings, judgment, disaster; that's the order. Thank God we can jump off the train at any point before it reaches its destination.

5. People can inherit mercy because of their family history.

"Therefore know that the Lord your God, He is God, the faithful God who keeps covenant and mercy for a thousand generations with those who love Him and keep His commandments. - **Deuteronomy 7:9(NKJV)**

Do any of your parents love The Lord? Do you have a praying grandmother? Has anyone in your family paved a pathway for you to follow in God's Kingdom? Do you know that because of your lineage you could be the beneficiary of inherited mercy? When people love God and keep His commandments, they trigger a *"Mercy Snowball"* that continues rolling for a thousand generations. If you're wondering why God is being especially merciful you might be caught up in the middle of one right now.

Great deliverance giveth he to his king; and sheweth mercy to his anointed, to David, and to his seed for evermore. - **Psalm 18:50(KJV)**

How could David's seed be shown mercy forevermore if his seed was not born yet? If mercy is only dependent on a person's actions, then that would have been completely impossible. Based on the actions of one man, the decision was made by God to show mercy to his descendants.

And his mercy is on them that fear him from generation to generation. - **Luke 1:50(KJV)**

If you fear God, the mercy of God you receive is generational. Not only are you going to benefit from it but so will your children and their children and their children, etc. This is like the ultimate *"Mercy Snowball"*. Wait… it gets better. Do you know that even if your parents messed it all up and their parents did and the disaster went all the way back until you found out your great, great, great, great… grandfather was Judas Iscariot or grandmother was Jezebel you can still inherit mercy? Here's how!

God's Mercy Extends for Generations

As he spake by the mouth of his holy prophets, which have been since the world began: That we should be saved from our enemies, and from the hand of all that hate us; To perform the mercy promised to our fathers, and to remember his holy covenant; The oath which he sware to our father Abraham, That he would grant unto us, that we being delivered out of the hand of our enemies might serve him without fear, In holiness and righteousness before him, all the days of our life. - **Luke 1:70-75(KJV)**

God made a covenant to show Abraham's seed mercy. He promised to save them from their enemies. As a result, the people of Israel remain God's chosen people regardless of what they've done. Even after they rebel against God and totally enrage Him, they seem to always end up right back in fellowship with Him. His mercy toward them is unbelievable. Now, here's where we fit in.

> *For ye are all the children of God by faith in Christ Jesus. For as many of you as have been baptized into Christ have put on Christ. There is neither Jew nor Greek, there is neither bond nor free, there is neither male nor female: for ye are all one in Christ Jesus. And if ye be Christ's, then are ye Abraham's seed, and heirs according to the promise.* - **Galatians 3:26-29(KJV)**

If you are a Christian, you are also Abraham's seed which means that you also inherit the mercy God awarded to him. Maybe that explains why, despite your family background, you too are in the middle of a *"Mercy Snowball."* Every time it looks like you're done and deservedly so, God always seems to pull you out of trouble. Even when you openly disobey, God still seems to give you another chance. He doesn't judge you because of your family name, He judges you based on your relationship with Christ. If you didn't grow up with parents who loved God or your grandmother was an atheist, you can still receive mercy due to your new family heritage.

> *But ye are a chosen generation, a royal priesthood, an holy nation, a peculiar people; that ye should shew forth the praises of him who hath called you out of darkness into his marvellous light; Which in time past were not a people, but are now the people of God: which had not obtained mercy, but now have obtained mercy.* - **1 Peter 2:9-10(KJV)**

Before you joined the family of God you did not have access to His generational mercy unless you inherited it from your earthly family. Some of us were blessed to come from Godly families but you may not have had the same experience. Still, to God be the glory for your new spiritual family. This connection has hooked you up with an everlasting flow of mercy.

It's the same mercy Saul received on the road to Damascus which changed his life and turned him into Apostle Paul. It's the same mercy Simon Peter received when he denied Jesus three times as Jesus carried the cross. Peter, the disciple, was forgiven and chosen by God to become Apostle Peter, the first leader of The Church. It's the same mercy I received as a young boy and still receive today. It's the best mercy on the market. It's the mercy you want to have. It's because of His mercy that you were taken out of the darkness and placed into His marvelous light. You are chosen. You are royal. You are holy. You are peculiar. You are a child of God. You have obtained mercy.

Even if you make a bad decision and disappoint God, ask for forgiveness, and tap into this mercy. It's always available. God's mercy extends for generations. Why not forget about your past and set things up for your future? Why not love God with all your heart and obey His commandments? That way, you can start rolling a *"Mercy Snowball"* in the direction of your descendants.

6. **God's decision to show mercy is affected by a person's relationship with Him. Certain people access more mercy than others.**

Delilah lulled Samson to sleep with his head in her lap, and then she called in a man to shave off the seven locks of his hair. In this way she began to bring him down, and his strength left him. Then she cried out, "Samson! The Philistines have come to capture you!" When he woke up, he thought, "I will do as before and shake myself free." But he didn't realize the Lord had left him. - **Judges 16:19-20(NLT)**

Samson knew what he was doing. He understood exactly how God's mercy worked. The story of his life was full of indiscretions, uncontrolled anger, and rebellion but through it all, God never left him. He thought he was invincible. He could do whatever he liked and still wake up each morning with the Spirit of Might on him. After all, he was chosen by God to be a judge of Israel. He just could not lose. Nonetheless, the Anointing on His life had one condition.

Finally, Samson shared his secret with her. "My hair has never been cut," he confessed, "for I was dedicated to God as a Nazirite from birth. If my head were shaved, my strength would leave me, and I would become as weak as anyone else." - **Judges 16:17(NLT)**

If Samson did not cut his hair, the Spirit of Might would have been upon him all the days of his life. If he kept that one vow, he would have been shown mercy regardless of what else he did wrong. Like we did earlier, let's again define the word *"mercy"* as it's used in the Bible. It appears many places in the Old Testament as the word *"chanan"* which means *"to show favor, be gracious or pity."* (Strong, The New Strong's Exhaustive Concordance of the Bible, 2003)

God showed grace, favor, and pity to Samson through all his shortcomings until the day he broke his Nazarite vow. Instantly, the party was over for Samson. As fast as the Holy Spirit had come upon him, the Holy Spirit was gone.

Whether or not we want to believe it, God's mercy is conditional. The Bible says in Romans 9:15; *"For he saith to Moses, I will have mercy on whom I will have mercy, and I will have compassion on whom I will have compassion."* Even though God's mercy is available to all mankind, everyone does not have the same access. Some enjoy more while others enjoy much less. As God said to Moses, it's His prerogative to do whatever He likes with His mercy. Thankfully, there's a standard of mercy available to all who are in Christ.

7. **God's mercy and truth go together. When people accept God's truth, they unlock His mercy.**

God forbid: yea, let God be true, but every man a liar; as it is written, That thou mightest be justified in thy sayings, and mightest overcome when thou art judged. - **Romans 3:4(KJV)**

There is no truth outside of God so every sincere search for truth will end up in one place: God! Everywhere you look in this world, people are constantly lying. Advertisers lie about the products they are selling so that people would buy them. Politicians lie to the electorate so they could get more votes. Pharmaceutical companies lie about their drugs so they could make money off gullible people looking for healing. Multi-level marketers lie to people about the money they could practically make in the long-term. Liars are everywhere.

But if our gospel be hid, it is hid to them that are lost: In whom the god of this world hath blinded the minds of them which believe not, lest the light of the glorious gospel of Christ, who is the image of God, should shine unto them. For we preach not ourselves, but Christ Jesus the Lord; and ourselves your servants for Jesus' sake. - **2 Corinthians 4:3-5(KJV)**

Why do ye not understand my speech? even because ye cannot hear my word. Ye are of your father the devil, and the lusts of your father ye will do. He was a murderer from the beginning, and abode not in the truth, because there is no truth in him. When he speaketh a lie, he speaketh of his own: for he is a liar, and the father of it. And because I tell you the truth, ye believe me not. - **John 8:43-45(KJV)**

Like father, like sons and daughters. The world is built on a system of lies because the god of this world is the father of lies. They are so saturated with lies that they squirm at the sound of truth. At the mention of the name Jesus, they lose their composure and get seriously offended. They have been blinded and have no idea that the one in whom they believe has been lying to them all along. It's impossible for him to tell the truth because it is not in him.

I trust nobody but God. People are liars and will break your heart over and over if you put your trust in them. However, I do trust God in people so only those people who have God in their hearts can be trusted. Again, without God inside of their hearts, all people are liars. Some want to be liars, but others can't help it. Even if they think they're telling the truth they can only tell "their truth" because without Jesus they do not know The Truth.

People look out for themselves and as my mother-in-law told my wife a long time ago; *"Baby, people will do whatever makes them happy."* Some of them will look you in the eye and lie with a straight face then sleep at night with a clear conscience. How do they do it? I don't know. Since they are unable to sense the conviction of the Holy Spirit who's going to tell them to stop lying? Not their father, the devil. I digress...

Surely His salvation is near to those who fear Him, That glory may dwell in our land. Mercy and truth have met together; Righteousness and peace have kissed. - **Psalm 85:9-10(NKJV)**

Mercy and truth go together. If you want God to shower His mercy on your life, you must accept His truth. You cannot reject God's truth and expect to receive His mercy. If you accept Jesus, who is The Truth, you will receive access to the mercy of God that was promised to Abraham. Additionally, if you accept God's Word, you accept His truth. Jesus said in John 17:17, *"Sanctify them through thy truth: thy word is truth."*

And Solomon said, Thou hast shewed unto thy servant David my father great mercy, according as he walked before thee in truth, and in righteousness, and in uprightness of heart with thee; and thou hast kept for him this great kindness, that thou hast given him a son to sit on his throne, as it is this day. - **1 Kings 3:6(KJV)**

According to the truth that David walked in, God showed Him "great" mercy. What does that mean? There was a direct correlation between David's acceptance of the truth and God's response with "great" mercy. God is no respecter of persons, but He is a respecter of principles (Acts 10:34). When God creates a system, if it works for one person, it will work for another. Do you want to be shown "great" mercy? Walk in truth. Walk in The Word of God.

On the other hand, what happens when people reject God's truth? Take a wild guess. If accepting the truth causes a release of God's mercy, rejecting the truth puts an end to it. Do you believe that? Do you believe that rejecting the truth could take someone outside of the range of God's mercy? It sounds impossible, doesn't it? Well, here's what The Word of God says about that.

> *But God shows his anger from heaven against all sinful, wicked people who suppress the truth by their wickedness. They know the truth about God because he has made it obvious to them. For ever since the world was created, people have seen the earth and sky. Through everything God made, they can clearly see his invisible qualities—his eternal power and divine nature. So they have no excuse for not knowing God. Yes, they knew God, but they wouldn't worship him as God or even give him thanks. And they began to think up foolish ideas of what God was like. As a result, their minds became dark and confused. Claiming to be wise, they instead became utter fools. And instead of worshiping the glorious, ever-living God, they worshiped idols made to look like mere people and birds and animals and reptiles. So God abandoned them to do whatever shameful things their hearts desired. As a result, they did vile and degrading things with each other's bodies. They traded the truth about God for a lie. So they worshiped and served the things God created instead of the Creator himself, who is worthy of eternal praise! Amen. That is why God abandoned them to their shameful desires. Even the women turned against the natural way to have sex and instead indulged in sex with each other. And the men, instead of having normal sexual relations with women, burned with lust for each other. Men did shameful things with other men, and as a result of this sin, they suffered within themselves the penalty they deserved. Since they thought it foolish to acknowledge God, he abandoned them to their foolish thinking and let them do things that should never be done.* - **Romans 1:18-28(NLT)**

Doesn't this story look like the world we live in today? People who have rejected the truth of God find themselves caught in a web of sin and silliness. It's gotten so bad that the people who stand for the truth are called "bigots" and "closed-minded" while those who have accepted lies are supposedly "progressive" and "open-minded." When people reject the truth, they have no choice but to accept foolishness and when they do so, God lets them do as they please. Eventually, their sin completely takes them over and reshapes their reality. Now they think a lie is true and the truth is a lie. Sadly, since they don't want God's truth, they won't enjoy God's mercy.

> *Let not mercy and truth forsake thee: bind them about thy neck; write them*

upon the table of thine heart: - **Proverbs 3:3(KJV)**

By mercy and truth iniquity is purged: and by the fear of the Lord men depart from evil. - **Proverbs 16:6(KJV)**

Don't let mercy and truth forsake you. Hold tight to the Word of God because by it you can be cleansed and set free. Truth is a person and His name is Jesus. Can you handle The Truth? I hope so. Your access to the mercy of God depends on it.

EVERLASTING

4 GOD'S LOVE AND NAME LAST FOREVER

God's Love is Everlasting

The Lord has appeared of old to me, saying: "Yes, I have loved you with an everlasting love; Therefore, with lovingkindness I have drawn you. - **Jeremiah 31:3 (NKJV)**

The everlasting love of God is something that must be experienced to be understood. Words in the English language are limited and can only capture so much of the vastness of God's love. His love is spiritual and that's why it exists outside of the limits of time and space. It has no beginning and will never end. It fits within no geographic boundary but is as personal as can be. When you experience God's love you can't help but feel like you're God's favorite. In our finite minds, it's just impossible for God to love billions of people on the earth the same when His love for each of us is so extravagant.

Love is patient and kind. Love is not jealous or boastful or proud or rude. It does not demand its own way. It is not irritable, and it keeps no record of being wronged. It does not rejoice about injustice but rejoices whenever the truth wins out. Love never gives up, never loses faith, is always hopeful, and endures through every circumstance. Prophecy and speaking in unknown languages and special knowledge will become useless. But love will last forever! - **1 Corinthians 13:4-8(NLT)**

Many years ago, I watched a documentary about an Australian man who lived his life as a rebel until he was poisoned. Still, just before he died, God gave him an opportunity to have his sins forgiven as a result of Jesus Christ's death on the cross. His mother was a Christian and interceded on his behalf all his life. So, while he lay dying in an ambulance, God brought the words of

The Lord's Prayer to his remembrance.

After this manner therefore pray ye: Our Father which art in heaven, Hallowed be thy name. Thy kingdom come, Thy will be done in earth, as it is in heaven. Give us this day our daily bread. And forgive us our debts, as we forgive our debtors. And lead us not into temptation, but deliver us from evil: For thine is the kingdom, and the power, and the glory, for ever. Amen. For if ye forgive men their trespasses, your heavenly Father will also forgive you: But if ye forgive not men their trespasses, neither will your Father forgive your trespasses.-
Matthew 6:9-15(KJV)

He literally saw the words of the prayer appear before his eyes as though they were written in thin air by the Hand of God. When the prayer got to the part where he was supposed to ask God for forgiveness, God asked him if he would first forgive those people who wronged him. Without any knowledge of how God's Kingdom worked, he refused, and the prayer remained stuck right there until he finally obliged.

Soon after that experience with God, he arrived at the hospital and died on a bed. In a moment, he could see his physical body lying motionless as he rose from the bed in spirit form. Suddenly, the room became completely dark. He thought he was still in the hospital. Though he was able to move around the room, he could not feel the walls nor the bed. If he reached out to touch something, his hands went right through it. His physical sense of feeling was gone.

In addition, he could not feel his own body because it was no longer made of physical matter. A few moments later, he started hearing eerie sounds and could see large eyes looking at him from the darkness. He could sense evil around him and knew that he was on his way to hell. The large evil creature in the darkness told him that he deserved to be there, and he knew that was the truth.

And this is the condemnation, that light is come into the world, and men loved darkness rather than light, because their deeds were evil. - **John 3:19(KJV)**

In him was life; and the life was the light of men. - **John 1:4(KJV)**

Out of nowhere, a light shone from the sky and he was drawn into the air by the light. As he ascended, he could see the darkness disappearing beneath him like a shrinking hole. He arrived in heaven and the most beautiful Person stood before him. Interestingly, even though he spent his entire life as a sinner, his spirit immediately recognized that he was standing before Jesus.

All the light he was seeing came out of Jesus and shone from His body because He was the source of all light. At that point, the guilt of a life dominated by sinful actions overwhelmed him and he started confessing all he had ever done. Then something happened that blew my mind.

He said that out of the body of Jesus emanated love. Jesus did not say; *"I love you!"* He did not do something nice to show the man that He loved him. He didn't wrap His arms around the man in a tight hug. He just beamed Love out of His own spiritual body into the spiritual body of the man. It revealed the fascinating truth that, in the spirit realm, love was something tangible that could be projected from one person to another.

He said that the Love of God pierced through his spiritual body removing all guilt the same way the beams of light expelled all darkness. God overwhelmed a man drowning in guilt by just standing there in front of him. Jesus didn't need to say a word or do a thing to demonstrate His Love. He exuded such Love that the man's spirit understood it completely without the existence of any other manifestation.

He that loveth not knoweth not God; for God is love. - **1 John 4:8(KJV)**

I'm no "love expert" and I don't claim to have ten steps to finding *"agape'"* love or anything like that. Nevertheless, one day, I needed spiritual love. I didn't need someone to do something nice for me. I needed more than a physical hug. I didn't need somebody to tell me that I was loved. I didn't need another scripture about the Love of God. I didn't need to memorize another verse.

There was a gap in my spirit that could not be filled with the love I had grown accustomed to thinking about. I needed a love that was deeper than anything ever explained to me. I didn't want one that was accessible to my physical senses, understandable by my mind or that could only be felt in my heart. I wanted that love that my dad has; that love that would break down all my defenses just by being there.

I didn't want to know that I was loved. I knew that already and something was still missing inside of me. I needed God's Love to go past my own effort to experience it because I wasn't getting it right. I practically stumbled into a church service and sat at the back of the section where I would usually sit with a desperate heart. I remembered the story of that man and it finally made sense to me.

What if spiritual love cannot be experienced by anything outside of the spirit? Maybe, I've missed it because I was focused on the manifestation or the symptoms of love and not on the source of the love itself. The *"agape'"* love I desperately needed was demonstrated in all of those ways I could see. Yet, I didn't really care that much because I could no longer trust my senses. Here's the interesting part.

I stood up in the pew during "Praise and Worship" and asked God to release from within Himself that same spiritual love He gave to the Australian guy He saved from hell. God alone understood what I was saying. I knew that unless I had seen that documentary, I would not have understood it the way I did even with all my knowledge of the Bible.

The truth is that even though spiritual love is manifested in the ways we describe; it cannot be truly experienced outside of the spirit realm. Yes, we are overwhelmed daily by the manifestation of the Love of God that we can see, touch, feel and understand. Yet, we do not truly experience the fullness of it unless we are in the spirit.

God is a Spirit: and they that worship him must worship him in spirit and in truth. - **John 4:24(KJV)**

For a couple of minutes, after I asked God for His Love, I felt nothing. Then suddenly something happened. The guilt of all my sin began to overwhelm me and I felt as dirty as I had ever felt. I cried out to God for forgiveness and I asked Him for help. There was no room for pride or excuses because in the spirit realm I was standing face to face with God. I didn't do anything special to get there and I was in no position to claim any more rights to be there than anyone else in the room. However, at that moment the people around me became obsolete.

I poured my heart out to God and honestly told Him how helpless I felt as a Christian. My efforts to get things right were worthless and I wasn't getting anywhere with my idea of righteousness. All my knowledge and all my gifts could not fill the void in my heart for the spiritual love of God. Consequently, I had tried to sense on a physical and mental level something that transcended either realm.

I thought that once I knew the Love of God with my mind that I had ascended to the heights of Christianity. I even thought that once I felt the Love of God in my heart, I had achieved the emotional height that I saw other faithful Christians reach. I discovered then that something was missing because I felt a void where I thought there was none. I still had a struggle within myself because I was not satisfied. At that point, God had me right where He wanted me. In my time of total desperation, His Love was about to explode in my spirit, and I was ready to receive it.

With my hands raised in the air (physical submission), my mind completely focused on God (mental submission) and a heart of total surrender (emotional submission) I got what I was looking for. I didn't feel anything physically. I didn't get any words of wisdom that touched my mind. I didn't respond from my heart emotionally to something I saw happen. I just had the spiritual experience that I yearned for that could change a man like me.

I don't know exactly how it happened and I'm happy about that. All I can say is I started crying and I thanked God for His love. It overwhelmed every facet of my being and for the first time I knew that I had experienced in my spirit, the Love that before that day I could only understand, sense, or feel.

For this reason I bow my knees to the Father of our Lord Jesus Christ, from whom the whole family in heaven and earth is named, that He would grant you, according to the riches of His glory, to be strengthened with might through His Spirit in the inner man, that Christ may dwell in your hearts through faith; that you, being rooted and grounded in love, may be able to comprehend with all the saints what is the width and length and depth and height— to know the love of Christ which passes knowledge; that you may be filled with all the fullness of God. - **Ephesians 3:14-19(NKJV)**

God's Love can manifest naturally but is deeper than our natural experience. It cannot be fully described with our intelligence because it is not mental. We cannot feel all of it in our hearts because it is not emotional. We cannot sense its fullness with our five senses because it is not physical. Still, it can manifest in every area of our lives.

What we have seen, felt, heard, and known all our lives is the manifestation necessary to assure us that His love was there. It's the difference between symptoms and the issue behind the symptoms. You might feel hurt in one part of your body, but the problem is somewhere else. The symptom tells you that a problem is there, but you may still have no idea what it really is.

And hope maketh not ashamed; because the love of God is shed abroad in our hearts by the Holy Ghost which is given unto us. - **Romans 5:5(KJV)**

I've seen the symptoms of God's love all my life, but I only fully experienced Him in person that day. It took the testimony of a man who got snatched from the jaws of hell for me to finally get there. I thought that signs of God's Love were enough but even that couldn't satisfy the empty spot inside of me. I needed a spiritual encounter with the only Spiritual Love that exists. His Love doesn't need to be compared to any other love because when it is experienced on a spiritual level it stands alone.

In sum, you will never be deceived by love if you desire the only love that is sourced in the Spirit of God. Every other love is an imitation. Some may look right with your eyes. Some may sound right with your ears. Some may all feel right when experienced with your body. Some may even taste and smell right. Nevertheless, a love that you can understand may feel right but also be wrong. It all depends on the level of your understanding.

Who also declared unto us your love in the Spirit. - **Colossians 1:8(KJV)**

Many types of love can be emotionally experienced. Yet, only one love is Spiritual and that's the Love of God. You don't need to be a "love expert" to recognize the right type of love. Even after you read all the best "love" books you might still get it wrong. People have so many great ideas that they use to evaluate love and almost go crazy when they somehow get deceived. Yet, to know if you're standing face to face with the Love of God you just need to be in the spirit. If God is before you, your spirit will recognize Him with relative ease.

I personally know a few people who walk daily in that type of love. Once I stand before them, my spirit recognizes God and if I'm in sin I just want to repent. They don't have to do one thing but stand there because God is Love and the light of God beams through these people. The Love of God pierces my body and removes the stain of guilt from my heart. That's the Spiritual Love we're all looking for. You think you find it when you find the symptoms, but your journey is not over until you encounter The Source.

God's Name is Everlasting

His name shall endure forever; His name shall continue as long as the sun. And men shall be blessed in Him; All nations shall call Him blessed. - **Psalm 72:17(NKJV)**

The name of God is more than just what we call Him to identify who He is or get His attention. It's so much more. When we typically think of someone's name, we think of it as a form of identification. That's why when we meet new people, we typically ask them to identify themselves by sharing their names. People have taken great liberty in naming their children. This is especially true in Western culture where names don't mean much more beyond what I just described. When you open the Bible and explore the naming convention of the people of Israel you enter a completely different world. In that culture, names mean something of significance and through those lenses, we experience the names of God.

> *And when they had set them in the midst, they asked, "By what power or by what name have you done this?"* - **Acts 4:7(NKJV)**

The name of God refers to the power of God and here is what that means. By what power or by what name? Very interesting. The words "name" and "power" were used interchangeably. Pay close attention to that and think about the implications. The power is in the name. Unlike what I assumed for many years; this is not referring to the Greek word *"Exousia"* but *"Dynamis"*.

Exousia (Strong, The New Strong's Exhaustive Concordance of the Bible, 2003)

> *Behold, I give unto you power to tread on serpents and scorpions, and over all the power of the enemy: and nothing shall by any means hurt you.* - **Luke 10:19(KJV)**

In this context, the Bible is referring to *"the power of authority (influence) and of right (privilege), the power of rule or government (the power of him whose will and commands must be submitted to by others and obeyed)."*

Dynamis (Strong, The New Strong's Exhaustive Concordance of the Bible, 2003)

> *But ye shall receive power, after that the Holy Ghost is come upon you: and ye shall be witnesses unto me both in Jerusalem, and in all Judaea, and in Samaria, and unto the uttermost part of the earth.* - **Acts 1:8(KJV)**

In this context, the word "power" means *"inherent ability, power residing in a thing by virtue of its nature, or which a person or thing exerts and puts forth, power for performing miracles."*

These are very different dimensions of power. The former denotes authority and the latter, inherent ability. I know that the name of Jesus gives us authority but that's not the type of power mentioned in Acts 1:8. While both types of power come from the same source there is an important distinction between them. I'll give you an illustration.

A policeman has two types of power. He has *"Exousia"* which is demonstrated when he sticks out his hand to stop the flow of traffic and cars screech to a halt. Can he physically stop the cars? No! The drivers of the cars recognize his authority and choose to respect it. That authority is not his own but is given to him by the Government that controls his jurisdiction. The power is not inherent within him and is only available to him because of his position. As a man, he does not have the authority to stop traffic so the day he quits the police force he no longer has access to that type of power.

He may also have a gun which gives him *"Dynamis"*. Therefore, even if a car does not stop when he sticks out his hand, he has another option. When his authority is compromised, he could pull out his gun and fire a couple of rounds at the driver. This power is also available to any other person with a gun and has nothing to do with his position as a policeman. The difference is that he is protected by law if he chooses to use it to correctly exercise his duty.

The gun also gives any person additional *"Exousia"* (authority) because of the potential *"Dynamis"* (the ability that can be exerted). In other words, you don't need to fire a gun to have power. You just need to show it. So, the officer has power (authority) because he is a policeman. He has additional power (authority) because he has a gun. He has even more power (ability) because he can fire the gun. *"Exousia"* power is a result of his position but *"Dynamis"* power is a result of what he can do. The same goes for The Body of Christ and the name of Jesus. It does not just give us *"Exousia"* but also *"Dynamis"*.

The Power of The Name of Jesus

> *And He said to them, "Go into all the world and preach the gospel to every creature. He who believes and is baptized will be saved; but he who does not believe will be condemned. And these signs will follow those who believe: In My name they will cast out demons; they will speak with new tongues; they will take up serpents; and if they drink anything deadly, it will by no means hurt them; they will lay hands on the sick, and they will recover."* - **Mark 16:15-18(NKJV)**

In the name of Jesus, we cast out demons, speak with new tongues, survive any danger, and cause people to receive their healing. Yet, the name of Jesus is not something we are as knowledgeable of as we probably should be. It's not exactly a popular teaching topic probably because we're not always sure what to say about it. It's one of those aspects of God's Kingdom that we just accept without really understanding how it works. There's nothing wrong with that but if God has more for us, let's get it.

Many of us use the name of Jesus and understand that it's important but do we have a true revelation of its power? I remember ending my prayers as a child with *"...in Jesus name, Amen."* I had no idea why we ended our prayers like that. I just believed it was important to make prayers work. Then over the years, the light of understanding shined brighter and brighter. Now, together we will discover another dimension of this truth.

> *Now Peter and John went up together to the temple at the hour of prayer, the ninth hour. And a certain man lame from his mother's womb was carried, whom they laid daily at the gate of the temple which is called Beautiful, to ask alms from those who entered the temple; who, seeing Peter and John about to go into the temple, asked for alms. And fixing his eyes on him, with John, Peter said, "Look at us." So he gave them his attention, expecting to receive something from them. Then Peter said, "Silver and gold I do not have, but what I do have I give you: In the name of Jesus Christ of Nazareth, rise up and walk." And he took him by the right hand and lifted him up, and immediately his feet and ankle bones received strength. So he, leaping up, stood and walked and entered the temple with them—walking, leaping, and praising God. And all the people saw him walking and praising God. Then they knew that it was he who sat begging alms at the Beautiful Gate of the temple; and they were filled with wonder and amazement at what had happened to him.* -
> **Acts 3:1-10(NKJV)**

Peter and John had two dimensions of power because of the name of Jesus. They had authority and inherent ability. The name of Jesus gave their words the ability to cause healing to take place. Therefore, they just told the man to rise and walk and that's exactly what happened immediately. There was nothing else they needed to do but speak.

> *And it came to pass, on the next day, that their rulers, elders, and scribes, as well as Annas the high priest, Caiaphas, John, and Alexander, and as many as were of the family of the high priest, were gathered together at Jerusalem. And when they had set them in the midst, they asked, "By what power or by what name have you done this?" Then Peter, filled with the Holy Spirit, said to them, "Rulers of the people and elders of Israel: If we this day are judged for a good deed done to a helpless man, by what means he has been made well, let it be known to you all, and to all the people of Israel, that by the name of Jesus Christ of Nazareth, whom you crucified, whom God raised from the dead, by Him this man stands here before you whole. This is the 'stone which was rejected by you builders, which has become the chief cornerstone.' Nor is there salvation in any other, for there is no other name under heaven given among men by which*

we must be saved." Now when they saw the boldness of Peter and John, and perceived that they were uneducated and untrained men, they marveled. And they realized that they had been with Jesus. And seeing the man who had been healed standing with them, they could say nothing against it. - **Acts 4:5-14(NKJV)**

The critics just could not believe it. The name of Jesus gave these men the same ability that Jesus had when He walked the earth. By His power, they were able to bring healing with just a word. There was no denying it because the man was standing right there. The name of Jesus also gave them boldness because of the authority that came with the name. This two-dimensional power of the name of Jesus is also available to the rest of The Body of Christ. We don't just walk in authority and command respect; we also can make things happen in the name of Jesus.

Now John answered Him, saying, "Teacher, we saw someone who does not follow us casting out demons in Your name, and we forbade him because he does not follow us." But Jesus said, "Do not forbid him, for no one who works a miracle in My name can soon afterward speak evil of Me. For he who is not against us is on our side. - **Mark 9:38-40(NKJV)**

Jesus said that the power to perform miracles is contained within His name. That's serious because if we want to see miracles happen at our hands we need to know where the power comes from. A man who was not even among the disciples but understood how to use the name of Jesus was able to unlock the same power that was available to the disciples. Though Jesus did make an important distinction. The man was on their side and that's why the name of Jesus worked for him. He had authority *(Exousia)* because he was positioned on the right side. He had the ability *(Dynamis)* because he understood how to use the name of Jesus. Even so, the power of the name of Jesus cannot be abused.

Then some of the itinerant Jewish exorcists took it upon themselves to call the name of the Lord Jesus over those who had evil spirits, saying, "We exorcise you by the Jesus whom Paul preaches." Also there were seven sons of Sceva, a Jewish chief priest, who did so. And the evil spirit answered and said, "Jesus I know, and Paul I know; but who are you?" Then the man in whom the evil spirit was leaped on them, overpowered them, and prevailed against them, so that they fled out of that house naked and wounded. This became known both to all Jews and Greeks dwelling in Ephesus; and fear fell on them all, and the name of the Lord Jesus was magnified. - **Acts 19:13-17(NKJV)**

The sons of Sceva had no relationship with Jesus so they did not have His authority. Consequently, they did not have the right to use the ability that came only from the name of Jesus. That's why the evil spirit had no respect for them. They were like regular men standing up in traffic and sticking their hands out expecting cars to stop. Nobody is going to stop because these men have no authority. Even if they claim the authority of policemen, nobody cares. They better get out of the street before someone hits them.

This brings us to a very important point. The power of the name of Jesus is two-dimensional and both dimensions must be in operation at the same time. In other words, if you don't have the authority to use the name of Jesus you won't have the ability that comes from it. You can't just use His name randomly and expect results. The spirit world operates by very strict rules that both the Kingdom of God and the kingdom of darkness must honor.

In the illustration of the policeman, his position gives him the authority to use the weapon in his possession. The weapon alone has power, but his authority allows him to use it lawfully. In the natural, illegal use of a firearm is a serious crime but it is still possible. It might be illegal, but the gun will still work in the hands of someone unlicensed. The spirit realm is different in most cases. When spiritual laws are broken, power becomes inaccessible.

The name of Jesus alone has power, but the authority we have through our relationship with Him allows us to use it. Yet, it's not so black and white in all situations. On rare occasions, God still allows people to use His name without the right relationship. See Matthew 7:21-23 for a better understanding of how that could happen. Unfortunately, situations like these don't end well for the people involved.

God's Kingdom is Everlasting

And do not lead us into temptation, But deliver us from the evil one. For Yours is the kingdom and the power and the glory forever. Amen. - **Matthew 6:13 (NKJV)**

Jesus said in John 18:36 that His Kingdom is not of this world. Then Apostle Paul describes the heroes of our faith in Hebrews 11:13 as strangers and pilgrims on this earth and Apostle Peter echoed the sentiment in 1 Peter 2:11. Jesus said in Matthew 16:19-20 not to lay up for yourselves treasures on earth but in heaven. In the same way, Apostle Paul said we should set our minds on things above and not on things on the earth in Colossians 3:2. All throughout the scriptures, we are instructed to stay focused on that which is everlasting, starting first and foremost with the Kingdom of God.

For our light affliction, which is but for a moment, is working for us a far more exceeding and eternal weight of glory, while we do not look at the things which are seen, but at the things which are not seen. For the things which are seen are temporary, but the things which are not seen are eternal. - **2 Corinthians 4:17-18(NKJV)**

As we bring this chapter to a close, let's remember that the natural realm is bound by the limits of time. Everything that physically exists has a physical beginning and a physical ending. Nothing physically lasts forever. Afflictions are seasonal, weeping endures for a night and tough times have an expiration date. They exist within the natural realm so at some point in time they must end. Never let what you see distract you from what God is doing in your life because what you see with your natural eyes is temporary. Keep your inner eyes fixed on eternity. There's an eternal weight of glory awaiting you if you choose to remain faithful to the God of the unseen.

5 CHRONOLOGICAL TIME

But when [in God's plan] the proper time had fully come, God sent His Son, born of a woman, born under the [regulations of the] Law, so that He might redeem and liberate those who were under the Law, that we [who believe] might be adopted as sons [as God's children with all rights as fully grown members of a family]. - **Galatians 4:4-5(AMP)**

So all the generations from Abraham to David are fourteen; from David to the Babylonian deportation (exile), fourteen generations; and from the Babylonian deportation to the Messiah, fourteen generations. - **Matthew 1:17(AMP)**

Jesus came to earth at a very specific moment in history. Though few understood ahead of time when that would be, God executed His plan to perfection. Like Jesus said in Matthew 24:36 that no man knows the day or the hour of His second coming, neither did many people know the exact timing of His first coming. Still, some did know the season when He would be born, and some will also know the season of His return.

In Luke 2:25-38, we learn of two prophets, Simeon, and Anna, who both anticipated the birth of Jesus and were present in the temple when He was dedicated to the Lord. They didn't know the exact moment it would all take place, but they knew they would see Him with their own eyes.

In this chapter, we will consider time as *"chrónos"* (Greek) which means *"a space of time (in general)"* and represents linear, sequential, chronological time; the time that's captured by clocks and calendars. (Strong, The New Strong's Exhaustive Concordance of the Bible, 2003)

51

In the beginning God created the heavens and the earth. - **Genesis 1:1(NKJV)**

And he said, "Look, I am making known to you what shall happen in the latter time of the indignation; for at the appointed time the end shall be. - **Daniel 8:19(NKJV)**

"Chrónos" has a precise beginning and a precise end. For as long as we are on earth governed by the systems of earth, we must submit to the laws of *"chrónos"*. Certain things must happen before other things can happen. Chronological time is what it is. You can't speed up chronological time and make a minute happen any faster than 60 seconds. You can't slow chronological time down and make a minute last longer than 60 seconds. You can't gain chronological time, nor can you lose this dimension of time.

You can't control chronological time. You can only control what you do with it. As I've said previously, one of my favorite college professors said that time is our only non-renewable resource. Once it's gone, it's gone, and we can never get it back. Nothing can be done to compensate for lost time. We can only learn from our mistakes and do better with the time we have left. However, this all relates to one dimension of time; chronological time and that's the focus of this chapter.

To everything there is a season, A time for every purpose under heaven: A time to be born, And a time to die; A time to plant, And a time to pluck what is planted; A time to kill, And a time to heal; A time to break down, And a time to build up; A time to weep, And a time to laugh; A time to mourn, And a time to dance; A time to cast away stones, And a time to gather stones; A time to embrace, And a time to refrain from embracing; A time to gain, And a time to lose; A time to keep, And a time to throw away; A time to tear, And a time to sew; A time to keep silence, And a time to speak; A time to love, And a time to hate; A time of war, And a time of peace. - **Ecclesiastes 3:1-8(NKJV)**

God created chronological time and He wove it into the fabric of every created thing. Hence, within the natural realm, timing is a God-given reality that cannot be overlooked. What God has planned will only work at the time and season He planned for it. If you align your efforts with His timing you will be like a fish swimming with the water current or a bird flying with the wind current. That doesn't mean your life will be a complete breeze (pun intended) if your timing is right. You will have the power of God behind you to provide the momentum you need to be successful. It took me a while, but I eventually learned that lesson. Now I embrace God's chronological timing.

Here's some of my story.

My final year of undergraduate studies completing the Dual Degree Engineering program at Morehouse College and the Georgia Institute of Technology was very exciting but mildly disconcerting at the same time. My excitement came from knowing how close I was to the completion of a very important season of my life. Though, at the same time, I didn't know exactly what would happen next. As I did for every other important decision in my life, I prayed and discussed it with my father.

During that season, I was amid a spiritual renaissance. I experienced angelic encounters, a vision of heaven, and developed the ability to finally hear God's Voice in a meaningful way. I was also active in my local church and lived with all my heart the words of Hebrews 10:25(KJV); *"Not forsaking the assembling of ourselves together, as the manner of some is; but exhorting one another: and so much the more, as ye see the day approaching."*

As a result of everything that was going on in my life, I had a decision to make. What should I do after graduation? At that time, I felt the righteous motivation to return to Trinidad and Tobago to serve in my parent's ministry. My grandfather was a preacher. My father is a preacher. My uncle is a preacher. My brother is a preacher. It was my turn to embrace the family business. I knew that God had called me to do His work, so I assumed that the next logical step after college was to accept a full-time ministry opportunity alongside my parents.

One day, when I felt especially motivated, I called my father and shared my grand plan. Since he was the pastor of a vibrant, growing church I assumed that he would be just as excited as I was that I was coming home to preach the gospel. Why wouldn't he? His oldest son was planning to leave the secular world behind and go into ministry just like he did. He listened while I shared my heart and even though I couldn't see his face, I could feel his warm smile. After that, he taught me my first profound lesson about timing. He started by explaining the importance of adhering to God's schedule.

Until the time that his word came: the word of the Lord tried him. - **Psalm 105:19(KJV)**

God has a master schedule in heaven in which every aspect of every person's life fits. It spans from the beginning of time to the end. It also shows the correlation between the circumstances of each person's life and how they fit into His grand plan for mankind. In God's plan for my life, certain things must happen at certain times for me to be most effective. In other words, living in God's Will is not just about what I do but when I do it.

If I choose to do something that God has called me to do but I start doing it outside of God's timing I have chosen the right thing at the wrong time. Because God's plan has a precise correlation between all our lives, when any of us get out of sequence, that decision adversely affects the lives of others. It was true that God had called me to the ministry, but it was not true that He called me to go into full-time ministry directly after college. He called me to go to graduate school and pursue my career as a structural engineer first. Then, at the right time, He would call me to the fivefold ministry with the full power of His anointing on my life.

If I stepped out before finishing my education I was destined to struggle through life. In fact, my ministry struggle would last until the right time came for me to be doing it in the first place. At that point, the grace for me to do what God called me to do would be clearly seen. Erroneously, I would have probably assumed that I was supposed to go through those rough years. I may have even used that testimony as a tool for ministry, when, it would have all been my fault. If I did what God said when God said to do it, it would have been so much easier.

He has made everything beautiful in its time. Also He has put eternity in their hearts, except that no one can find out the work that God does from beginning to end. - **Ecclesiastes 3:11(NKJV)**

My wife and I frequent a Caribbean restaurant near our home in Georgia where they sell some of the best Jamaican food. Sometimes, after an early morning workout, we would buy ackee and saltfish for breakfast. Ackee is a West African fruit that became the national fruit of Jamaica and it's delicious. However, there's an interesting fact about ackee that's relevant to this study. Ackee can only be eaten and enjoyed when it's ripe. Until it's fully ripe, it doesn't just taste bad, it's poisonous. The same fruit that blesses your life with good taste can put you in a coma or even kill you if eaten before it's ripe. It doesn't matter how hungry you are, how much of a rush you are in or how desperate you are, you cannot enjoy ackee before its time.

The Lord wants to teach us a valuable Kingdom principle through the example of ackee. Many important things in life are chronological time-dependent. They cannot be rushed. They cannot be manipulated. They cannot be forced. They only happen when they're supposed to happen. It doesn't matter what you do, certain things won't happen right until the time is right. Even if you find a way to force them to happen early, they won't happen right. I can think of several real-life examples that fit perfectly into this scenario including the following.

The full-term of a human baby in the womb is targeted for nine months. If a mother wants to have natural childbirth under normal circumstances, she typically must wait until around that time for the baby to be delivered. If she simply gets tired of being pregnant after two months, she can't decide to give birth on her own schedule. Premature childbirth comes with serious health risks. A mother must understand where she is in her pregnancy and act accordingly for the sake of her child's life. On the other hand, at the end of nine months, ready or not, when a baby is ready to leave the womb, the mother typically has only one logical choice: push. In the same way, when the chronological time comes for anything ordained by God to happen, there can be no delay, it must happen.

With Chronological Time Comes Expectations

> *For though by this time you ought to be teachers [because of the time you have had to learn these truths], you actually need someone to teach you again the elementary principles of God's word [from the beginning], and you have come to be continually in need of milk, not solid food.* - **Hebrews 5:12(AMP)**

It is expected that after a certain amount of chronological time, certain things should happen. For example, if you're in church for a long time you should be able to teach others. Obviously, that's not always the case but it's a reasonable expectation. With the passage of time, you're supposed to learn a few things that you can teach someone else.

My wife, Angel and I once had a conversation with a lady at a social event who genuinely loved her church. She had been there for over eight years and considered herself to be one of the founding members. She especially loved her pastor and raved about how he skillfully wove pop culture phenomena into his Sunday sermons. Yet, in the same conversation, she admitted that she didn't know The Bible even on a basic level. Unfortunately, she didn't think anything was wrong with that.

She explained that she held an important mid-level leadership role in the church and was once asked by her pastor to share a quick, encouraging word during a Sunday service. Instead of studying the scriptures and presenting something solid, she stood up and shared from her heart a few thoughts on a cliché she assumed was from The Bible. After receiving rave reviews from other members for what she shared, the pastor pulled her aside to thank her personally. Yet, he did let her know that what she shared was not Biblical.

Again, the assumption was that after eight years in the church she would know enough to stand before the congregation and share a simple thought that was scripturally based. Unfortunately, that was an incorrect assumption.

When I was a child, I talked like a child, I thought like a child, I reasoned like a child; when I became a man, I did away with childish things. - 1 **Corinthians 13:11(AMP)**

There's an expectation that maturity increases with age. Therefore, childishness or immaturity is associated with childhood. At a very young age, human beings are supposed to make impulsive decisions that are not based on logic or deep thought. Children are expected to be disciplined by their parents to help them learn how to make better decisions, develop the right attitude toward life and grow in character. Therefore, the legal age for adulthood ranges somewhere between 18 and 21 in most Western societies and is supposed to coincide with mental and emotional maturity. Those are some of the typical expectations that come with chronological time.

Respect God's Chronological Timing

You made all the delicate, inner parts of my body and knit me together in my mother's womb. Thank you for making me so wonderfully complex! Your workmanship is marvelous—how well I know it. You watched me as I was being formed in utter seclusion, as I was woven together in the dark of the womb. You saw me before I was born. Every day of my life was recorded in your book. Every moment was laid out before a single day had passed. - **Psalm 139:13-16(NLT)**

The immeasurable complexity and precision of creation continue to baffle the most advanced scientists. From the precise orbit and rotation of the earth for the sustenance of human life to the mind-boggling electrical impulses in the human brain that translate into thoughts God has established His inventive superiority. His creative genius is beyond our understanding and His attention to detail cannot be understated. He didn't just create simple beings. He created the most complex ecosystems, then placed the most complex beings within them with the ability to replicate themselves.

This begs the question; *"If God is so detail-oriented in His approach to the physical makeup of created systems and beings, would He not be similarly detailed about time itself?"* Before you were born, God laid your life out in His book with daily entries. Even when things appear to be random, they're not. God operates by a schedule. Remember, He's the same God who created the heavens and the earth as well as every living creature living within them. He wasn't random with anything else so why would He be random with the circumstances of your life?

Imagine God has a large control room in heaven with Supervisory Control and Data Acquisition (SCADA) systems, multiple switchboards, screens, sensors, and timers. From that room, He monitors the lives of each human being, constantly evaluating them against pre-set sequences of events that He designed. The circumstances He planned for each person fits into His eternal plan for all of mankind. These circumstances also interact in predetermined ways with His plans for all other people.

> *And we know that God causes everything to work together for the good of those who love God and are called according to his purpose for them.* - **Romans 8:28(NLT)**

As we go through life and make decisions to obey or disobey God's directions He is constantly adjusting and re-adjusting the controls to ensure that everything works out the right way in the end. Due to His omniscience, He can restore what was lost during seasons of disobedience or ignorance. Not just that, He knows how to place people right back to the place they are supposed to be in His plan at any given time. He doesn't need to move us back to where we strayed from His Will, He can reconcile our past, stabilize our present and fast forward to the future where we would be, had we done everything right. This is what I refer to later in the book as redeeming our time.

6 GOD'S SET TIME

Then the Lord answered me and said: "Write the vision And make it plain on tablets, That he may run who reads it. For the vision is yet for an appointed time; But at the end it will speak, and it will not lie. Though it tarries, wait for it; Because it will surely come, It will not tarry. - **Habakkuk 2:2-3(NKJV)**

In Habakkuk 2:2-3, the Hebrew word used to represent time is *"mow`ed"* (pronounced *mo-ade'*) which means *"appointed place, time or meeting."* (Strong, The New Strong's Exhaustive Concordance of the Bible, 2003) I would further describe it as a time that's appointed, like the time set on your alarm clock. It is the moment ordained by God for something specific to happen. It's non-negotiable and cannot change. When God speaks a Word over your life or gives you a vision, He sets an appointment on the calendar that will not be altered. If you make it to the appointed place, time, or meeting, you will see the word come to pass just like He said.

Then they said to him, "Where is Sarah your wife?" So he said, "Here, in the tent." And He said, "I will certainly return to you according to the time of life, and behold, Sarah your wife shall have a son." (Sarah was listening in the tent door which was behind him.) Now Abraham and Sarah were old, well advanced in age; and Sarah had passed the age of childbearing. Therefore Sarah laughed within herself, saying, "After I have grown old, shall I have pleasure, my lord being old also?" And the Lord said to Abraham, "Why did Sarah laugh, saying, 'Shall I surely bear a child, since I am old?' Is anything too hard for the Lord? At the appointed time I will return to you, according to the time of life, and Sarah shall have a son." But Sarah denied it, saying, "I did not laugh," for she was afraid. And He said, "No, but you did laugh!" - **Genesis 18:9-15(NKJV)**

Why did Sarah laugh at the Word of The Lord? The same reason anyone of us would laugh. It was physically impossible for her to have a child at her age which we can safely assume was long after menopause. Yet, to God, it was nothing special. That's why He asked a pointed question of her that He asks of all of us who struggle to believe His promises; *"Is there anything too hard for the Lord?"* The answer is no. With complete assurance, God declared that at the appointed time He would return to see the fulfillment of His promise. Those were His words to Sarah back then and those are His words to you now.

> *And the Lord visited Sarah as He had said, and the Lord did for Sarah as He had spoken. For Sarah conceived and bore Abraham a son in his old age, at the set time of which God had spoken to him. And Abraham called the name of his son who was born to him—whom Sarah bore to him—Isaac. Then Abraham circumcised his son Isaac when he was eight days old, as God had commanded him. Now Abraham was one hundred years old when his son Isaac was born to him. And Sarah said, "God has made me laugh, and all who hear will laugh with me." She also said, "Who would have said to Abraham that Sarah would nurse children? For I have borne him a son in his old age."* - **Genesis 21:1-7 (NKJV)**

At the set time, God did exactly what He said even though it took a miracle for it to happen. While Sarah laughed with doubt when she first heard God's promise, she laughed with joy when the promise was fulfilled. This is the reality of God's set time. When God puts an appointment on your calendar for you to receive the fulfillment of a promise, He always shows up on time. However, you also need to show up to receive it regardless of how impossible it may seem. You need to believe what God says then be in the place He tells you to be at the time He tells you to be there to receive what He has for you.

Jesus Knew His Set Time

> *The next day there was a wedding celebration in the village of Cana in Galilee. Jesus' mother was there, and Jesus and his disciples were also invited to the celebration. The wine supply ran out during the festivities, so Jesus' mother told him, "They have no more wine." "Dear woman, that's not our problem," Jesus replied.* **"My time has not yet come."** *But his mother told the servants, "Do whatever he tells you." Standing nearby were six stone water jars, used for Jewish ceremonial washing. Each could hold twenty to thirty gallons. Jesus told the servants, "Fill the jars with water." When the jars had been filled, he said, "Now dip some out, and take it to the master of ceremonies." So the*

servants followed his instructions. When the master of ceremonies tasted the water that was now wine, not knowing where it had come from (though, of course, the servants knew), he called the bridegroom over. "A host always serves the best wine first," he said. "Then, when everyone has had a lot to drink, he brings out the less expensive wine. But you have kept the best until now!" This miraculous sign at Cana in Galilee was the first time Jesus revealed his glory. And his disciples believed in him. - **John 2:1-11(NLT) (Emphasis mine)**

Studying the words of Jesus is always a fascinating experience. If we were to project upon Him what we would expect Him to say in every circumstance, we would be completely off base. For instance, when His mother approached Him concerning the lack of wine at the wedding, He initially resisted. First, He said that it was not their problem and He was right about that. The people putting on the wedding should have planned better and ensured that they had an adequate supply of wine. That's logical, isn't it? Yet, that had nothing to do with the basis of His hesitation. For Him, it was all about respecting God's timing. He said, *"My time has not yet come."* That's the real reason why He did not want to get involved.

Jesus operated on a strict schedule that was defined by His Father in heaven. He had the ability to do miracles at the time of His mother's request, but He knew that the time was not right for Him to reveal His glory in public. Think about it. The scripture says in Colossians 2:9-10(NLT); *"For in Christ lives all the fullness of God in a human body. So you also are complete through your union with Christ, who is the head over every ruler and authority."* This means that all of God existed within Him as He walked the earth. Still, even though He created time, He chose to be constrained by it. His own mother didn't understand that and neither did His brothers.

*After this, Jesus traveled around Galilee. He wanted to stay out of Judea, where the Jewish leaders were plotting his death. But soon it was time for the Jewish Festival of Shelters, and Jesus' brothers said to him, "Leave here and go to Judea, where your followers can see your miracles! You can't become famous if you hide like this! If you can do such wonderful things, show yourself to the world!" For even his brothers didn't believe in him. Jesus replied, **"Now is not the right time for me to go, but you can go anytime.** The world can't hate you, but it does hate me because I accuse it of doing evil. You go on. I'm not going to this festival, because my time has not yet come." After saying these things, Jesus remained in Galilee.* - **John 7:1-9(NLT) (Emphasis mine)**

Jesus had brothers who meant well but didn't understand the importance of God's set time. To them, it made perfect sense for Jesus to go to the Jewish Festival of Shelters and showcase His power. If He was going to be seen by the world, He needed to take advantage of the opportunity before Him. In their eyes, He should have jumped at the prospect of readymade publicity. Still, Jesus stuck to God's set time. He waited thirty years before launching into public ministry, so He wasn't about to let His brothers talk Him into jumping ahead of His Father's schedule. While they thought His miracles would make Him famous, He knew God's plan was much bigger. If He did things God's way, He would change eternity and that's exactly what He did.

> *Let this mind be in you which was also in Christ Jesus, who, being in the form of God, did not consider it robbery to be equal with God, but made Himself of no reputation, taking the form of a bondservant, and coming in the likeness of men. And being found in appearance as a man, He humbled Himself and became obedient to the point of death, even the death of the cross. Therefore God also has highly exalted Him and given Him the name which is above every name, that at the name of Jesus every knee should bow, of those in heaven, and of those on earth, and of those under the earth, and that every tongue should confess that Jesus Christ is Lord, to the glory of God the Father.* - **Philippians 2:5-11(NKJV)**

While His brothers were thinking about a festival, Jesus was thinking about the cross. He didn't need to put on a show at the festival to make Himself famous. He was God in the flesh walking the earth among the same people He created with His own hands. He didn't need their approval. He knew that the cross would be the most effective tool of marketing and publicity for His ministry that the world had ever seen. When God's plan was fully executed, the world would be changed forever and people from everywhere on earth would follow Him for eternity. Therefore, it was worth the wait. Acknowledging the power of the cross, He said in John 12:32-33(NLT); *"And when I am lifted up from the earth, I will draw everyone to myself." He said this to indicate how he was going to die."* Speaking of death, Jesus knew exactly when His time would come and embraced it.

> *Now before the Passover Feast,* **Jesus knew that His hour had come [and it was time] for Him to leave this world and return to the Father.** *Having [greatly] loved His own who were in the world, He loved them [and continuously loves them with His perfect love] to the end (eternally). It was during supper, when the devil had already put [the thought of] betraying Jesus into the heart of Judas Iscariot, Simon's son, that Jesus, knowing that the Father had put everything into His hands, and that He had come from God and was [now] returning to God got up from supper, took off His [outer] robe, and taking a [servant's] towel, He tied it around His waist. Then He*

poured water into the basin and began washing the disciples' feet and wiping them with the towel which was tied around His waist. - **John 13:1-5(AMP) (Emphasis mine)**

"I am the good shepherd. The good shepherd gives His life for the sheep. But a hireling, he who is not the shepherd, one who does not own the sheep, sees the wolf coming and leaves the sheep and flees; and the wolf catches the sheep and scatters them. The hireling flees because he is a hireling and does not care about the sheep. I am the good shepherd; and I know My sheep, and am known by My own. As the Father knows Me, even so I know the Father; and I lay down My life for the sheep. - **John 10:11-15 (NKJV)**

In the same way that Jesus knew the right time to reveal Himself to the world, He knew the right time to bring His earthly ministry to a glorious end on the cross. That's one good reason why He could take the betrayal of Judas in stride. Not only did He know it was supposed to happen, He knew exactly when. In fact, at the precise moment, in John 13:27, Jesus told Judas to go ahead and do what he was planning to do quickly. Like the scriptures say in Psalm 37:23(KJV); *"The steps of a good man are ordered by the Lord: and he delighteth in his way."* The Lord orders the type of steps we take but He also orders the timing of those steps.

Contrary to what it looked like at the time; nobody took the life of Jesus. He laid His life down. In John 18:11, Jesus rebuked Peter for fighting back when the soldiers came to arrest Him. Even worse, earlier in Mark 8:33, Jesus rebuked the devil behind Peter who was trying to dissuade him from accepting God's plan for His death and resurrection.

The prophet in Isaiah 53:7 said that like a lamb being led to the slaughter He was silent. From all indications, Jesus never resisted death and would have given up His life at any moment. Yet, that was not entirely true. He knew when the time of His death would come so He didn't resist at that time but before then, nobody could touch Him. Check this out.

"Where is your father?" they asked. Jesus answered, "Since you don't know who I am, you don't know who my Father is. If you knew me, you would also know my Father." Jesus made these statements while he was teaching in the section of the Temple known as the Treasury. **But he was not arrested, because his time had not yet come.** - **John 8:19-20(NLT) (Emphasis mine)**

Some of the people who lived in Jerusalem started to ask each other, "Isn't this the man they are trying to kill? But here he is, speaking in public, and they say nothing to him. Could our leaders possibly believe that he is the Messiah? But how could he be? For we know where this man comes from. When the Messiah comes, he will simply appear; no one will know where he comes from." While Jesus was teaching in the Temple, he called out, "Yes, you know me, and you know where I come from. But I'm not here on my own. The one who sent me is true, and you don't know him. But I know him because I come from him, and he sent me to you." Then the leaders tried to arrest him; **but no one laid a hand on him, because his time had not yet come.** - **John 7:25-30(NLT) (Emphasis mine)**

Yes, Jesus humbly accepted the cross but that didn't mean He could be killed at any moment. Whether they knew it or not, every human being on the earth at the time that Jesus lived had to respect God's set time for His death. Who had the power to take the life of Jesus before His time had come? Nobody. They couldn't even arrest Him before His time had come. He was the giver of life and until He was ready to give His own life nobody could take it.

At the time of His arrest, He said to Peter in Matthew 26:52-54(NLT); *"Put away your sword," Jesus told him. "Those who use the sword will die by the sword. Don't you realize that I could ask my Father for thousands of angels to protect us, and he would send them instantly? But if I did, how would the Scriptures be fulfilled that describe what must happen now?"*

In John 7:1-9, Jesus knew His "set" time and refused to let His brothers talk Him into getting ahead of His Father's schedule. The time had not come for Him to reveal Himself to the masses so instead of going to the festival He stayed home. That's a perfect example of how we should apply our own understanding of our "set" time. If you know that your time has not come for something, don't get ahead of God. How can you be so sure? First, listen to God's Voice. If He doesn't tell you it's time to move, it's not time to move. Second, look for God's open door. He won't ask you to do something without first opening the door for you to do it. When He opens the door and tells you to walk through it, it's your "set" time. Until then, wait.

And let us not grow weary while doing good, for in due season we shall reap if we do not lose heart. - **Galatians 6:9(NKJV)**

Keep doing good. Keep praying. Keep serving. Keep obeying God. Keep worshiping. Keep walking in God's Will. Don't give up. Don't lose heart. Don't get tired. Don't be weary. Stick it out until your due season comes because those who sow and care for their crops while they develop will reap when harvest time comes around. You can't force your set time to come ahead of God's schedule so all you can do is be faithful to God long enough to see it happen during your lifetime. As the psalmist said in Psalm 27:13(NKJV); *"I would have lost heart, unless I had believed That I would see the goodness of the Lord In the land of the living."*

> *Thou shalt arise, and have mercy upon Zion: for the time to favour her, yea, the set time, is come.* - **Psalm 102:13(KJV)**

When it's your set time for God's favor, it's your set time. God set it and nobody can change the setting, not even you. Until it comes, wait for it but when it comes, embrace it. God keeps all His appointments that He makes with you so you should too.

GOD'S SET TIME

7 A TIMELINE OF EXPERIENCES

Therefore do not cast away your confidence, which has great reward. For you have need of endurance, so that after you have done the will of God, you may receive the promise: - **Hebrews 10:35-36(NKJV)**

Chronological timelines don't apply to all of God's promises. Certain promises from God aren't fulfilled based on the time on the clock or the calendar but on a timeline of obedience. When you do what God has asked you to do, He will do what He promised He will do. There are things God is waiting to do in our countries, cities, churches, families, and personal lives that will not happen until we do His Will.

When He opened the fifth seal, I saw under the altar the souls of those who had been slain for the word of God and for the testimony which they held. And they cried with a loud voice, saying, "How long, O Lord, holy and true, until You judge and avenge our blood on those who dwell on the earth?" - **Revelation 6:9-10(NKJV)**

The martyrs asked God a very specific question. How long would it take before God executes judgment on those who did them wrong? A simple answer would have been something like, "Two days, two months, two years, etc." That's typically how you answer a question that asks how long before something happens. You use chronological time. Here's the answer.

Then a white robe was given to each of them; and it was said to them that they should rest a little while longer, until both the number of their fellow servants and their brethren, who would be killed as they were, was completed. - **Revelation 6:11(NKJV)**

The martyrs asked a question about time and received a response that had nothing to do with a clock or calendar. God said, *"You want to know how long it will take for me to execute judgment? It will take as long as it takes for a pre-determined number of your fellow servants and brethren to die in the Great Tribulation."* This type of time is measured by a pre-determined sequence of events. In this case, it is the Great Tribulation. (See Revelation 7:9-17)

> *To everything there is a season, A time for every purpose under heaven: A time to be born, And a time to die; A time to plant, And a time to pluck what is planted; A time to kill, And a time to heal; A time to break down, And a time to build up; A time to weep, And a time to laugh; A time to mourn, And a time to dance; A time to cast away stones, And a time to gather stones; A time to embrace, And a time to refrain from embracing; A time to gain, And a time to lose; A time to keep, And a time to throw away; A time to tear, And a time to sew; A time to keep silence, And a time to speak; A time to love, And a time to hate; A time of war, And a time of peace.* - **Ecclesiastes 3:1-8(NKJV)**

To every purpose, there is an associated time. The converse is also true. To every time there is an associated purpose. Though time is typically measured by the clock or the calendar, it should always be associated with a purpose. In other words, if I ask, *"What time is it?"* The answer is not just 9:00 PM or 10:00 PM. Tell me the purpose. It's time to write; for promotion; to heal; to sow, etc. This fits into a pattern in scripture where in certain cases, God's schedule is based on an associated purpose rather than chronological time.

> *My times are in Your hand; Deliver me from the hand of my enemies, And from those who persecute me.* - **Psalm 31:15(NKJV)**

The Hebrew word for *"time"* used in these scriptures is *"`eth"* (pronounced *ayth*) which means, *"time (of an event), time (usual), experiences, fortunes, occurrence, occasion."* (Pierce) It's a fascinating depiction of a simple word. Yet, as you can see, it's a loaded word. Without question, two words in this definition stand out the most to me: experiences and fortunes. The Bible translators interpreted a Hebrew word that also means experiences and fortunes as the English word, time. The moment I understood that, was the moment God revealed an entirely new perspective of time to me. My experiences and fortunes are in God's hands. That's profound.

In Ecclesiastes 3, the word `eth is translated into time. Each mention of time is tied to a particular purpose or experience; birth, death, sowing, reaping, killing, healing, breaking down, building up, weeping, laughing, mourning, etc. Since there's a time for every purpose or experience under heaven, you can use those experiences to represent the time they are associated with.

Esther's Timely Intervention

Then the king's scribes were called on the thirteenth day of the first month, and a decree was written according to all that Haman commanded—to the king's satraps, to the governors who were over each province, to the officials of all people, to every province according to its script, and to every people in their language. In the name of King Ahasuerus it was written, and sealed with the king's signet ring. And the letters were sent by couriers into all the king's provinces, to destroy, to kill, and to annihilate all the Jews, both young and old, little children and women, in one day, on the thirteenth day of the twelfth month, which is the month of Adar, and to plunder their possessions. - **Esther 3:12-13(NKJV)**

Haman, the son of *Hammedatha* the *Agagite*, had a historical vendetta against the Jews. He was a descendant of King Agag of the Amalekites, whom King Saul refused to kill at the direction of the prophet Samuel as recorded in 1 Samuel 15. Not only did this oversight cost Saul his kingdom, but it also created this bad situation for the Jews generations later. Haman convinced Medo-Persian King Ahasuerus to go along with his evil plan to kill them all.

When Mordecai learned all that had happened, he tore his clothes and put on sackcloth and ashes, and went out into the midst of the city. He cried out with a loud and bitter cry. He went as far as the front of the king's gate, for no one might enter the king's gate clothed with sackcloth. And in every province where the king's command and decree arrived, there was great mourning among the Jews, with fasting, weeping, and wailing; and many lay in sackcloth and ashes. - **Esther 4:1-3(NKJV)**

At the time, Queen Esther, who was also a Jew, was married to the king. She was strategically placed in the palace by God after a sequence of unfortunate events for former Queen Vashti. Her cousin Mordecai (see Esther 2:7), who raised her as his own daughter, when he heard of Haman's plot, led the Jewish people in a time of great public mourning. Yet, while all her Jewish counterparts were crying out before God, Esther, in the comfort of the palace, was totally oblivious to what was going on.

So Esther's maids and eunuchs came and told her, and the queen was deeply distressed. Then she sent garments to clothe Mordecai and take his sackcloth away from him, but he would not accept them. Then Esther called Hathach, one of the king's eunuchs whom he had appointed to attend her, and she gave him a command concerning Mordecai, to learn what and why this was. So Hathach went out to Mordecai in the city square that was in front of the king's gate. And Mordecai told him all that had happened to him, and the sum of money that Haman had promised to pay into the king's treasuries to destroy the Jews. He also gave him a copy of the written decree for their destruction, which was given at Shushan, that he might show it to Esther and explain it to her, and that he might command her to go in to the king to make supplication to him and plead before him for her people. So Hathach returned and told Esther the words of Mordecai. - **Esther 4:4-9(NKJV)**

After first attempting to console Mordecai to no avail, Esther inquired of him, the circumstances responsible for his sorrow. He quickly brought Esther up to speed on what was going on by providing the king's eunuch with all the details. Not only that, he provided physical evidence to prove that everything he said was the truth. He then did what was expected of him as Esther's only known father, he asked her to intervene. Well, he didn't exactly ask. He commanded her to go to the king on behalf of the Jews and ask for mercy. After all, she was a Jew just like the rest of them and by God's providence was in a position of influence at that time.

Then Esther spoke to Hathach, and gave him a command for Mordecai: "All the king's servants and the people of the king's provinces know that any man or woman who goes into the inner court to the king, who has not been called, he has but one law: put all to death, except the one to whom the king holds out the golden scepter, that he may live. Yet I myself have not been called to go in to the king these thirty days." So they told Mordecai Esther's words. - **Esther 4:10-12(NKJV)**

Esther had some legitimate concerns, so she felt scared when she heard Mordecai's request. She understood the risk of approaching the king without an invitation. Even though the situation was desperate, she didn't want to lose her life by barging into the inner court. Thank God, there was one caveat: the golden scepter. If the king stuck out his golden scepter, any uninvited guest was spared death. There was a very small window of opportunity, but Esther thought it was worth noting in her message to Mordecai.

And Mordecai told them to answer Esther: "Do not think in your heart that you will escape in the king's palace any more than all the other Jews. For if you remain completely silent at this time, relief and deliverance will arise for the Jews from another place, but you and your father's house will perish. Yet who knows whether you have come to the kingdom for such a time as this?" - **Esther 4:10-12(NKJV)**

Mordecai explained to Esther how time works in God's Kingdom. It's always attached to a specific purpose. In his explanation, he repeatedly used the word `eth to denote time. It was not by chance that God had brought her to the kingdom at that time and it didn't happen because it was on a chronological schedule. He had a purpose for her to carry out at that time and that's the only reason why he allowed her to become queen.

Then Esther told them to reply to Mordecai: "Go, gather all the Jews who are present in Shushan, and fast for me; neither eat nor drink for three days, night or day. My maids and I will fast likewise. And so I will go to the king, which is against the law; and if I perish, I perish!" So Mordecai went his way and did according to all that Esther commanded him. - **Esther 4:15-17(NKJV)**

Mordecai's explanation had the desired effect. Esther understood the purpose associated with the time and accepted her God-ordained responsibility to do something about Haman's plot. She made up her mind that even if it cost her life, she was only in the position of the queen at that time to approach the king and seek mercy for the Jews. Nothing else! She didn't take it lightly and called a fast for the Lord to intervene. The plan worked and the rest is history. Her time had a purpose and her purpose had a time. What about you? What's the purpose of your time?

Joseph's Timeline of Experiences

He sent a man before them— Joseph—who was sold as a slave. They hurt his feet with fetters, He was laid in irons. Until the time that his word came to pass, The word of the Lord tested him. The king sent and released him, The ruler of the people let him go free. He made him lord of his house, And ruler of all his possessions, To bind his princes at his pleasure, And teach his elders wisdom. - **Psalm 105:17-22(NKJV)**

The word Joseph received did not manifest until he went through certain experiences. His time was not just chronological, nor was there only a set time. Whenever he finished the process, his time was done and the word concerning God's ultimate plan for his life came to pass. Sometimes, a Word from God will not come to pass until you go through certain experiences. It doesn't matter how long it takes. That specific word is on a timeline of experiences, not a chronological timeline. This means you have no choice but to embrace the process and make the most of the required experiences.

Now Israel loved Joseph more than all his children, because he was the son of his old age. Also he made him a tunic of many colors. But when his brothers

saw that their father loved him more than all his brothers, they hated him and could not speak peaceably to him. Now Joseph had a dream, and he told it to his brothers; and they hated him even more. So he said to them, "Please hear this dream which I have dreamed: There we were, binding sheaves in the field. Then behold, my sheaf arose and also stood upright; and indeed your sheaves stood all around and bowed down to my sheaf." And his brothers said to him, "Shall you indeed reign over us? Or shall you indeed have dominion over us?" So they hated him even more for his dreams and for his words. Then he dreamed still another dream and told it to his brothers, and said, "Look, I have dreamed another dream. And this time, the sun, the moon, and the eleven stars bowed down to me." So he told it to his father and his brothers; and his father rebuked him and said to him, "What is this dream that you have dreamed? Shall your mother and I and your brothers indeed come to bow down to the earth before you?" And his brothers envied him, but his father kept the matter in mind. -
Genesis 37:3-11 NKJV)

At the tender age of 17 years old, God revealed His plan for Joseph's life through two dreams. While Joseph innocently shared his dreams with his family, their negative responses must have surprised him. At first, he didn't seem to understand what they meant. Nonetheless, by sharing his dreams, he received the understanding he needed. It was his brothers who interpreted the first dream and his father who interpreted the second one. As Joseph would discover later, dream interpretation ran in the family.

From that moment, a timeline of experiences began which would culminate 22 years later with Joseph's brothers bowing before him as the 2nd most powerful man in the world. What mattered most was not the 22 years it took to get Joseph to his position in Egypt but the different circumstances he had to experience. It was due to those experiences that he ended up in the right place at the right time to save his family from famine and certain death.

Experience #1: Human Trafficking

So it came to pass, when Joseph had come to his brothers, that they stripped Joseph of his tunic, the tunic of many colors that was on him. Then they took him and cast him into a pit. And the pit was empty; there was no water in it. And they sat down to eat a meal. Then they lifted their eyes and looked, and there was a company of Ishmaelites, coming from Gilead with their camels, bearing spices, balm, and myrrh, on their way to carry them down to Egypt. So Judah said to his brothers, "What profit is there if we kill our brother and conceal his blood? Come and let us sell him to the Ishmaelites, and let not our hand be upon him, for he is our brother and our flesh." And his brothers listened. Then Midianite traders passed by; so the brothers pulled Joseph up and lifted him out of the pit, and sold him to the Ishmaelites for twenty shekels of silver. And they took Joseph to Egypt... Now the Midianites had sold him in Egypt to Potiphar, an officer of Pharaoh and captain of the guard. - **Genesis 37:23-28, 36(NKJV)**

Joseph's brothers sold him into the hands of human traffickers who were on their way to Egypt. That was step 1 in God's plan to save the Children of Israel. Even though it was a despicable act worthy of the highest level of disdain, that is what it took to get Joseph into position in Egypt over two decades before his services would be needed. Not just that, the human traffickers sold him to Potiphar who was the captain of Pharaoh's guard. This placed Joseph in the perfect position for his future role in the palace. He had to be in a position of authority in Egypt to save his own family from starvation during the worst famine they ever experienced. As an added benefit, he saved the lives of countless Egyptians as well as people from neighboring territories who came to buy food.

Experience #2: Slavery in Egypt

Now Joseph had been taken down to Egypt. And Potiphar, an officer of Pharaoh, captain of the guard, an Egyptian, bought him from the Ishmaelites who had taken him down there. The Lord was with Joseph, and he was a successful man; and he was in the house of his master the Egyptian. And his master saw that the Lord was with him and that the Lord made all he did to prosper in his hand. So Joseph found favor in his sight, and served him. Then he made him overseer of his house, and all that he had he put under his authority. So it was, from the time that he had made him overseer of his house and all that he had, that the Lord blessed the Egyptian's house for Joseph's sake; and the blessing of the Lord was on all that he had in the house and in the field. Thus he left all that he had in Joseph's hand, and he did not know what he had except for the bread which he ate. Now Joseph was handsome in form and appearance. - **Genesis 39:1-6(NKJV)**

Joseph made the most of his experience in Potiphar's house. Though he was a slave with nothing of value to his name, his relationship with The Lord caused him to be successful and prosperous. This also confirmed that even though his circumstances were unfortunate, God wanted him there. The same Lord that caused Joseph to prosper as a slave could have freed him in an instant but chose not to.

Potiphar got blessed not because of anything he did right but because God included him in the timeline of experiences for Joseph's march to the throne. As God blessed Joseph, he blessed the house he lived in and at the time, it happened to be Potiphar's house. Thus, Potiphar did what any good manager would do. He promoted Joseph to oversee everything under his control.

Experience #3: False Accusation

And it came to pass after these things that his master's wife cast longing eyes on Joseph, and she said, "Lie with me." But he refused and said to his master's wife, "Look, my master does not know what is with me in the house, and he has committed all that he has to my hand. There is no one greater in this house than I, nor has he kept back anything from me but you, because you are his wife. How then can I do this great wickedness, and sin against God?" So it was, as she spoke to Joseph day by day, that he did not heed her, to lie with her or to be with her. But it happened about this time, when Joseph went into the house to do his work, and none of the men of the house was inside, that she caught him by his garment, saying, "Lie with me." But he left his garment in her hand, and fled and ran outside… So she kept his garment with her until his master came home. Then she spoke to him with words like these, saying, "The Hebrew servant whom you brought to us came in to me to mock me; so it happened, as I lifted my voice and cried out, that he left his garment with me and fled outside." So it was, when his master heard the words which his wife spoke to him, saying, "Your servant did to me after this manner," that his anger was aroused. - **Genesis 39:7-12, 16-19(NKJV)**

When it was time for Joseph to move on from Potiphar's house God knew exactly what it would take to get him out of there. With a work ethic that was beyond reproach and knowing that Potiphar didn't have to pay Joseph for his services, it was highly unlikely that Potiphar would ever have wanted to part with his prized slave. Yet, there was one prize in Potiphar's life that was totally off-limits: his wife.

She knew that, and she was willing to abuse his trust by attempting to seduce Joseph. When it didn't work, she falsely accused Joseph of attempted rape which her gullible husband believed. Since Potiphar could not get Joseph directly to Pharaoh for the final step of God's plan, he could only last a little longer in Joseph's timeline of experiences. God used Potiphar's wife to create a legitimate exit for Joseph.

Experience #4: Prison

Then Joseph's master took him and put him into the prison, a place where the king's prisoners were confined. And he was there in the prison. But the Lord was with Joseph and showed him mercy, and He gave him favor in the sight of the keeper of the prison. And the keeper of the prison committed to Joseph's hand all the prisoners who were in the prison; whatever they did there, it was his doing. The keeper of the prison did not look into anything that was under Joseph's authority, because the Lord was with him; and whatever he did, the Lord made it prosper. – **Genesis 39:20-23(NKJV)**

Even in prison, The Lord was with Joseph. If God wanted Joseph out of prison, He would have freed him instead of joining him there. Lest we forget, God knows how to break people out of prison. In Acts 12, God sent an angel that took Peter by the hand directly out of a locked prison cell. Then in Acts 16, God did the same thing again for Paul and Silas, breaking them out of prison at midnight while they worshiped. Hence, it was God's choice for Joseph to be in prison because it was no ordinary prison.

It was the place where the king's prisoners were kept, and God was positioning Joseph for a face to face encounter with the king. For Joseph, the number of days, weeks, months, or years from his dream to its fulfillment didn't matter but the experiences he had to go through did. With each experience, God brought Joseph closer and closer to where he needed to be. Like God did in Potiphar's house, He didn't just visit Joseph in prison but stayed with him throughout the entire experience. With the presence of The Lord evident in the prison because of Joseph, there was prosperity in a place typically associated with misery.

Experience #5: Interpreting the Dreams of the King's Butler and Baker

It came to pass after these things that the butler and the baker of the king of Egypt offended their lord, the king of Egypt. And Pharaoh was angry with his two officers, the chief butler and the chief baker. So he put them in custody in the house of the captain of the guard, in the prison, the place where Joseph was confined. And the captain of the guard charged Joseph with them, and he served them; so they were in custody for a while. Then the butler and the baker of the king of Egypt, who were confined in the prison, had a dream, both of them, each man's dream in one night and each man's dream with its own interpretation. And Joseph came in to them in the morning and looked at them, and saw that they were sad. So he asked Pharaoh's officers who were with him in the custody of his lord's house, saying, "Why do you look so sad today?" And they said to him, "We each have had a dream, and there is no interpreter of it." So Joseph said to them, "Do not interpretations belong to God? Tell them to me, please." - **Genesis 40:1-8(NKJV)**

In this experience, we see clearly how God set things up for Joseph to inch closer and closer to the palace. After a timely disagreement, Pharaoh sent two of his most important servants to the same prison with Joseph. Fortunately, the keeper of the prison assigned Joseph to serve them. This put him in position to hear their dreams and interpret them. Even though Joseph asked the butler to remember him and put in a good word when he was restored to the palace from the prison, the butler did not. Yet, even that disappointment was all in God's plan. It then took two more years for Joseph to get his final experience which would lead him to a face-to-face encounter with the king.

Experience #6 – Interpreting Pharaoh's Dreams

> *Then it came to pass, at the end of two full years, that Pharaoh had a dream; and behold, he stood by the river… And the seven thin heads devoured the seven plump and full heads. So Pharaoh awoke, and indeed, it was a dream. Now it came to pass in the morning that his spirit was troubled, and he sent and called for all the magicians of Egypt and all its wise men. And Pharaoh told them his dreams, but there was no one who could interpret them for Pharaoh. Then the chief butler spoke to Pharaoh, saying: "I remember my faults this day. When Pharaoh was angry with his servants, and put me in custody in the house of the captain of the guard, both me and the chief baker, we each had a dream in one night, he and I. Each of us dreamed according to the interpretation of his own dream. Now there was a young Hebrew man with us there, a servant of the captain of the guard. And we told him, and he interpreted our dreams for us; to each man he interpreted according to his own dream. And it came to pass, just as he interpreted for us, so it happened. He restored me to my office, and he hanged him." Then Pharaoh sent and called Joseph, and they brought him quickly out of the dungeon; and he shaved, changed his clothing, and came to Pharaoh. And Pharaoh said to Joseph, "I have had a dream, and there is no one who can interpret it. But I have heard it said of you that you can understand a dream, to interpret it." So Joseph answered Pharaoh, saying, "It is not in me; God will give Pharaoh an answer of peace." -* **Genesis 41:1,7-16 (NKJV)**

God gave Pharaoh two dreams knowing full well that nobody, but Joseph would be poised to interpret them. God also had Pharaoh's butler in the right place at the right time in the palace to conveniently remember how Joseph interpreted his own dream, two years earlier. Suddenly, Joseph was summoned to the palace to meet with the King and his timeline of experiences began closing in on the manifestation of his dream. This is when everything started pointed in a much more positive direction.

Experience #7 – Promotion to the Palace

> *So the advice was good in the eyes of Pharaoh and in the eyes of all his servants.*

And Pharaoh said to his servants, "Can we find such a one as this, a man in whom is the Spirit of God?" Then Pharaoh said to Joseph, "Inasmuch as God has shown you all this, there is no one as discerning and wise as you. You shall be over my house, and all my people shall be ruled according to your word; only in regard to the throne will I be greater than you." And Pharaoh said to Joseph, "See, I have set you over all the land of Egypt." Then Pharaoh took his signet ring off his hand and put it on Joseph's hand; and he clothed him in garments of fine linen and put a gold chain around his neck. And he had him ride in the second chariot which he had; and they cried out before him, "Bow the knee!" So he set him over all the land of Egypt. Pharaoh also said to Joseph, "I am Pharaoh, and without your consent no man may lift his hand or foot in all the land of Egypt." And Pharaoh called Joseph's name Zaphnath-Paaneah. And he gave him as a wife Asenath, the daughter of Poti-Pherah priest of On. So Joseph went out over all the land of Egypt. Joseph was thirty years old when he stood before Pharaoh king of Egypt. And Joseph went out from the presence of Pharaoh, and went throughout all the land of Egypt. - **Genesis 41:37-46 NKJV)**

At 30 years old, a total of 13 years into the timeline of experiences which began with his own dreams, Joseph was promoted to 2nd in command in Egypt. If I was producing a movie about his life, this would have been a fitting end to the story. Here's the rags-to-riches story of a man who went from human trafficking victim to world leader all while remaining faithful to God and maintaining his integrity. Joseph was faithful to God, so God promoted him. What a beautiful story.

Yet, God wasn't finished. Becoming the leader of Egypt was not the destination but a means to an even greater end. Against popular opinion, Pharaoh didn't promote Joseph because he interpreted his dreams. He promoted him because he had a plan for what Egypt should do as a result of the dreams. His ability to interpret dreams got him an audience with the king but it was his ability to do something with the information that convinced the king to trust him with the kingdom.

Experience #8 – Saving the World from Starvation

Now in the seven plentiful years the ground brought forth abundantly. So he gathered up all the food of the seven years which were in the land of Egypt, and laid up the food in the cities; he laid up in every city the food of the fields which surrounded them. Joseph gathered very much grain, as the sand of the sea, until he stopped counting, for it was immeasurable… Then the seven years of plenty which were in the land of Egypt ended, and the seven years of famine began to come, as Joseph had said. The famine was in all lands, but in all the land of

Egypt there was bread. So when all the land of Egypt was famished, the people cried to Pharaoh for bread. Then Pharaoh said to all the Egyptians, "Go to Joseph; whatever he says to you, do." The famine was over all the face of the earth, and Joseph opened [l]all the storehouses and sold to the Egyptians. And the famine became severe in the land of Egypt. So all countries came to Joseph in Egypt to buy grain, because the famine was severe in all lands. – **Genesis 41:47-49, 53-57(NKJV)**

God used Joseph to save the world from starvation. As the leader of Egypt's affairs, he had the authority to execute the brilliant plan he received from God. If any of the experiences Joseph went through had not taken place, this happy ending would have been impossible. Though this story is typically shared with Joseph as the central figure, it was so much bigger. It's true that God used Joseph to execute the plan but what makes it so special is the perspective of the people that Joseph saved from starvation because of his journey. They lived to tell the story of how one man's incredible experience with God saved the world.

Experience #9 – Fulfillment: Brothers Bowing Before Joseph

When Jacob saw that there was grain in Egypt, Jacob said to his sons, "Why do you look at one another?" And he said, "Indeed I have heard that there is grain in Egypt; go down to that place and buy for us there, that we may live and not die." So Joseph's ten brothers went down to buy grain in Egypt... Now Joseph was governor over the land; and it was he who sold to all the people of the land. And Joseph's brothers came and bowed down before him with their faces to the earth. - **Genesis 42:1-3, 6(NKJV)**

Dream fulfilled! Since Joseph began leading Egypt at 30 years old and the 7 years of plenty had already passed, Joseph was already in his late 30s by the time he saw his brothers again. It may have taken over 20 years but when the timeline of experiences was complete, Joseph witnessed with his own eyes what he had only seen in his dreams as a precocious 17-year-old. With age and responsibility, came personal growth, increased maturity, and remarkable insight. So much so, that with the help of hindsight, which is 20-20, he was able to clearly articulate what happened during this timeline of experiences.

Experience #10 - Joseph Summed Up His Experiences

Then Joseph could not restrain himself before all those who stood by him, and he cried out, "Make everyone go out from me!" So no one stood with him while Joseph made himself known to his brothers. And he wept aloud, and the Egyptians and the house of Pharaoh heard it. Then Joseph said to his brothers,

"I am Joseph; does my father still live?" But his brothers could not answer him, for they were dismayed in his presence. And Joseph said to his brothers, "Please come near to me." So they came near. Then he said: "I am Joseph your brother, whom you sold into Egypt. But now, do not therefore be grieved or angry with yourselves because you sold me here; for God sent me before you to preserve life. For these two years the famine has been in the land, and there are still five years in which there will be neither plowing nor harvesting. And God sent me before you to preserve a posterity for you in the earth, and to save your lives by a great deliverance. So now it was not you who sent me here, but God; and He has made me a father to Pharaoh, and lord of all his house, and a ruler throughout all the land of Egypt. - **Genesis 45:1-8(NKJV)**

Then his brothers also went and fell down before his face, and they said, "Behold, we are your servants." Joseph said to them, "Do not be afraid, for am I in the place of God? But as for you, you meant evil against me; but God meant it for good, in order to bring it about as it is this day, to save many people alive. Now therefore, do not be afraid; I will provide for you and your little ones." And he comforted them and spoke kindly to them. – **Genesis 50:18-21(NKJV)**

God sent Joseph to Egypt two decades early to save his family and the world from famine. His brothers were not responsible. Midianite human traffickers were not responsible. Potiphar, nor his lying wife were responsible. They were all tools in the hands of God. What a fascinating story! A timeline of experiences spanning over two decades for a singular purpose; preserving the lineage of the Children of Israel while saving the world. With that understanding, let's take a second look at how the psalmist described Joseph's timeline of experiences in Psalm 105. You will see it from an entirely different perspective.

And He called for a famine upon the land [of Egypt]; He cut off every source of bread. He sent a man before them, Joseph, who was sold as a slave. His feet they hurt with shackles; He was put in chains of iron, Until the time that his word [of prophecy regarding his brothers] came true, The word of the Lord tested and refined him. The king sent and released him, The ruler of the peoples [of Egypt], and set him free. He made Joseph lord of his house And ruler of all his possessions, To imprison his princes at his will, That he might teach his elders wisdom. Israel also came into Egypt; Thus Jacob sojourned in the land of Ham. There the Lord greatly increased [the number of] His people, And made them more powerful than their enemies. - **Psalm 105:16-23(AMP)**

The psalmist saw Joseph's life through his experiences. He made the very specific connection between the famine that hit the land of Egypt and God's plan to strategically send Joseph there two decades before it happened. He then connected Joseph's experience to Israel's sojourn to Egypt. It's there that Israel became a great nation. Last, but not least, here's how God instructed Israel concerning migrating to Egypt in the famine to be in Joseph's care.

> *So Israel set out with all that he had, and came to Beersheba [where both his father and grandfather had worshiped God], and offered sacrifices to the God of his father Isaac. And God spoke to Israel in visions of the night and said, "Jacob, Jacob!" And he said, "Here I am." And He said, "I am God, the God of your father; do not be afraid to go down to Egypt, for I will make you (your descendants) a great nation there. I will go down with you to Egypt, and I will also surely bring you (your people) up again; and Joseph will put his hand on your eyes [to close them at the time of your death]."* - **Genesis 46:1-4(AMP)**

While the people of Israel entered Egypt as a small, dysfunctional family trying to escape famine, they flourished there and became the great nation we know today. This was only possible because of Joseph's experiences. God set the parameters of Joseph's journey with such precision that it all makes sense when observed through 20-20 hindsight.

Without such perspective to keep him encouraged, Joseph drew his confidence from the presence of The Lord. As we can see in the scriptures, God accompanied him from the day he received his dream to the day it was fulfilled and thereafter. This journey was not measured with chronological time but with 10 key experiences and many more in between. That's Joseph's story, what timeline of experiences are you on?

> *I will bless the Lord at all times; His praise shall continually be in my mouth.* - **Psalm 34:1(NKJV)**

The word translated as time is `eth. It doesn't matter what experiences you have, good or bad. Bless The Lord in all of them.

> *Trust in Him at all times, you people; Pour out your heart before Him; God is a refuge for us. Selah* - **Psalm 62:8(NKJV)**

The word translated as time is also `eth. In all your experiences, trust in The Lord. Pour out your heart to Him and let Him be your refuge. If your life is on a timeline of experiences, you should make the most of each experience and enjoy the ride.

And we know that all things work together for good to those who love God, to those who are the called according to His purpose. - **Romans 8:28(NKJV)**

God doesn't waste experiences, whether good or bad. He uses them to position us for bigger and better things. Through experiences, He teaches us valuable lessons we could use later in our lives. Most importantly, He wants us to help others by sharing our testimonies. So, think like God, don't waste your experiences.

A TIMELINE OF EXPERIENCES

8 CYCLICAL (REPEATED) TIME

Then Elijah said to all the people, "Come near to me." So all the people came near to him. And he repaired the altar of the Lord that was broken down. And Elijah took twelve stones, according to the number of the tribes of the sons of Jacob, to whom the word of the Lord had come, saying, "Israel shall be your name." Then with the stones he built an altar in the name of the Lord; and he made a trench around the altar large enough to hold two seahs of seed. And he put the wood in order, cut the bull in pieces, and laid it on the wood, and said, "Fill four waterpots with water, and pour it on the burnt sacrifice and on the wood." Then he said, "Do it a second time," and they did it a second time; and he said, "Do it a third time," and they did it a third time. So the water ran all around the altar; and he also filled the trench with water. - **1 Kings 18:30-35(NKJV)**

Elijah was so confident that God would respond to his sacrifice that he took additional steps to prove it. Instead of simply placing the sacrifice on the altar like they usually did, he asked the people with him to pour water on the sacrifice multiple times. Their repeated action made it practically impossible to light the wood on fire without a miracle from heaven. This was his exact intention. If you continue to read the account of what happened in 1 Kings 18, you will see how The Lord sent fire from heaven to consume the sacrifice, altar and all the water to prove Elijah's point.

The repeated soaking of the sacrifice with water during a devastating drought was a sign of Elijah's supreme confidence in God to respond to his prayer. They didn't have water to waste, so if they were going to throw it all over the sacrifice and fill up a trench with it, they better have had something of significance to show for it in the end. On top of that, Elijah had no Plan B. It was clear to him that if this plan didn't work, he would face certain death along with the people of Israel who supported him. Fortunately, the name of the Lord was glorified, so the false prophets of Baal were defeated and put to death.

Three times, Elijah led the Israelites in an unusual sacrifice of the most coveted resource at the time; water. Yes, they sacrificed a bull unto The Lord, which was valuable but amid the drought, what was more valuable to them was water. Most importantly, God responded to the extravagant sacrifice of water by ending the drought and sending rain to the earth. The Hebrew word used for *"time"*, in this case, was *"shanah"* (pronounced *shaw-naw'*) which means, *"to repeat, do again, change, alter."* (Strong, The New Strong's Exhaustive Concordance of the Bible, 2003)

> *As a dog returns to his own vomit, So a fool repeats his folly.* - **Proverbs 26:11(NKJV)**

The word *"shanah"* is translated as *"repeats"* in this verse. When you repeat bad decisions, you place your life in holding patterns. You might feel stuck in one place waiting on God to move but because you're in a holding pattern, He's waiting on you to move on from your repeated folly. On the other hand, you might feel like you're moving but instead of making progress, you keep going in circles. That was the experience of the Israelites in the wilderness.

> *"Every commandment which I command you today you must be careful to observe, that you may live and multiply, and go in and possess the land of which the Lord swore to your fathers. And you shall remember that the Lord your God led you all the way these forty years in the wilderness, to humble you and test you, to know what was in your heart, whether you would keep His commandments or not. So He humbled you, allowed you to hunger, and fed you with manna which you did not know nor did your fathers know, that He might make you know that man shall not live by bread alone; but man lives by every word that proceeds from the mouth of the Lord. Your garments did not wear out on you, nor did your foot swell these forty years. You should know in your heart that as a man chastens his son, so the Lord your God chastens you.* - **Deuteronomy 8:1-5(NKJV)**

For 40 years, the Israelites kept going around the same mountain until the generation that left Egypt died and the generation born in the wilderness was ready to finally enter the Promised Land. Thankfully, as is God's custom, the time in the wilderness was not wasted. God used it as a time of processing for His people. After their failure to enter the Promised Land in 11 days, God humbled, tested, and tried them for 40 years so that there would not be a repeat of the same mistake. Since Romans 15:4 states that historical accounts like these were written in scripture for our learning, what can we learn to avoid making the same mistakes over and over? What tools are there in scriptures like these to address our challenges with habitual sins? Let's find out together.

Why Can't I Stop Going Back to the Same Sin?

So the trouble is not with the law, for it is spiritual and good. The trouble is with me, for I am all too human, a slave to sin. I don't really understand myself, for I want to do what is right, but I don't do it. Instead, I do what I hate. But if I know that what I am doing is wrong, this shows that I agree that the law is good. So I am not the one doing wrong; it is sin living in me that does it. And I know that nothing good lives in me, that is, in my sinful nature. I want to do what is right, but I can't. I want to do what is good, but I don't. I don't want to do what is wrong, but I do it anyway. But if I do what I don't want to do, I am not really the one doing wrong; it is sin living in me that does it. I have discovered this principle of life—that when I want to do what is right, I inevitably do what is wrong. I love God's law with all my heart. But there is another power within me that is at war with my mind. This power makes me a slave to the sin that is still within me. Oh, what a miserable person I am! Who will free me from this life that is dominated by sin and death? - **Romans 7:14-24(NLT)**

The Apostle Paul, who wrote most of the New Testament by the inspiration of The Holy Ghost knew exactly what it felt like to struggle against sinful desires. In his heart he wanted to do what was right but constantly found himself doing what was wrong. It bothered him so much that he cried out to God for help in Romans 7. I don't know about you, but I thank God for this level of transparency in the scriptures. Let me quickly touch on a few highlights from that scripture.

First, The Apostle Paul wrote this after he became a Christian. He was not speaking from the position of a sinner. He spoke as one who knew what was right but was in a battle to live right daily. He knew who God had created him to be and understood the difference between his identity and the sin he struggled with. He did not let the sin define him. He looked at the sinful desire as an intruder that was in his life and he wanted it gone. That's the example he set for us. With that perspective, he then offered the solution.

Thank God! The answer is in Jesus Christ our Lord. So you see how it is: In my mind I really want to obey God's law, but because of my sinful nature I am a slave to sin. - **Romans 7:25(NLT)**

Our answer is in Jesus Christ. It is in Him that we find our freedom from the power of the sinful nature that tries to choke the life out of us. We cannot fight the desire for sin with our own will. We are not strong enough to resist our human nature. We must take on the new spiritual nature of Christ. He is our victory. Apostle Paul continued to elaborate on this in Romans 8.

So now there is no condemnation for those who belong to Christ Jesus. And because you belong to him, the power of the life-giving Spirit has freed you from the power of sin that leads to death. The law of Moses was unable to save us because of the weakness of our sinful nature. So God did what the law could not do. He sent his own Son in a body like the bodies we sinners have. And in that body God declared an end to sin's control over us by giving his Son as a sacrifice for our sins. He did this so that the just requirement of the law would be fully satisfied for us, who no longer follow our sinful nature but instead follow the Spirit. - **Romans 8:1-4(NLT)**

Don't feel condemned because of what you've been through. I know it's shameful to be a Christian who struggles in any area, but God does not condemn you. He presents the solution and sets you free. The power of the Spirit of God through Jesus has freed you from the power of sin. When He died on the cross, He ended the grip of sin over your life. So how do you receive that freedom?

You are spirit, soul, and body. Once you accept Jesus Christ as your savior, your spirit is set free. If there is any remnant of a spiritual stronghold in your life, you can go to your pastor for spiritual deliverance. He will cast out that spirit in the name of Jesus. Once you receive your spiritual deliverance there are more steps to be taken. The struggle then becomes one with your soul (mind, will, and emotions) and your body.

Your soul is where you develop habits and foster desires. It's there where the bondage to sin can still influence your life even when your spirit has been made free. You must retrain your mind to think the right way and your body to crave the right things. If you're accustomed to doing certain things, it's difficult to just stop "cold turkey" even if you know you don't have to do them anymore. Here's some advice from the scriptures. Take this from my heart to yours.

How Sin Works

Blessed is the man who endures temptation; for when he has been approved, he will receive the crown of life which the Lord has promised to those who love Him. Let no one say when he is tempted, "I am tempted by God"; for God cannot be tempted by evil, nor does He Himself tempt anyone. But each one is tempted when he is drawn away by his own desires and enticed. Then, when desire has conceived, it gives birth to sin; and sin, when it is full-grown, brings forth death. - **James 1:12-15(NKJV)**

1. Sinful desires exist in our hearts.
2. We are presented with temptation that matches those sinful desires.
3. We act out those sinful desires in response to the temptation.

Once you've completed the sinful action, you open the door for the curse of sin and death to enter your life. The temptation is not entirely something the enemy creates. It's also not entirely external to you. As the scripture says, it's the result of the enemy exploiting a desire that's already in your heart. You can only be enticed by something if you already have a desire in your heart for it. As a result, the problem with temptation is not gone if you can eliminate the external portion of the temptation. If that desire remains in your heart you can be enticed again.

I'll give you a simple illustration. People who think addiction is entirely physical, think that if you separate the person from the addiction you have set the person free. However, the addiction is not just on the outside. It's directly connected to a stronghold in the person's mind and heart. Accordingly, the person can stay clean for a long period of time but if the stronghold is not dealt with, in its entirety, the person is still in bondage. The next time the person is given free access to the object of desire, that temptation will rise again.

Therefore let him who thinks he stands take heed lest he fall. No temptation has overtaken you except such as is common to man; but God is faithful, who will not allow you to be tempted beyond what you are able, but with the temptation will also make the way of escape, that you may be able to bear it. - **1 Corinthians 10:12-13(NKJV)**

Everybody is tempted and anybody can fall. That's why we all must be careful. Whether you win or lose when you're tempted has much less to do with what you do when you're tempted and much more to do with what you did before you were tempted. You should look at temptation like you look at a test. Your preparation for the test is much more important than what you do during the test because it determines what you can do. Therefore, the devil can't take all the credit for someone giving in to temptation. He only exploits desires that are already in the person and is opportunistic enough to catch the person off-guard.

Let me say this one more time with a bit more balance. Even though it's true that what you do during the test is what really matters in the end, your options during the test are limited by your preparation for the test. If you are well prepared you have a chance to pass the test. Once you're in the test you can rely on your preparation and do exactly what you know so you can pass the test.

On the other hand, if you are not prepared for the test you fail the test before you even start. In that case, it doesn't really matter what you do during the test unless you plan to cheat. Even though both are very important, since execution depends on preparation, preparation is more important. You can't execute what you didn't prepare.

This is where the devil really traps many Christians. We do not prepare for temptation ahead of time and we think that we can just figure it out in the middle of the temptation. While that's possible it's not very probable. In the natural, it's possible to pass one exam after not studying but it's impossible to pass every exam in your life if you never study. At some point, you're going to fail. Hence the saying; *"If you fail to prepare, prepare to fail."* Preparation does not guarantee success, but a lack of preparation guarantees failure. When you're prepared and face temptation, you'll be able to decipher the way of escape that God has already laid out for you. Once you find a way out of the temptation, you'll have the option to take it.

Never overestimate yourself. Every chain is as strong as its weakest link. Even if you're strong in most areas but have one weakness, the enemy won't waste time with temptation in those strong areas. He'll focus on just your weakness. Thankfully, others have been through it before and there's a roadmap for success already published. It doesn't matter how weak you are in any area of your life, you're not too weak to win.

Fortuitously, God enables us to stop sin at any one of the three stages of sin with decreasing effectiveness:

1. Sinful Desires: The Word of God, Prayer, and Submission to the Holy Spirit
2. Temptation: Avoid Certain Situations and People
3. Sinful Action: Personal Discipline and Accountability

How Do You Prepare for Temptation?

Seeing then that we have a great High Priest who has passed through the heavens, Jesus the Son of God, let us hold fast our confession. For we do not have a High Priest who cannot sympathize with our weaknesses, but was in all points tempted as we are, yet without sin. Let us therefore come boldly to the throne of grace, that we may obtain mercy and find grace to help in time of need. - **Hebrews 4:14-16(NKJV)**

Jesus was tempted just like the rest of us and did not sin. Why? He was prepared. How did He do it and what advice did He leave so that we could follow in His footsteps? That's what the next part of this chapter is all about. We know that Jesus is God, so He's supposed to defeat temptation. Yet, when He came to earth as a man, He demonstrated the possibilities for our human existence. What He could do while walking the earth, we can do also, by the power of His Spirit. Let's follow His example of defeating temptation.

Hide The Word of God in Your Heart!

Your word I have hidden in my heart, That I might not sin against You. - **Psalm 119:11(NKJV)**

Sin is conceived in your heart so the first step to defeating sin is to attack its roots with The Word of God. As you spend time filling your heart and mind with The Word of God it changes the way you think and feel about things. The Word of God in your heart is directly proportional to your ability to resist temptation.

One of the first signs that I'm running low on God's Word in my heart is my lack of resistance to temptation. Without fail, I recognize the need to adjust my schedule to spend more time with God through His Word. Hence, Psalm 119:11 is one of the most powerful scriptures to have in your knowledge base. You cannot wait to store God's Word in your heart in order to resist a certain temptation in the middle of the temptation. You must do it before.

Pay close attention to where The Word of God needs to be for you to be able to resist sin. It needs to be in your heart. Why your heart? Your heart is where your desires are. If you put The Word of God in your mind only you will know what's right and wrong but that doesn't mean you'll want to do what's right. The Pharisees had God's Word in their minds and that did nothing for their hearts.

When The Word of God is in your heart it controls your Will and your emotions. You're never tempted by logic; you're tempted by desires. If your logic doesn't line up with your desires unless you're exceptionally disciplined, you will do what you desire against your logic. People who give in to temptations know that what they're doing is wrong but still do it anyway. The

89

Word in your head makes you aware of what's right. The Word in your heart gives you the power to do it. When you have a true love for God's Word you will open your heart and let it in. When it's in your heart you'll do what it says. Still, there's more. The power of The Word of God itself will evoke change.

> *For the word of God is alive and powerful. It is sharper than the sharpest two-edged sword, cutting between soul and spirit, between joint and marrow. It exposes our innermost thoughts and desires. Nothing in all creation is hidden from God. Everything is naked and exposed before his eyes, and he is the one to whom we are accountable.* - **Hebrews 4:12-13(NLT)**

The Word of God gets past your pretenses and exposes your true heart. It cuts you open and shows you how different you are from God's ideal. It separates the desires of your spirit from your flesh and forces you to choose. It reveals the truth about how you think and lets you be honest about your desires. That's how powerful it is.

By itself, The Word of God impacts your heart. The truth of God's Word brings light to every dark area on the inside of your heart and has the power to bring even unintentional change. Consistently feeding your soul with The Word causes genuine transformation to take place. The moment The Word enters your heart, it goes to work on changing your heart.

The Word of God is a precision instrument in God's hands that He uses to carry out His Will in your life. Even when you try to hide sin deep in your heart, a timely Word from God knows how to find and expose it. Thus, if you do nothing else, always be in an environment where you are fed with the authentic Word of God. It will do what you can't do for yourself. It will fix your heart. Yet, there's even more to the story.

> *Then Jesus was led up by the Spirit into the wilderness to be tempted by the devil. And when He had fasted forty days and forty nights, afterward He was hungry. Now when the tempter came to Him, he said, "If You are the Son of God, command that these stones become bread." But He answered and said, "It is written, 'Man shall not live by bread alone, but by every word that proceeds from the mouth of God.' " Then the devil took Him up into the holy city, set Him on the pinnacle of the temple, and said to Him, "If You are the Son of God, throw Yourself down. For it is written: 'He shall give His angels charge over you,' and, 'In their hands they shall bear you up, Lest you dash your foot against a stone.' " Jesus said to him, "It is written again, 'You shall not tempt the Lord your God.' " Again, the devil took Him up on an exceedingly high mountain, and showed Him all the kingdoms of the world and their glory. And he said to Him, "All these things I will give You if You will*

fall down and worship me." Then Jesus said to him, "Away with you, Satan! For it is written, 'You shall worship the Lord your God, and Him only you shall serve.' " Then the devil left Him, and behold, angels came and ministered to Him. - **Matthew 4:1-11(NKJV)**

How did Jesus defeat the devil when He was tempted? Most people say that He quoted scripture. Right? Wrong! The devil quoted scripture too. The scripture alone did not give Jesus the victory. If that's true, most Christians in "Word of Faith" and charismatic churches would be spiritual giants. They quote a lot of scriptures but that doesn't mean they're living right. Every time a Bible scholar falls into sin the question remains; *"Why didn't the knowledge of all those scriptures guarantee victory over sin?"* Simply put; they don't live by what they quote.

> *"Now the parable is this: The seed is the word of God. Those by the wayside are the ones who hear; then the devil comes and takes away the word out of their hearts, lest they should believe and be saved. But the ones on the rock are those who, when they hear, receive the word with joy; and these have no root, who believe for a while and in time of temptation fall away. Now the ones that fell among thorns are those who, when they have heard, go out and are choked with cares, riches, and pleasures of life, and bring no fruit to maturity. But the ones that fell on the good ground are those who, having heard the word with a noble and good heart, keep it and bear fruit with patience.* - **Luke 8:11-15(NKJV)**

Unless you're keeping The Word and bearing fruit which can be seen in your life, mindlessly repeating The Word of God alone doesn't unlock its true power. Jesus said that the people who receive The Word with joy but don't allow it to form roots and penetrate their hearts will fall away in the time of temptation.

> *But be doers of the word, and not hearers only, deceiving yourselves. For if anyone is a hearer of the word and not a doer, he is like a man observing his natural face in a mirror; for he observes himself, goes away, and immediately forgets what kind of man he was.* - **James 1:22-24(NKJV)**

When you speak The Word it only has power if you really believe it. If you believe The Word, you will let it change you. If The Word does not change you it has not taken root in your heart. Thus, you are not able to use it when faced with temptation. Jesus was a doer of The Word so when He said The Word it had power. That's how it works.

> *Because thou hast kept the word of my patience, I also will keep thee from the*

hour of temptation, which shall come upon all the world, to try them that dwell upon the earth. - **Revelation 3:10(KJV)**

If you keep God's Word, He'll keep you from the hour of temptation. That's a promise that you can hold on to with all your heart.

Watch and Pray

Keep watch and pray, so that you will not give in to temptation. For the spirit is willing, but the body is weak!" - **Matthew 26:41(NLT)**

Jesus had a vibrant prayer life and encouraged His disciples to follow His lead. Prayer prepares your heart to defeat the enemy by strengthening your spirit man. It's your spirit that desires to do what's right in God's sight. Since prayer is a spiritual action, your spirit benefits the most from prayer. It's tough to continue in sin when you're continuing in prayer. You can't have both. You always must choose one.

One sign that I haven't been spending enough time with The Lord in prayer is my lack of resistance to temptation. If I unplug from God's presence, I lose the power to fight temptation. You can try to fight temptation with your mind or train your body to respond differently to tempting circumstances, but you will eventually fail. Your flesh is too weak to resist temptation on its own.

Even if you're strong enough some of the time you won't be able to resist all the time. Your strength to live right must come from the power of the Holy Spirit. That's why an active, consistent prayer life is essential to every believer. You need to pray before you are tempted so that when you are tempted you don't fall.

In this manner, therefore, pray: Our Father in heaven, Hallowed be Your name. Your kingdom come. Your will be done On earth as it is in heaven. Give us this day our daily bread. And forgive us our debts, As we forgive our debtors. And do not lead us into temptation, But deliver us from the evil one. For Yours is the kingdom and the power and the glory forever. Amen. - **Matthew 6:9-13(NKJV)**

Have you ever wondered why Jesus said to ask God not to lead us into temptation but deliver us from evil? He didn't waste words and He told His disciples to say those words for a reason. Why? God would never lead us into temptation so why do we need to even pray that? That sounds right, doesn't it? Well, check this out. Jesus was speaking out of His personal experience.

Then was Jesus led up of the Spirit into the wilderness to be tempted of the devil. - **Matthew 4:1(KJV)**

Who led Jesus into the wilderness to be tempted of the devil? The Holy Spirit! So, if Jesus says to ask The Father not to do that to you, do exactly what Jesus says because He knows why He said it. Let's pray; *"Lord, lead us not into temptation but deliver us from evil. We know we can't make You do anything but the least we could do is ask. Those were the instructions we received from Jesus."*

The temptation is a test. If you learn something, then you're supposed to be tested so you can receive a reward and promotion. When God sees that you're ready to be tested that's exactly what He'll allow. Even if you end up in the middle of a strong temptation that you never expected, it's just a test. Your success in that test will result in your promotion.

"Blessed is the man who endures temptation; for when he has been approved, he will receive the crown of life which the Lord has promised to those who love Him." - **James 1:12(NKJV)**

Since it's inevitable, you can think of temptation as an opportunity to demonstrate your spiritual development. God also rewards those who endure temptation. Beat your strongest temptation and receive your crown.

Now unto him that is able to keep you from falling, and to present you faultless before the presence of his glory with exceeding joy, To the only wise God our Saviour, be glory and majesty, dominion and power, both now and ever. Amen. - **Jude 24-25(KJV)**

You don't have to fall. The Lord can keep you standing strong if you humble yourself and let Him. He knows the weakness of your flesh because He created you. He also knows how to strengthen those areas of weakness with His supernatural power. Submit to Him and allow Him to do what only He can do.

But you, beloved, building yourselves up on your most holy faith, praying in the Holy Spirit, keep yourselves in the love of God, looking for the mercy of our Lord Jesus Christ unto eternal life. - **Jude 20-21(NKJV)**

A person who speaks in tongues is strengthened personally, but one who speaks a word of prophecy strengthens the entire church. - **1 Corinthians 14:4(NLT)**

Jesus said to pray even though your spirit is willing, and your flesh is weak. Jude and Apostle Paul, however, provided a remedy for your weakness; pray in the spirit. Don't settle for weakness in the face of temptation when you can get stronger through prayer in the spirit. In Matthew 4:1-11, you will notice first that fasting and prayer prepared Jesus for the temptation He faced at the hands of the devil.

The enemy knew Jesus was hungry, so He first tempted Him with food. Then he tempted Jesus to prove Himself by jumping off a cliff and letting the angels save Him. Last, He offered Jesus the kingdoms of the world as an easy alternative to the Father's plan for His ascension through the cross according to Philippians 2:1-11. In each situation, Jesus responded to the temptation with the Word of God that was hidden in His heart and He defeated the enemy. His example is the one we should all follow.

Submit to The Holy Spirit

> *Therefore submit to God. Resist the devil and he will flee from you. Draw near to God and He will draw near to you. Cleanse your hands, you sinners; and purify your hearts, you double-minded.* - **James 4:7-8(NKJV)**

You must submit to God first before you can resist the devil and expect him to flee. The connection between submission to God and the authority to resist the devil is not a popular topic. Regrettably, that explains why even though many of us use the name of Jesus, plead the Blood of Jesus, pray in tongues, fast, call on The Holy Spirit and quote scripture, the devil would not leave us alone. If we cannot submit to God, we cannot expect the devil to flee.

> *I can of Myself do nothing. As I hear, I judge; and My judgment is righteous, because I do not seek My own will but the will of the Father who sent Me.* - **John 5:30(NKJV)**

Jesus did not seek His own Will but did the Will of His Heavenly Father. In that way, Jesus was totally submitted to His Father. Therefore, when He resisted the devil, He had the power of The Father behind Him. For that reason, the devil had no choice but to flee. Are you totally submitted to God? Do you seek only His Will? Do you keep His Word?

> *The Lord knoweth how to deliver the godly out of temptations, and to reserve the unjust unto the day of judgment to be punished:* - **2 Peter 2:9(KJV)**

If you're Godly, God will deliver you out of temptation. It's a promise that He is committed to keeping. Yet, none of this is possible in your own strength. Even if you commit to The Word of God and a lifestyle of prayer, the power to live right comes only from The Holy Spirit.

> *But I say, walk habitually in the [Holy] Spirit [seek Him and be responsive to His guidance], and then you will certainly not carry out the desire of the sinful nature [which responds impulsively without regard for God and His precepts]. For the sinful nature has its desire which is opposed to the Spirit, and the [desire of the] Spirit opposes the sinful nature; for these [two, the sinful nature and the Spirit] are in direct opposition to each other [continually in conflict], so that you [as believers] do not [always] do whatever [good things] you want to do.* - **Galatians 5:16-17(AMP)**

As you submit to the Holy Spirit, He will do the one thing that permanently adjusts your posture against temptation. He will curb the desires of your sinful nature. He will take the Word of God that you sow in your heart, combine it with the impact of your prayers and finish the process of transforming your inner man. He will wage war against your flesh and defeat it for good. By His strength, you will receive victory over temptation that will last a lifetime. All you need to do is habitually seek Him and be responsive to His guidance. He will take it from there.

Don't Set Yourself Up

> *Can a man take fire to his bosom, And his clothes not be burned? Can one walk on hot coals, And his feet not be seared?* - **Proverbs 6:27-28(NKJV)**

It takes a long time for your heart and mind to be purged of certain sinful desires through prayer, fasting and God's Word. Accordingly, as you go through the process, avoid situations where you're weak and are vulnerable to fall into sin. Don't set yourself up to fail.

> *Stay away from every kind of evil.* - **1 Thessalonians 5:22(NLT)**

There's no need to test whether you have overcome a sinful desire. If you have the power to avoid temptation, avoid it. What can't be stopped at the first stage of sin, can be stopped at the second. Even if you're not yet delivered from a sinful desire, without a temptation, you cannot sin.

> *Do not be deceived: "Evil company corrupts good habits."* - **1 Corinthians 15:33(NKJV)**

As you walk along the journey of holiness, the right friendships are priceless. Having the wrong people in your life can derail your efforts to avoid temptation. You can control what you do, but you can't control other people's actions. Avoid people who will draw you away from God.

Personal Discipline

> *Don't you realize that in a race everyone runs, but only one person gets the prize? So run to win! All athletes are disciplined in their training. They do it to win a prize that will fade away, but we do it for an eternal prize. So I run with purpose in every step. I am not just shadowboxing. I discipline my body like an athlete, training it to do what it should. Otherwise, I fear that after preaching to others I myself might be disqualified.* - **1 Corinthians 9:24-27(NLT)**

After you've started the process of eliminating sinful desires and avoiding tempting situations, you still need personal discipline. You can't control every environment so there is no way to avoid all temptations. You need to know how to stop yourself from responding to temptations even when your sinful desires want to fall for them. The more you do what's right, the easier it becomes to do right. The more you do what's wrong, the easier it becomes to do wrong.

> *Confess your sins to each other and pray for each other so that you may be healed. The earnest prayer of a righteous person has great power and produces wonderful results.* - **James 5:16(NLT)**

Having an accountability partner doesn't change your sinful desires, nor does it eliminate temptation but it's a good first step to take. You don't have to go through temptation alone when God has placed others around you to provide support. All Christians need at least one person to be accountable to. In this way, you can ensure that you're not the reason behind certain cycles in your life. Life is too short for you to be going around the same mountain over and over like the Children of Israel in the wilderness. When you pass the character test, you can end the cycle and move forward.

When God Repeats Himself

> *And the dream was repeated to Pharaoh twice because the thing is established by God, and God will shortly bring it to pass.* - **Genesis 41:32(NKJV)**

> *This will be the third time I am coming to you. "By the mouth of two or three witnesses every word shall be established."* - **2 Corinthians 13:1(NKJV)**

Pharaoh had the same dream from God twice. Several scriptures in the Bible say the same thing. Sometimes, when God repeats Himself, it's a good thing. In the face of difficult life decisions, you need confirmation that you're making the right choices. When God confirms a Word by repeating it, that Word is established. You can have confidence that you heard God correctly. Don't waste time, run with it. While reading this book, God will confirm many things in your life. Don't question Him, boldly follow His directions. His Word has been confirmed by the mouth of two or three witnesses. It is established.

Cyclical/ Seasonal Time

Certain things take place after regular intervals of time; the sun sets and rises in one day; spring, summer, fall, and winter repeat in one year. Many trees only bear fruit during certain times of the year. With each season comes associated expectations. They are predictable and can be maximized with proper planning.

> *"While the earth remains, Seedtime and harvest, Cold and heat, Winter and summer, And day and night Shall not cease."* - **Genesis 8:22(NKJV)**

Spring comes after winter. If you're tired of winter, you can't force spring to come any faster, you must wait for it. That's just the way it is and there's nothing you can do about it while the earth remains. You are also subject to cyclical time. When the sun rises, it's morning time and when the sun sets, it's evening time. The sun won't set in the morning or rise in the evening. That's how time works, and you're bound to it. Certain things don't happen unless the season is right for them to happen.

> *Blessed is the man Who walks not in the counsel of the ungodly, Nor stands in the path of sinners, Nor sits in the seat of the scornful; But his delight is in the law of the Lord, And in His law he meditates day and night. He shall be like a tree Planted by the rivers of water, That brings forth its fruit in its season, Whose leaf also shall not wither; And whatever he does shall prosper.*
> - **Psalm 1:1-3(NKJV)**

You can only bring forth fruit in the season designated for that fruit. A revelation of that will change your life for the better. It will help you to curb your expectations to match the season of your life. It will save you from disappointment and frustration. It will cause you to focus your energy in the right direction. There's a season to sow and a season to reap. If you sow during your planting season you can be confident that you will reap in your harvest season. Also, depending on what you sowed you can set your expectations for the appropriate harvest at the appropriate time.

There's a season to work and a season to rest. If you work during your resting season you won't make it through your working season. There's a season to start certain things and a season to end them. There's a season to go to certain places and a season to leave them forever. Since there's a season for everything, you're always in the season for something. What season are you in right now? Live like you're in that season.

9 DUE TIME

Daniel answered and said: "Blessed be the name of God forever and ever, For wisdom and might are His. And He changes the times and the seasons; He removes kings and raises up kings; He gives wisdom to the wise And knowledge to those who have understanding. He reveals deep and secret things; He knows what is in the darkness, And light dwells with Him. - **Daniel 2:20-22(NKJV)**

God is sovereign and He created all things including time. At *"kairós"* or due time, God changes times and seasons to match His heavenly agenda. He speeds things up and slows things down to favor His plans, purpose, and people. He throws the proper order of events out the window and takes over. The Greek word, *"kairós"* means, *"a fixed and definite time, the time when things are brought to crisis, the decisive epoch waited for, opportune or seasonable time, the right time."* (Strong, The New Strong's Exhaustive Concordance of the Bible, 2003)

Then Joshua spoke to the Lord on the day when the Lord handed over the Amorites to the sons of Israel, and Joshua said in the sight of Israel, "Sun, stand still at Gibeon, And moon, in the Valley of Aijalon." So the sun stood still, and the moon stopped, Until the nation [of Israel] took vengeance upon their enemies. Is it not written in the Book of Jashar? So the sun stood still in the middle of the sky and was in no hurry to go down for about a whole day. There has not been a day like that before it or after it, when the Lord listened to (heeded) the voice of a man; for the Lord was fighting for Israel. - **Joshua 10:12-14(AMP)**

What really happened that day? Did Joshua's words stop the sun from moving? One of the basic lessons we learn in the study of Classical Mechanics is that, as it relates to the earth, the sun is not moving. It's the earth that's moving. What about the moon? Did it stop moving? Did the moon's lack of movement affect the force of gravity or the tides? Do you understand the collateral impact or unintended consequences that a situation like that would have had on the earth's ecosystem? If the earth stopped rotating for several hours so that the sun remained directly above the battlefield, what happened on the other side of the earth? Did they remain in darkness?

The Bible was written by men under the inspiration of The Holy Spirit, so they communicated the truth from their perspective. From the perspective of the people watching this event in real-time and looking up to the sky, it seemed like the sun stood still. They didn't know how or why it happened, but the sun did not move. That's what they saw and that's how they passed the story down through each successive generation. It wasn't a statement of science, but the true account of a physical observation recorded in the Book of *Jashar*. Of course, with our current understanding of the Cosmos, we know that it would have been more accurate to state that the earth stood still relative to the sun. Yet, none of that matters in terms of the miraculous nature of the event. Even if the earth stood still, that would have been a scientific anomaly.

This situation defies all logic and cannot be explained by natural phenomena. On the other hand, what if there's a Kingdom explanation for this? God inserted His supernatural power to save Israel and took control of natural time. His *"kairós"* was imposed upon earth's *"chrónos"* long enough for His people to defeat their enemies. God also overrode the reality of cyclical time, stopping the earth's daily movement. It was the set time for Israel to defeat the Amorites whose wickedness against God and His children reached its fullness of time.

"Kairós" has no limitation nor schedule and is not subject to any earthly laws. It's the time that represents God's sovereignty. It's the time when God imposes the power of infinite eternity on finite time. Whenever He feels like breaking into a situation with His power, He will do so. He created time and can do whatever He pleases with it. Any time is a good time for the *"kairós"* of God and if it's good for Him, it's good for us.

Case Study: Moses and the Children of Israel

One day, after Moses had grown [into adulthood], it happened that he went to his countrymen and looked [with compassion] at their hard labors; and he saw an Egyptian beating a Hebrew, one of his countrymen. He turned to look around, and seeing no one, he killed the Egyptian and hid him in the sand. He went out the next day and saw two Hebrew men fighting with each other;

and he said to the aggressor, "Why are you striking your friend?" But the man said, "Who made you a prince and a judge over us? Do you intend to kill me as you killed the Egyptian?" Then Moses was afraid and said, "Certainly this incident is known." - **Exodus 2:11-14(AMP)**

In Exodus 2:11-14, we read the account of Moses killing an Egyptian to save a Hebrew slave. At that point, he was forty years old. He did it out of compassion for his people, but it didn't work out the way he thought it would. To Moses, it seemed like the right *"chrónos"* to do something drastic because any time was good to be free from slavery. Yet, it wasn't God's *"kairós"*. Predictably, God did not break in and help Moses free his people in response to killing the Egyptian. It wasn't the set time for freedom because we read in Genesis 15:13(AMP); *"God said to Abram, "Know for sure that your descendants will be strangers [living temporarily] in a land (Egypt) that is not theirs, where they will be enslaved and oppressed for four hundred years."*

The Hebrews had to be enslaved for four hundred years and would not be free any earlier than that. It also was not the fullness of time. Look at the response of the Hebrew man when Moses told him to stop fighting his brother. He obviously wasn't ready for the leadership of Moses, and neither was Moses. Their freedom would only happen after a process and it was a threefold process that was just getting started.

Moses had to go through a developmental process in the wilderness with God for forty years. After that, Egypt had to go through the punitive process of ten plagues. Most importantly, the Hebrews had to finish their process of learning to trust God for their salvation and freedom. Unfortunately, for most of them, they never completed their process so even though they made it out of Egypt, they didn't make it into the Promised Land. They died in the wilderness and their fullness of time never came.

"Every commandment which I command you today you must be careful to observe, that you may live and multiply, and go in and possess the land of which the Lord swore to your fathers. And you shall remember that the Lord your God led you all the way these forty years in the wilderness, to humble you and test you, to know what was in your heart, whether you would keep His commandments or not. So He humbled you, allowed you to hunger, and fed you with manna which you did not know nor did your fathers know, that He might make you know that man shall not live by bread alone; but man lives by every word that proceeds from the mouth of the Lord. - **Deuteronomy 8:1-3(NKJV)**

The *"set"* time for freedom from slavery was four hundred years from the start. The *"chrónos"* for entering the promised land was eleven days from breaking camp at Mt. Sinai. They had *"chrónos"* and God's set time on their side, but they still didn't see the promise. Why? They didn't reach the fullness of time. They didn't complete the process of mental and spiritual transformation in the wilderness after eleven days or even forty years. Hence, they never experienced God's *"kairós"* and died in the wilderness. While God was dealing with the Children of Israel as a group, He was also working on Moses as an individual.

God worked with Moses in forty-year cycles. At forty years old Moses felt sudden compassion for the Hebrew slaves and killed an Egyptian to save one of his brethren. It was not the *"set"* time for their freedom, so he was forced to run into the wilderness. There he spent another forty years before God showed up to call him back to Egypt. He returned at eighty years old and at that time, The Lord was supporting him. When Moses was done in Egypt not only did every firstborn in Egypt die, their entire army was drowned in the Red Sea and the Children of Israel were set free. Forty years after that, at the age of 120, Moses finally saw the Promised Land. Unfortunately, he couldn't enter because he didn't do so forty years earlier. He wasn't weak, sick or impaired, but he died at 120 at the end of his *"chrónos"*.

What Happens at *"Kairós"*?

> *Now after John was put in prison, Jesus came to Galilee, preaching the gospel of the kingdom of God, and saying, "The time is fulfilled, and the kingdom of God is at hand. Repent, and believe in the gospel."* - **Mark 1:14-15(NKJV)**

When Jesus launched His public ministry, He declared that it was officially *"kairós"*. He meant it was God's opportune or right time to intervene in a big way in the world's affairs. Here are just a few things that happen at *"kairós"*.

1. God Fulfills His Word
2. Heavenly Visitation
3. Restoration
4. Supernatural Harvests
5. God's Judgment

Let's now take a more detailed look at each one.

God Fulfills His Word

> *And the whole multitude of the people was praying outside at the hour of incense. Then an angel of the Lord appeared to him, standing on the right side*

of the altar of incense. And when Zacharias saw him, he was troubled, and fear fell upon him. But the angel said to him, "Do not be afraid, Zacharias, for your prayer is heard; and your wife Elizabeth will bear you a son, and you shall call his name John. And you will have joy and gladness, and many will rejoice at his birth. For he will be great in the sight of the Lord, and shall drink neither wine nor strong drink. He will also be filled with the Holy Spirit, even from his mother's womb. And he will turn many of the children of Israel to the Lord their God. He will also go before Him in the spirit and power of Elijah, 'to turn the hearts of the fathers to the children,' and the disobedient to the wisdom of the just, to make ready a people prepared for the Lord." And Zacharias said to the angel, "How shall I know this? For I am an old man, and my wife is well advanced in years." And the angel answered and said to him, "I am Gabriel, who stands in the presence of God, and was sent to speak to you and bring you these glad tidings. But behold, you will be mute and not able to speak until the day these things take place, because you did not believe my words which will be fulfilled in their own time." - **Luke 1:10-20(NKJV)**

In Luke 1, the miraculous birth of John the Baptist was recorded. After years of asking God for their first child, an angel appeared to Zacharias with a message from God about John. At first, Zacharias didn't believe and was made dumb until the eighth day when his son was to be circumcised and given a name. Elizabeth, his wife, broke tradition by calling her son John. An angel told Zacharias the same thing earlier, so when he agreed with the name, people were astonished. At that moment, he received his voice again and declared God's goodness. Gabriel told Zacharias that the miraculous birth of John the Baptist would come at *"kairós"* because that's when God's Word would be fulfilled.

But it is not that the word of God has taken no effect. For they are not all Israel who are of Israel, nor are they all children because they are the seed of Abraham; but, "In Isaac your seed shall be called." That is, those who are the children of the flesh, these are not the children of God; but the children of the promise are counted as the seed. For this is the word of promise: "At this time I will come and Sarah shall have a son." - **Romans 9:6-9(NKJV)**

The miraculous birth of Isaac also came at *"kairós"*. It's a time when miracles take place scheduled by God's prophetic Word. When God first told Abraham, that Sarah would have a son, she laughed because she could not believe it. Yet, God put a timeline of one year on the prophetic Word and promised to return at that time to verify the outcome. It was an ambitious proclamation by all standards with the added constraint of a specific timeline. Nevertheless, since it came from God it was already done. That's what due time is all about. It's an opportune time for God to move in our favor. It doesn't take place on any other schedule but God's.

Heavenly Visitation

Now as He drew near, He saw the city and wept over it, saying, "If you had known, even you, especially in this your day, the things that make for your peace! But now they are hidden from your eyes. For days will come upon you when your enemies will build an embankment around you, surround you and close you in on every side, and level you, and your children within you, to the ground; and they will not leave in you one stone upon another, because you did not know the time of your visitation." - Luke 19:41-44(NKJV)

God shows up at *"kairós"*. Yet, Israel completely missed their time of visitation. Had they known their Messiah had come, they would have experienced peace. A few years later, the Roman army literally flattened Jerusalem including their beloved temple just like Jesus said. (Chabad-Lubavitch Media Center)

After this there was a feast of the Jews, and Jesus went up to Jerusalem. Now there is in Jerusalem by the Sheep Gate a pool, which is called in Hebrew, Bethesda, having five porches. In these lay a great multitude of sick people, blind, lame, paralyzed, waiting for the moving of the water. For an angel went down at a certain time into the pool and stirred up the water; then whoever stepped in first, after the stirring of the water, was made well of whatever disease he had. Now a certain man was there who had an infirmity thirty-eight years. When Jesus saw him lying there, and knew that he already had been in that condition a long time, He said to him, "Do you want to be made well?" The sick man answered Him, "Sir, I have no man to put me into the pool when the water is stirred up; but while I am coming, another steps down before me." Jesus said to him, "Rise, take up your bed and walk." And immediately the man was made well, took up his bed, and walked. And that day was the Sabbath. - John 5:1-8(NKJV)

At *"kairós"*, angels show up to do God's bidding. God sent an angel to trouble the water in the pool of Bethesda, releasing the power of healing. Whenever you see increased angelic activity, know that it's your day of visitation. Get your miracle! Let's break it down a little more so it's easier to understand. Once a year, an angel would visit the Pool of Bethesda and stir the water. That immediately triggered a release of God's miraculous healing power. Anybody needing healing had one job. Step in the water first.

Hence, people simply hung out around the pool waiting for their opportunity. If they missed it, they had to wait a full year for their next chance. Things changed when Jesus, the Living Water, showed up at the pool. For the man with the 38-year sickness, his Day of Visitation had come on a completely different schedule. He didn't have to wait for the angel to show up anymore, God Himself was there. Again, the man had one job; believe. He demonstrated that belief when he received his healing. For the first time in his life, he took up his bed and walked.

God is troubling the water. Our day of visitation has come. We are in a season of miracles and answered prayer. These are all statements we hear from time to time in charismatic Christian church circles. They help to motivate us and increase our intensity during corporate worship. They encourage church attendance, inspire devotion, prayer, and scripture reading. They heighten our spiritual expectations. However, are they even true?

Be honest. If every time I see you, I say that it's your day of visitation or your season of miracles, at what point will you start questioning the veracity of my statements? That's why I strongly resist the urge to make frivolous declarations even if they're positive. I know it doesn't hurt to speak good things over your life, but the scripture says in Proverbs 13:12(NKJV); *"Hope deferred makes the heart sick, But when the desire comes, it is a tree of life."* You should always be encouraged to believe God, but you shouldn't get your hopes up about promises that God didn't make to you. That will make your heart sick.

Au contraire, when the day of visitation is really coming, I feel like it's my duty to shout it from the mountain tops. As 2018 was ending I knew something was going on in the spiritual atmosphere around me. God was gearing up to do some new things and my spiritual sensitivity was heightened. We're long past that now so I can confidently confirm that what I felt officially happened. The season for miracles was not on its way, it was already there. How do I know? I saw it happen before my eyes throughout 2019 and beyond.

> *But Jesus looked at them and said, "With people [as far as it depends on them] it is impossible, but with God all things are possible." -* **Matthew 19:26(AMP)**

One by one, God answered prayers for our family and church, some of which we figuratively threw at the wall hoping they would stick. Things we couldn't see possibly happening with our natural eyes happened and they continued to happen one after the other. We posted a list early in the year and crossed items off the moment God delivered. Once we realized that our Day of Visitation had begun, we added a few more items to our prayer list that would only be possible with miracles. Then, God started answering those prayers also.

The wind blows where it wishes and you hear its sound, but you do not know where it is coming from and where it is going; so it is with everyone who is born of the Spirit." - **John 3:8(AMP)**

It's impossible to predict how the Spirit of God will move unless He tells us. Without a prophetic unction, I couldn't tell you long in advance that 2019 would have been a special year but I'm telling you now. It was an unusual year. I don't fully know what went on in the spirit, but the atmosphere was stirred, and God did something amazing. Not only was the water troubled to allow one person to get a miracle, but Jesus, the Living Water, showed up, allowing anyone who believed in Him to access whatever they needed.

Jesus said to him, "[You say to Me,] 'If You can?' All things are possible for the one who believes and trusts [in Me]!" Immediately the father of the boy cried out [with a desperate, piercing cry], saying, "I do believe; help [me overcome] my unbelief." - **Mark 9:23-24(AMP)**

Do you want to see impossible things become possible in your life? Can you believe God for a miracle? If yes, submit all unbelief to God then expect Him to do what only He can do. Don't miss your hour of visitation like the Jews. They brought Jesus to tears in Luke 19:41-44. Even though He proved Himself when He rose from the dead, some still wouldn't believe. Many of them are still waiting for God to do what He has already done. Let that never be said of you. He is releasing angels. He is answering prayer. He is doing miracles. He is opening doors. He is inspiring repentance. He is moving. You have one job; believe God.

Restoration

So repent [change your inner self—your old way of thinking, regret past sins] and return [to God—seek His purpose for your life], so that your sins may be wiped away [blotted out, completely erased], so that times of refreshing may come from the presence of the Lord [restoring you like a cool wind on a hot day]; and that He may send [to you] Jesus, the Christ, who has been appointed for you, whom heaven must keep until the time for the [complete] restoration of all things about which God promised through the mouth of His holy prophets from ancient time. - **Acts 3:19-21(AMP)**

"Kairós" is the time of refreshing and restoration. God knows when we need rest. He provides times of refreshing in His presence according to Acts 3:19. He can pluck us out of storms and put us beside still waters when we need

Him to act. Sometimes, He slows our lives down for our own good. We must not complain because it's only in those seasons that our souls can be restored.

Jesus said in Matthew 11:28-29(KJV); *"Come unto me, all ye that labour and are heavy laden, and I will give you rest. Take my yoke upon you, and learn of me; for I am meek and lowly in heart: and ye shall find rest unto your souls."* In His own words, Jesus declared that He came at the time of refreshing and restoration of God's people. Fortunately, what began with the first coming of Jesus did not end with His death and resurrection but continues until His triumphant return.

> *So He came to Nazareth, where He had been brought up. And as His custom was, He went into the synagogue on the Sabbath day, and stood up to read. And He was handed the book of the prophet Isaiah. And when He had opened the book, He found the place where it was written: "The Spirit of the Lord is upon Me, Because He has anointed Me To preach the gospel to the poor; He has sent Me to heal the brokenhearted, To proclaim liberty to the captives And recovery of sight to the blind, To set at liberty those who are oppressed; To proclaim the acceptable year of the Lord." Then He closed the book, and gave it back to the attendant and sat down. And the eyes of all who were in the synagogue were fixed on Him. And He began to say to them, "Today this Scripture is fulfilled in your hearing."* - **Luke 4:16-21(NKJV)**

"Kairós" is God's RIGHT time for restoration. Jesus confirmed that it was the time to give good news to the poor, restore freedom to captives, restore sight to the blind and freedom to the oppressed. For centuries, the Jews would read from Isaiah 61 in their synagogues. They looked forward to the day when God would fulfill His promise of sending the Messiah to earth. When Jesus walked into the synagogue in Nazareth on the Sabbath day, He announced that the time they had been waiting for had finally come. Some believed Him, some didn't, but it happened anyway because it was God's right time. It was *"kairós"*.

Supernatural Harvests

> *Then Peter began to say to Him, "See, we have left all and followed You." So Jesus answered and said, "Assuredly, I say to you, there is no one who has left house or brothers or sisters or father or mother or wife or children or lands, for My sake and the gospel's, who shall not receive a hundredfold now in this time—houses and brothers and sisters and mothers and children and lands, with persecutions—and in the age to come, eternal life.* - **Mark 10:28-30(NKJV)**

In Mark 10:17-25, the rich young ruler did not just have money, but money had him. Jesus knew that and put him to the test. Jesus told him to sell everything and give the money to the poor not because that's what every rich person is supposed to do but to prove a point. What point? That it's hard to trust in riches and trust in God. When Jesus told the rich young ruler to get rid of his money, Jesus was asking the young man to trust Him.

Unfortunately, he could not. That's the same test Jesus put His twelve disciples through, in Luke 9:1-6 and His seventy disciples in Luke 10:1-12. He asked them all to leave their money behind and trust Him to provide for them. They did it and guess what happened? In Luke 22:35-36, they testified that they lacked nothing while they walked in the power of God and were free to get their money back.

When Jesus told the disciples that they would reap a hundredfold harvest in *"this time"* in Mark 10:30, the word He used was *"kairós"*. He wasn't just referring to an arbitrary time but God's opportune or due time. That was His promise to them then and that's His promise to you now. If you sacrifice anything for His sake you can be assured that at *"kairós"*, your harvest will come, and it will be incredibly huge.

> *"Behold, the days are coming," says the Lord, "When the plowman shall overtake the reaper, And the treader of grapes him who sows seed; The mountains shall drip with sweet wine, And all the hills shall flow with it.* - **Amos 9:13(NKJV)**

At *"kairós"*, you will sow and reap in record time. How? Your harvest will be on its way before you sow so (pun intended) by the time you sow, it will be right there waiting for you. This is one of the supernatural ways that God brings restoration to your life. I've experienced this in my life already. Between the years 2018 and 2019 I saw God compress the time between seedtime and harvest in many areas of my life. It's surreal to think about it in hindsight but I know firsthand that God can do this because He did it for me. My due time came and with it came miraculous harvests both in amount and promptness. It took a long period for harvest time to come but when it started, everything happened quickly.

God's Judgment

> *Another parable He put forth to them, saying: "The kingdom of heaven is like a man who sowed good seed in his field; but while men slept, his enemy came and sowed tares among the wheat and went his way. But when the grain had sprouted and produced a crop, then the tares also appeared. So the servants of*

108

the owner came and said to him, 'Sir, did you not sow good seed in your field? How then does it have tares?' He said to them, 'An enemy has done this.' The servants said to him, 'Do you want us then to go and gather them up?' But he said, 'No, lest while you gather up the tares you also uproot the wheat with them. Let both grow together until the harvest, and at the time of harvest I will say to the reapers, "First gather together the tares and bind them in bundles to burn them, but gather the wheat into my barn." - **Matthew 13:24-30(NKJV)**

Judgment, due or harvest time can be both positive and negative because at that time you reap whatever you have sown. In the parable, both the wheat and the tares are harvested at the same time. The good harvest is kept while the bad harvest is burned. When considered in the context of our lives, it's an illustration of how God's Kingdom works. Until judgment time, it may look like God is unjust for allowing the wicked to thrive alongside the righteous.

Why wouldn't He just pluck them out of the way the moment they first spring up? Why not judge wicked people at the first sign of their wickedness? In our minds, it should be easy for God to selectively judge people. It shouldn't take that much effort to kill the firstborn in Egypt and protect the firstborn in Goshen. (Exodus 12) Doesn't The Bible say that a thousand will fall at our side and ten thousand at our right hand, but it will not come near us? (Psalm 91) Then why was the master of the field in the parable so concerned about collateral damage?

God sends rain on the just and unjust (Matthew 5:45) and when judgment comes, it affects everyone. For instance, when people call for judgment on a nation, don't they understand that everyone in the nation is affected including the faithful Christians? Yes, God will protect us but that doesn't mean we won't be impacted. That's why God waits until the right time to execute His judgment. He waits for a time when He can separate the righteous from the wicked. Since judgment impacts all present, He understands the need to keep His people out of the line of fire. In Genesis 19, God sent angels to rescue Lot and his family from the destruction of Sodom and Gomorrah. He waited until they were out of town before unleashing fire and brimstone from heaven.

The nations were angry, and Your wrath has come, And the time of the dead, that they should be judged, And that You should reward Your servants the prophets and the saints, And those who fear Your name, small and great, And should destroy those who destroy the earth." - **Revelation 11:18(NKJV)**

"Kairós" is a time of celebration for God's servants, the prophets and the saints who fear His name because we will receive our rewards. At the same time, it's a period of great sorrow and dread for our enemies because they will be destroyed. It's important that we don't celebrate too early. It's the mercy of God that He waits for as many as could be saved from His punishment to be saved before He executes judgment. (2 Peter 3:9) We're still living in a season of grace and mercy but when *"Kairós"* comes, it's all over. Let's make the most of it and call anyone we can reach to join us in God's ark of safety.

Therefore judge nothing before the time, until the Lord comes, who will both bring to light the hidden things of darkness and reveal the counsels of the hearts. Then each one's praise will come from God. - **1 Corinthians 4:5 (NKJV)**

Some Christians are a bit trigger-happy with God's judgment. We want God to judge people now and if He won't do it, we will do it. For some reason, some of us want Him to show us mercy, but we don't want that same mercy extended to others. We're like Jonah who would rather see God destroy Nineveh instead of prophesying and giving them a chance to repent. Don't be anxious to judge ahead of God's schedule. Be patient and let God judge in His time. Even if it takes a while, *"kairós"* is coming. At that time, God will separate the wheat from the tares.

Vengeance is Mine, and recompense; Their foot shall slip in due time; For the day of their calamity is at hand, And the things to come hasten upon them.' - **Deuteronomy 32:35(NKJV)**

It may seem long in coming but God will judge your enemies. Vengeance is the Lord's. You don't need to keep score because The Lord is the ultimate score-keeper. He might be merciful and forget the sins of all who accept His salvation, but He remembers in minute detail the offenses of those who don't. Let your enemies do what they do and watch God take care of them at the right time.

When He had come to the other side, to the country of the Gergesenes, there met Him two demon-possessed men, coming out of the tombs, exceedingly fierce, so that no one could pass that way. And suddenly they cried out, saying, "What have we to do with You, Jesus, You Son of God? Have You come here to torment us before the time?" Now a good way off from them there was a herd of many swine feeding. So the demons begged Him, saying, "If You cast us out, permit us to go away into the herd of swine." And He said to them, "Go." So when they had come out, they went into the herd of swine. And suddenly the whole herd of swine ran violently down the steep place into the sea, and perished in the water. - Matthew 8:28-32(NKJV)

What a riveting exchange! The conversation between Jesus and the demons revealed that God's judgment was already established and understood by all in the spirit realm. The demons knew that their final judgment in hell was coming at *"kairós"* so they questioned why Jesus would torment them before then. They also knew that they didn't have a right to possess people, so when Jesus cast them out, He allowed them to possess some pigs. He could have sent them directly to hell, but they appealed to Him for mercy. Hell is obviously a place of torment for them also. As a result, they asked to remain on earth until they are forced to go there. (Matthew 12:43-45)

> *And they will fall by the edge of the sword, and be led away captive into all nations. And Jerusalem will be trampled by Gentiles until the times of the Gentiles are fulfilled.* - **Luke 21:24(NKJV)**

At the end of time, God will allow His enemies to have "free reign" for a short while. It's called the time of the Gentiles. As you read all the Biblical accounts of the events that will happen during that time, it's clear that God will choose to delay His judgment. It's not a question of if God will bring an end to all the evil in this world but when. Now is their time but *"kairós"* is God's time.

> *For the time has come for judgment to begin at the house of God; and if it begins with us first, what will be the end of those who do not obey the gospel of God?* - **1 Peter 4:17(NKJV)**

At *"kairós"*, God will also judge His own people. In fact, He will judge us first, then He'll judge our enemies. With that in mind, we must prepare for the time of judgment. In addition, if we're not prepared at this time, we should be appealing daily to God's mercy so that He would delay what He has planned. Perhaps, that would buy us some time to get ourselves ready. God is sovereign and will do whatever He wants but it doesn't hurt to ask for Him to wait a bit.

How to Prepare for *"Kairós"*

> *So Jesus said to them, "My time has not yet come; but any time is right for you. The world cannot hate you [since you are part of it], but it does hate Me because I denounce it and testify that its deeds are evil. Go up to the feast yourselves. I am not going up to this feast because My time has not yet fully come."* - **John 7:6-8(AMP)**

Jesus waited until it was God's opportune time to launch into public ministry. That didn't happen until after His baptism by John the Baptist at the Jordan River (Matthew 3:13-17). He was willing to endure thirty years of relative obscurity just so that He would not get ahead of His Father's heavenly schedule. In hindsight, it seems like an easy feat but when you think about it from His perspective you'll realize how challenging it was.

As you read Luke 12:41-50, you will receive insight into the wisdom of Jesus as a twelve-year-old boy. He went to the temple in Jerusalem on His own and engaged the Hebrew scholars in deep conversation. When challenged by His mother, He made it clear that He was about His Father's business. This demonstrated His supernatural wisdom and strong sense of purpose from a very young age. It's not like He didn't know His identity nor was He unsure of His spiritual authority at that age. He just understood that He needed to wait until the time was right for Him to step out in a big way.

How was He able to contain Himself for another eighteen years before revealing His identity to the world? The writer of Hebrews 4:15 said that Jesus understands our weaknesses because He faced the same temptations that we do. Hence, we must all understand that it was also a struggle for Jesus. He had to tamp down His emotions and keep His ego in check while waiting on His turn for glory. Like Jesus and all who came after Him, you also must wait for your time. Since that's easier said than done, what should you do until then?

1. **Repent**
2. **Watch and Pray**
3. **Keep Doing Well**
4. **Stay Humble**
5. **Stay Faithful**

Repent

> *Now after John [the Baptist] was arrested and taken into custody, Jesus went to Galilee, preaching the good news of [the kingdom of] God, and saying, "The [appointed period of] time is fulfilled, and the kingdom of God is at hand; repent [change your inner self—your old way of thinking, regret past sins, live your life in a way that proves repentance; seek God's purpose for your life] and believe [with a deep, abiding trust] in the good news [regarding salvation]." -* **Mark 1:14-15(AMP)**

As you await your time of visitation from The Lord, change your mindset.

Live like you know God is about to show up in your life; live with purpose. When used in a Biblical context the word "repent" should not be confused with the word "apologize". While an apology is simply something that's said, in this context, repentance is a complete change of heart, renewal of the mind, rejection of what was previously accepted, lifestyle change and a new sense of God-given purpose.

For me, that understanding has been a big help. Apart from growing up in a family of prominent ministers, I've received a myriad of prophetic words from both people and angels concerning my destiny. I know where my life will end up, but God did not reveal to me all the details of the journey. I must trust Him for every step. For instance, I've had a complete change of heart pertaining to the ministry. I'm no longer driven by numbers or the response of people to anything I do for The Lord. Until my time comes to be pushed to the front, I've learned to be satisfied with my portion. If I'm doing something for The Lord, His response alone should be my motivation.

After turning my back on my previous mindset, God gave me a renewed sense of purpose and fresh energy to run this race. That's exactly what He wants to do for you if you would choose to repent. It doesn't mean you've done anything wrong. It simply means that you're ready to do something new and you're choosing to think differently. Nobody wins when a child of God gets ahead of God's schedule. It didn't work for Moses and it won't work for you. If you have a Word from God for your life, your time is coming. Repent and do what you're supposed to do while you wait for it.

Watch and Pray

> *Take heed, watch and pray; for you do not know when the time is.* - **Mark 13:33(NKJV)**

> *Be anxious for nothing, but in everything by prayer and supplication, with thanksgiving, let your requests be made known to God; and the peace of God, which surpasses all understanding, will guard your hearts and minds through Christ Jesus.* - **Philippians 4:6-7(NKJV)**

Pray with your eyes open while you wait for your due season. Since you have no idea when God will deliver on His promises, don't just pray, watch and pray. Look around at what God is doing and keep the lines of communication accessible. At any moment, He could open the window of opportunity for you to make your next move. Jesus had a lifestyle of prayer and the effects of it could be seen in every area of His life. (Matthew 26:36, Luke 9:18&28, John 17, etc.) It gave Him confidence, He walked in peace and most importantly,

He understood the times and seasons He lived in. Wouldn't it be amazing to live like that today?

The antidote to anxiety in Philippians 4:6-7 is prayer with thanksgiving. People who are always in God's face, placing their needs at His altar and giving Him thanks for what He's already done, experience God's supernatural peace. He keeps their hearts secure along their journey to destiny. They never feel forsaken nor abandoned by God. They know He's right there with them because they talk to Him all the time. While you wait on The Lord to fulfill His promises, instead of becoming anxious about when it all will take place, sit before Him, and get to know Him better.

Prayer doesn't just change your situation; it changes your perspective on your situation. When a promise from God seems like it's taking forever, prayer helps you to endure until the end. As your relationship with God grows stronger you will find joy just in being with Him. His presence will become everything to you. As you seek His Kingdom and righteousness first, all the things you pray about will be added unto you. (Matthew 6:33)

Keep Doing Well

And let us not grow weary while doing good, for in due season we shall reap if we do not lose heart. - **Galatians 6:9(NKJV)**

You have no idea when your due season will come but if God says it, you know it's coming. While you wait, don't grow weary while doing what's good in His sight. In Luke 8:11, Jesus said that The Word of God is seed. After it's sown in your heart, you should expect a period of germination and growth before it fully develops into a tree that bears fruit. Furthermore, the length of that period depends on the type of seed. While some seeds grow quickly in a matter of weeks or months, others take several years before there's even a sign of fruit. Like any good farmer, who would cultivate crops until they are sufficiently fruitful, a good Christian should cultivate the Word of God until it comes to pass. One way to do so is through a lifestyle of doing good.

I don't know what God has promised you so I can't say exactly what you should be doing in your case. What I do know is that there is much good to be done in service to God right where you are and that's what He expects. For instance, I received a prophetic word that The Body Church would be the fastest growing church in Atlanta a few years ago. At the time that I'm writing this, it hasn't happened yet. My responsibility is to keep showing up to the church each week and keep doing what God called me to do regardless of how many people are in the building. I can't grow weary nor can I lose heart. I must cultivate the seed of The Word of God until it's due for manifestation. What about you? How can you keep doing good until your due season? If you don't lose heart, you will reap when your due time comes.

Stay Humble

Therefore humble yourselves under the mighty hand of God, that He may exalt you in due time, casting all your care upon Him, for He cares for you. - **1 Peter 5:6-7(NKJV)**

Let this mind be in you which was also in Christ Jesus, who, being in the form of God, did not consider it robbery to be equal with God, but made Himself of no reputation, taking the form of a bondservant, and coming in the likeness of men. And being found in appearance as a man, He humbled Himself and became obedient to the point of death, even the death of the cross. Therefore God also has highly exalted Him and given Him the name which is above every name, that at the name of Jesus every knee should bow, of those in heaven, and of those on earth, and of those under the earth, and that every tongue should confess that Jesus Christ is Lord, to the glory of God the Father. - **Philippians 2:5-11(NKJV)**

Because you have a Word from The Lord doesn't mean you can be prideful. Stay humble until your due time comes. Jesus knew that He was the Son of God but demonstrated meekness throughout His life on earth. From His birth in a manger to His death on the cross, He humbled Himself and walked in full obedience to His Father. He paid the ultimate price and earned the right to have the most prominent name that will ever exist. That's the example God wants you to follow. Even when you feel like God is taking too long to act on your behalf, never give in to the temptation to exalt yourself before God exalts you.

Humility is a master key to supernatural exaltation. While it may appear to the natural eye that humility and exaltation are contradictory, in the spirit realm they are complementary. God wants you to bring yourself low so that He can lift you up. When that happens, not only does He get the glory, but you get the benefit of being lifted without having to do it in your own strength. Depending on your personal situation, trying to make things happen on your own could be overwhelming. It may sound impressive to be a self-made success but it's so much better to be God-made. When God does something, He does it right and He defends it with all the power of heaven. Let the mind of Christ be in you so that you can experience the type of exaltation that only comes from God.

Stay Faithful

Remember, dear brothers and sisters, that few of you were wise in the world's eyes or powerful or wealthy when God called you. Instead, God chose things the world considers foolish in order to shame those who think they are wise. And he chose things that are powerless to shame those who are powerful. God chose things despised by the world, things counted as nothing at all, and used them to bring to nothing what the world considers important. As a result, no one can ever boast in the presence of God. God has united you with Christ Jesus. For our benefit God made him to be wisdom itself. Christ made us right with God; he made us pure and holy, and he freed us from sin. Therefore, as the Scriptures say, "If you want to boast, boast only about the Lord." - **1 Corinthians 1:26-31(NLT)**

The smallest family will become a thousand people, and the tiniest group will become a mighty nation. At the right time, I, the Lord, will make it happen." **- Isaiah 60:22(NLT)**

Several years ago I remember walking into a Chinese "all-you-can-eat" buffet with my wife Angel. I was hungry and excited to eat large, unhealthy portions of cheap, tasty food. As we were being seated by the hostess, I noticed a local, well-known pastor that I recognized from Christian television having lunch on a table close by. Not wanting to waste a good opportunity, I took Angel with me to say hello. I told him how much I appreciated his ministry and let him know that we know him from television. He then asked me who I was. I told him that I was nobody; just a guy who saw him on television.

Being the pastor of a very small church I felt insignificant. I didn't think I even needed to mention the church to this man because it didn't matter. His response took me by surprise, but I knew it was God speaking through him. He looked me in my eyes and said, *"Nobody is a nobody. When it's your time, it's your time."* Believe me, that simple statement sent chills down my spine because The Holy Ghost knew that I needed to hear that. I walked away and that was the end of our conversation. For the rest of the day and perhaps a few more days thereafter, I couldn't stop thinking about those words.

When it's your time, it's your time. My God, that still ministers to my spirit every time I even think of it. At the right time, God will transform the smallest, tiniest, most insignificant person into a mighty voice for His Kingdom. He chooses regular people to do great things. Apostle Paul was careful to say in 1 Corinthians 1:26 that not many of them were wise, wealthy, or powerful in the world's eyes when God called them. He never said that they didn't become wise, wealthy of powerful after God called them. They may have been relative unknowns when they were called by God but that doesn't mean they stayed that way.

God handpicks people who are despised by the world and counted out just to prove that the world's standards of value are nothing in comparison to His. Why would that be God's approach? He wants to get all the glory. He knows how people think so he ensures that no human being can take the credit for something only He could do. He likes flipping the script on people and upending our natural expectations. He is sovereign and we need to accept that He will do what He wants to do whether we agree with Him or not.

Nevertheless, what is one of the most important qualities God looks for in the simple people He selects for His service? What does He expect to see in us as we carry out our calling on the earth? He wants faithfulness.

> *Then He said, "Hear now My words: If there is a prophet among you, I, the Lord, make Myself known to him in a vision; I speak to him in a dream. Not so with My servant Moses; He is faithful in all My house. I speak with him face to face, Even plainly, and not in dark sayings; And he sees the form of the Lord. Why then were you not afraid To speak against My servant Moses?"* - **Numbers 12:6-8(NKJV)**

Moses was the most faithful person in all of Israel, so he had an unusual relationship with God. While God would speak to prophets in visions, dreams, and parables God spoke directly and clearly to Moses. Furthermore, God did not just speak to him on the inside of his heart, God spoke to him face to face. That's something no other human in history but Jesus or perhaps Adam and Eve could have ever claimed. It's true that Moses was flawed and needed a lot of work when God called him but even God could not deny his faithfulness.

> *"Who then is a faithful and wise servant, whom his master made ruler over his household, to give them food in due season?* - **Matthew 24:45(NKJV)**

> *He who is faithful in what is least is faithful also in much; and he who is unjust in what is least is unjust also in much. Therefore if you have not been faithful in the unrighteous mammon, who will commit to your trust the true riches? And if you have not been faithful in what is another man's, who will give you what is your own?* - **Luke 16:10-12(NKJV)**

God may not care much about your prominence, wealth, or reputation when He calls you, but He does care about your faithfulness. He chooses faithful people to make rulers over His household. He takes those who are faithful over a little and significantly increases their portion. Until your due time comes, remain faithful and committed to what God has placed in your charge. It might be a small family, business, church, ministry, non-profit, etc. in the world's eyes but in God's eyes, it's your breeding ground for faithfulness.

10 UNDERSTANDING GOD'S TIMING

"For My thoughts are not your thoughts, Nor are your ways My ways," says the Lord. "For as the heavens are higher than the earth, So are My ways higher than your ways, And My thoughts than your thoughts. - **Isaiah 55:8-9(NKJV)**

God is omniscient and we are not, so He made it clear in Isaiah 55:8-9 that His thoughts and ways are much higher than our own. If we attempt to explain every decision God makes, every action He takes and His reasoning behind them all, our minds would be overloaded quickly. Even when we think we understand Him, we really don't. He used the gap between the heavens and the earth to illustrate the size of the gap between His intelligence and ours. It cannot be measured because it's limitless.

Taking that into consideration, it would be a lot to ask a human being to understand God's timing. Why is it that when we think God should do something He sometimes doesn't and when we think He shouldn't, He sometimes does? I've heard it said within Christian circles that God doesn't come when you want Him but He's always right on time. When I first heard it, I thought it was a cop-out used to justify unanswered prayer. God didn't respond to your prayer so let's use His sovereignty to explain it away. Then I matured as a Christian and realized that they were right all along. Here's a perfect example from the life of Jesus.

A man named Lazarus was sick. He lived in Bethany with his sisters, Mary and Martha. This is the Mary who later poured the expensive perfume on the Lord's feet and wiped them with her hair. Her brother, Lazarus, was sick. So the two sisters sent a message to Jesus telling him, "Lord, your dear friend is very sick." But when Jesus heard about it he said, "Lazarus's sickness will not end in death. No, it happened for the glory of God so that the Son of God will receive glory from this." So although Jesus loved Martha, Mary, and Lazarus, he stayed where he was for the next two days. - **John 11:1-6(NLT)**

Jesus clearly understood the emergency at hand. Lazarus was terribly sick and the message that came from his sisters stated such. Yet, instead of immediately rushing to His friend's aid as Martha and Mary were expecting, Jesus purposefully waited for two days. He knew that they didn't understand the reason behind His two-day delay and neither did His disciples. Nonetheless, He told His disciples that Lazarus' sickness would not end in death. In other words, even if it included death, that was just an intermediate step and not the end of it. What was certain to come out of the situation was glory for God and His Son, Jesus.

Finally, he said to his disciples, "Let's go back to Judea." But his disciples objected. "Rabbi," they said, "only a few days ago the people in Judea were trying to stone you. Are you going there again?" Jesus replied, "There are twelve hours of daylight every day. During the day people can walk safely. They can see because they have the light of this world. But at night there is danger of stumbling because they have no light." Then he said, "Our friend Lazarus has fallen asleep, but now I will go and wake him up." The disciples said, "Lord, if he is sleeping, he will soon get better!" They thought Jesus meant Lazarus was simply sleeping, but Jesus meant Lazarus had died. So he told them plainly, "Lazarus is dead. And for your sakes, I'm glad I wasn't there, for now you will really believe. Come, let's go see him."- **John 11:7-15(NLT)**

Jesus proved once again that His two-day delay was purposeful. He waited until He was assured of Lazarus' death before deciding to move. To further emphasize His position on the purposeful delay, Jesus made the bold statement that He was glad He wasn't there to intervene prior to the death of Lazarus. That's shocking! How were the disciples supposed to take that statement? Yet, Jesus explained that His delay was justified because it would create the opportunity for people to really believe in a way they could not believe otherwise. The obvious question is, *"Believe what?"* In a subsequent conversation with Martha, Jesus answered that question with a simple explanation. Here's how that conversation went.

When Martha got word that Jesus was coming, she went to meet him. But Mary stayed in the house. Martha said to Jesus, "Lord, if only you had been here, my brother would not have died. But even now I know that God will give you whatever you ask." Jesus told her, "Your brother will rise again." "Yes," Martha said, "he will rise when everyone else rises, at the last day." Jesus told her, "I am the resurrection and the life. Anyone who believes in me will live, even after dying. Everyone who lives in me and believes in me will never ever die. Do you believe this, Martha?" "Yes, Lord," she told him. "I have always believed you are the Messiah, the Son of God, the one who has come into the world from God." - **John 11:20-27(NLT)**

Jesus was delayed for two days to ensure that Lazarus was dead before He arrived. Why? He wanted to debut as the resurrection and the life. Martha knew that Jesus had the power to heal Lazarus which was the reason why she sent for Him while Lazarus was sick. That's why she confronted Jesus the moment she saw Him and said that if He only had been on time, He could have saved Lazarus. She was right but her perspective was limited. Jesus had already proven Himself as a healer, so Martha already believed that. Martha also already believed in the Resurrection on the last day when everyone will rise again. Two down, one to go.

Jesus delayed His arrival so that she, as well as everyone else present, could believe something new by showing them what they had never witnessed before. Just like Jesus would later say that He is the way, truth, and life in John 14:6, He introduced Himself on that day as the resurrection and the life. If people could believe in Him, the power of death would be defeated in their lives. Those who die would live again and those who live would never die. Martha believed and her belief was rewarded a few moments later.

Then Jesus shouted, "Lazarus, come out!" And the dead man came out, his hands and feet bound in graveclothes, his face wrapped in a headcloth. Jesus told them, "Unwrap him and let him go!" - **John 11:43-44(NLT)**

Was Jesus late? Absolutely not! It looked to everyone like two days was an unnecessary delay but to Jesus, it was perfect timing. The people around Him had no real idea of who He was and did not know that His power was limitless. Hence, He orchestrated a situation that would allow God to be glorified through His Son, Jesus by demonstrating His resurrection power. Until then, they believed that the resurrection was an event, but it took Him raising Lazarus from the dead for them to believe that the Resurrection is a person and His name is Jesus. What looked like a delay in the eyes of people was precise timing in the eyes of God.

What do you think Martha's response would have been if she understood what Jesus was doing ahead of time? What if she knew that His delay was a good thing and could grasp His timing? As the saying goes, *"hindsight is 20-20"*. So, as we read the account of what happened in the scriptures thousands of years after the fact it makes sense to us. On the other hand, if we were experiencing it in real-time we would have felt just like Martha, disappointed and confused that Jesus took so long to show up. What if we had the ability to understand God's timing? How would that change our perspective? Is it even possible for that to happen? Yes!

How to Know God's Timing

> *Then the Pharisees and Sadducees came, and testing Him asked that He would show them a sign from heaven. He answered and said to them, "When it is evening you say, 'It will be fair weather, for the sky is red'; and in the morning, 'It will be foul weather today, for the sky is red and threatening.' Hypocrites! You know how to discern the face of the sky, but you cannot discern the signs of the times.* - **Matthew 16:1-3(NKJV)**

Jesus scolded the Pharisees and Sadducees for not understanding God's timing. With that statement, He revealed that it's humanly possible to do so. Since Jesus verified that it's possible to know God's timing, I believe it's worth the effort to discover how to make that happen in our lives. The psalmist David said that our times are in God's hands (Psalm 31:15). Fortunately, God wants to open His hands to show His children what's in there. Yes, God's ways and thoughts are higher than our thoughts. Yes, God's wisdom is unlimited. Yet, God has created ways for people to access the wisdom only He possesses.

> *Of the tribe of Issachar, men who understood the times, with knowledge of what Israel should do, two hundred chiefs; and all their relatives were at their command;* - **1 Chronicles 12:32(AMP)**

There was one tribe among the Children of Israel, called Issachar, which understood God's timing. This gave them the ability to know what Israel should do, which likewise, brings up an interesting point. If you understand the timing of anything you will know what to do. Joseph understood the timing of the famine in Egypt and knew what to do during the times of plenty. Investors who understood the timing of the Great Recession were able to adjust their investments accordingly. People who know the timing of weather conditions can prepare themselves as needed. In much the same way, when people understand God's timing, they always know what to do.

> *Thus says the Lord, The Holy One of Israel, and his Maker: "Ask Me of things to come concerning My sons; And concerning the work of My hands, you command Me.* - **Isaiah 45:11(NKJV)**

If you're like me and can guarantee that you're not from the tribe of

Issachar, how can we understand the times? How can we know what to do? Should we try to identify the modern descendants of Issachar and ask them for directions? Otherwise, what are we supposed to do? Well, I have some good news to share. God's message to us is simple, *"just ask"*. Ask Him of things to come and make requests concerning the work of His hands. He doesn't want to keep His own children in the dark because He knows the value of this information to our success in life. Before we dig into specifics let's recap a bit.

> *He has made everything beautiful and appropriate in its time. He has also planted eternity [a sense of divine purpose] in the human heart [a mysterious longing which nothing under the sun can satisfy, except God]—yet man cannot find out (comprehend, grasp) what God has done (His overall plan) from the beginning to the end.* - **Ecclesiastes 3:11(AMP)**

God's plan is eternal. It spans from before time began through the fullness of time to eternity. Still, God planted His divine purpose in the human heart. This means that inside each of us is the need to fit into eternity. We know that our lives don't exist in a vacuum and that's without anybody ever telling us that. That sense of divine purpose is innate to our humanity. We want to know where we fit in God's plan and where His plan for us fits into His eternal plan. That's why we need to grasp God's timing. It's important to know the why, what and how of life but that's not enough. It's also important to know when. God's timing is inextricably tied to God's eternal plan within which we must fit God's purpose for each of us.

Here are five ways God reveals His timing to people.

1. The Word of God
2. Prayer
3. Signs
4. Dreams and Visions
5. Prophecy

Let's now explore each of these ways through which God communicates His timing and take the next steps toward knowing what to do in every situation we face. We may not all be descendants of the tribe of Issachar, but we can use the tools provided by God to know the times and seasons of God. We can then know what to do in our own lives and like that special tribe, we can use our access to God's wisdom to guide the decisions of others. Let's now dig deeper into the first item on our list, "The Word of God".

11 GOD'S TIMING THROUGH HIS WORD

But as for you, teach the things which are in agreement with sound doctrine [which produces men and women of good character whose lifestyle identifies them as true Christians]. Older men are to be temperate, dignified, sensible, sound in faith, in love, in steadfastness [Christlike in character]. Older women similarly are to be reverent in their behavior, not malicious gossips nor addicted to much wine, teaching what is right and good, so that they may encourage the young women to tenderly love their husbands and their children, to be sensible, pure, makers of a home [where God is honored], good-natured, being subject to their own husbands, so that the word of God will not be dishonored. In a similar way urge the young men to be sensible and self-controlled and to behave wisely [taking life seriously]. And in all things show yourself to be an example of good works, with purity in doctrine [having the strictest regard for integrity and truth], dignified, sound and beyond reproach in instruction, so that the opponent [of the faith] will be shamed, having nothing bad to say about us. -
Titus 2:1-8(AMP)

As a young man, I was taught that experience is one of the greatest teachers. As I've grown older and matured in the faith I couldn't agree more. Until principles are put into practice, their value is not fully realized. However, who says that the only experience we benefit from must be our own? It's entirely possible to learn from the experience of others. That's the saving grace for younger people. They may not have the life experience necessary to make the best decisions, but they do have access to the experience of their parents, teachers, mentors, and other older counterparts.

In contrast to the popular saying, youth does not have to be wasted on the young. Through direct or indirect mentorship, the emotional energy and physical strength that's typically associated with youth can be combined with the experience and wisdom that's typically associated with age. Apostle Paul admonished Titus to use his platform as a preacher of the gospel to encourage the older women of the church to mentor the younger women in the area of Godly living. The same should be expected of the men of the church. Those who are older should be examples to those you are younger. That's direct mentorship and it's effective when done correctly from both sides.

> *For whatever things were written before were written for our learning, that we through the patience and comfort of the Scriptures might have hope.* - **Romans 15:4(NKJV)**

The Scriptures allow us to learn from the experiences of others. When we read the Bible, we see how God operates in the lives of people and gain insight into the possibilities of His engagement with us. We see the mistakes of the Children of Israel, but we see God's redemptive hand in their lives. We see the passion and effectiveness of the early church, but we see the challenges they faced as they matured in the faith. It would take many lifetimes for any of us to personally experience everything we read in the scriptures but fortunately, we don't have to. Included in the many life lessons available in the Bible are God's instructions about time.

Daniel Used God's Word to Know God's Timing

> *Hope deferred makes the heart sick, But when the desire comes, it is a tree of life.* - **Proverbs 13:12(NKJV)**

I once heard a story on public radio about a US prisoner of war who survived years as a captive in a foreign country. He was one of many soldiers who were brought into the enemy's camp but only one of the few who walked out. They were tortured, abused, and mistreated, sometimes to the point of death for so long that it became nearly impossible to survive. When he was asked to share his story of survival, he revealed some fascinating principles of human psychology. He said that even though he was essentially helpless and at the mercy of his captors, hope was the fuel that kept him alive. They controlled what he did and when he did it, but they did not control his mind.

Even so, he clarified that all types of hope are not the same. They aren't equally effective when one is in bondage long-term. He said that there were four types of captives. The first group woke up each day believing that was the day they would be free. The second group manufactured specific dates in their mind and looked forward to being set free on those dates. The third group thought they would be set free quickly and didn't expect to be in bondage for too long. The fourth believed they would be free one day but didn't know when and accepted that. To put it bluntly, the first three groups of prisoners died in captivity.

The first group would wake up expecting to be free each day and when nothing happened their hope would be shattered. That took place over and over and over until they essentially gave up on even the thought of freedom. The second group would imagine the dates when the US army would show up to the prison to rescue them. In their heads, they would come up with random reasons why they would be rescued on Christmas, New Year's Day, or Independence Day, etc.

When these dates came and nothing happened, they also lost hope. The third group was not prepared for the long haul. In their minds, they would be released quickly. The war would be over soon, and they were going home. That's what they believed strongly at the beginning until days turned into weeks, weeks turned into months and months turned into years. As expected, when their hope ran out, they eventually gave up.

The last group comprised of the survivors. They never gave up hope, not because they knew when they would be free or how they would be free but only that they would be free. They woke up each day not expecting to be free that day. They entered captivity not expecting to be freed soon. They faced each milestone of time not thinking that those dates held any significance to their captors or their home country. They just believed in freedom and kept hope alive in their hearts while their fellow prisoners died around them. The prophet Daniel was that kind of prisoner. Then one day God showed him the truth about the imminent freedom of his people.

In the third year of the reign of Jehoiakim king of Judah, Nebuchadnezzar king of Babylon came to Jerusalem and besieged it. The Lord gave Jehoiakim king of Judah into his hand, along with some of the articles of the house of God; and he brought them into the land of Shinar, to the house of his god, and brought the articles into the treasury of his god. And the [Babylonian] king told Ashpenaz, the chief of his officials, to bring in some of the sons of Israel, including some from the royal family and from the nobles, young men without blemish and handsome in appearance, skillful in all wisdom, endowed with intelligence and discernment, and quick to understand, competent to stand [in the presence of the king] and able to serve in the king's palace. He also ordered

Ashpenaz to teach them the literature and language of the Chaldeans. The king assigned a daily ration for them from his finest food and from the wine which he drank. They were to be educated and nourished this way for three years so that at the end of that time they were [prepared] to enter the king's service. Among them from the sons of Judah were: Daniel, Hananiah, Mishael, and Azariah. The commander of the officials gave them [Babylonian] names: Daniel he named Belteshazzar, Hananiah he named Shadrach, Mishael he named Meshach, and Azariah he named Abed-nego. - **Daniel 1:1-6(AMP)**

In the timeline of Bible history, Daniel lived in a very interesting period. His time of recorded prophetic ministry and political leadership spanned around seventy years. He witnessed the fall of Jerusalem and was brought into the land of Shinar by the Babylonians to serve the King. From the beginning of their tenure in the King's palace, he and his friends separated themselves from their peers. Over the years, he rose through the ranks to become a trusted advisor to four different kings. He demonstrated the skill of prospering in a foreign land as well as excelling as a Godly person in hostile secular environments.

Still, with all his success, he was still living in bondage. The people of Judah were captives to Babylon first, then the Medes and the Persians. He yearned to be free and didn't know when it would happen until the year that Babylon fell. That year, God revealed to Daniel the exact schedule of His plan for their freedom using a very simple tool, a book. I once heard a famous preacher say that the easiest way to hide something from a black man is to put it in a book. Thankfully, that's not true for all black men and though Daniel was Jewish, that was not true for him either. He was a reader and God spoke to Him through books.

It was the first year of the reign of Darius the Mede, the son of Ahasuerus, who became king of the Babylonians. During the first year of his reign, I, Daniel, learned from reading the word of the Lord, as revealed to Jeremiah the prophet, that Jerusalem must lie desolate for seventy years. So I turned to the Lord God and pleaded with him in prayer and fasting. I also wore rough burlap and sprinkled myself with ashes. - **Daniel 9:1-3(NLT)**

Seventy years total was the prescribed duration of Jewish captivity in Babylon. That was it! After seventy years, the people of Judah would be free. Daniel read the Word of God in a book written by the prophet Jeremiah and knew exactly what God was doing and when. He was able to count exactly how long they had been in bondage at the time and realized that his freedom was about one year away. It completely blew his mind, so he immediately went into a time of prayer and fasting to get a better understanding of what he was reading. Were they truly at the end of their bondage? That was amazing. He didn't know how God would set them free, but he finally knew when and that was enough to completely change his countenance. One year later, Cyrus, the Persian captured Babylon, and everything changed. Here's a summary of how it all took place.

> *So the Lord brought the king of Babylon against them. The Babylonians killed Judah's young men, even chasing after them into the Temple. They had no pity on the people, killing both young men and young women, the old and the infirm. God handed all of them over to Nebuchadnezzar. The king took home to Babylon all the articles, large and small, used in the Temple of God, and the treasures from both the Lord's Temple and from the palace of the king and his officials. Then his army burned the Temple of God, tore down the walls of Jerusalem, burned all the palaces, and completely destroyed everything of value. The few who survived were taken as exiles to Babylon, and they became servants to the king and his sons until the kingdom of Persia came to power. So the message of the Lord spoken through Jeremiah was fulfilled. The land finally enjoyed its Sabbath rest, lying desolate until the seventy years were fulfilled, just as the prophet had said. In the first year of King Cyrus of Persia, the Lord fulfilled the prophecy he had given through Jeremiah. He stirred the heart of Cyrus to put this proclamation in writing and to send it throughout his kingdom: "This is what King Cyrus of Persia says: "The Lord, the God of heaven, has given me all the kingdoms of the earth. He has appointed me to build him a Temple at Jerusalem, which is in Judah. Any of you who are his people may go there for this task. And may the Lord your God be with you!"*
> - **2 Chronicles 36:17-23(NLT)**

Isn't it amazing how the scripture encapsulated seventy years of intense action in seven verses? For years, Jeremiah prophesied that captivity was coming, and many people didn't listen. In fact, false prophets rose to contradict the truth he was telling the people until the day came that exactly what he said became a sad reality. Jeremiah's prophecy was so accurate that Daniel was able to use it as a script to predict what would happen next.

At the seventy-year mark, God moved on the heart of Cyrus, a Persian, to release God's people to return to Jerusalem. He considered himself called by God to let the people of Judah rebuild the temple that his Babylonian predecessors had destroyed. Not just that, Chapter 1 of the Book of Ezra outlined how they left Babylon the same way the Children of Israel left Egypt; loaded with gold, silver, and other gifts from their "neighbors".

To us, this is a Bible story but to Daniel, this was his life. We know how the story ends so we can fast forward to see the end then use that to provide context for the beginning. In doing so, we may not fully appreciate the process. Prophet Jeremiah provided with such precision, God's timeline for the people of Judah. Yet, it took 69 years for it to click in Daniel's mind. For 69 years he was the prisoner who knew he would be free but just didn't know when and accepted it. Then, after reading the Word of God, he became the prisoner who knew exactly when his freedom was about to take place. This is the power of the Word of God to reveal God's timing.

Jesus Used God's Word as the Script for His Life

> *So He came to Nazareth, where He had been brought up. And as His custom was, He went into the synagogue on the Sabbath day, and stood up to read. And He was handed the book of the prophet Isaiah. And when He had opened the book, He found the place where it was written: "The Spirit of the Lord is upon Me, Because He has anointed Me To preach the gospel to the poor; He has sent Me to heal the brokenhearted, To proclaim liberty to the captives And recovery of sight to the blind, To set at liberty those who are oppressed; To proclaim the acceptable year of the Lord." Then He closed the book, and gave it back to the attendant and sat down. And the eyes of all who were in the synagogue were fixed on Him. And He began to say to them, "Today this Scripture is fulfilled in your hearing."* - **Luke 4:16-21(NKJV)**

Jesus was the Christ, the Anointed One. That's the point of what Isaiah prophesied concerning Him. He was the one empowered and set apart by God to preach the good news to the less fortunate. His words would be so powerful that they would change people's lives forever. With this anointing, He would heal broken hearts and set captives free. He would remove the burden of blindness and destroy the yoke of oppression. He also came to announce the acceptable year of The Lord. If it was His intention to make a grand entrance. What an entrance!

Jesus found Himself in the scriptures and took the liberty to share the good news in the synagogue in Nazareth. He let them know that Isaiah 61 was a prophetic word about Him. I can only imagine the expressions on the faces of all who heard what Jesus said that day. While it's evident to us that He was speaking the truth, many of them did not believe, and they eventually forced Him out of the synagogue. Regardless, this was indicative of how He operated. His life on earth consisted of a multitude of fulfilled prophecies starting from the Book of Genesis.

Then He said to them, "These are the words which I spoke to you while I was still with you, that all things must be fulfilled which were written in the Law of Moses and the Prophets and the Psalms concerning Me." And He opened their understanding, that they might comprehend the Scriptures. Then He said to them, "Thus it is written, and thus it was necessary for the Christ to suffer and to rise from the dead the third day, and that repentance and remission of sins should be preached in His name to all nations, beginning at Jerusalem. And you are witnesses of these things. Behold, I send the Promise of My Father upon you; but tarry in the city of Jerusalem until you are endued with power from on high." - **Luke 24:44-49(NKJV)**

Jesus used the scriptures as the script (pun intended) for His life. He didn't just do whatever He felt like doing. It wasn't by chance that every dimension of his life was a fulfillment of specific prophetic words recorded throughout the Old Testament. Jesus was intentional. He searched the scriptures to find what it said about Him then He deliberately fulfilled each prophetic Word. Had the disciples listened to what Jesus was telling them all along, they would have known exactly what was going to happen to Him and when. That's how we must live if we are to take advantage of the wisdom offered in God's Word.

Like the script for a movie, the disciples simply needed to follow the details of the scriptures that pertained to Jesus. This was especially important as the time of His death and resurrection got closer and closer. It was a traumatic experience for them all, but they should have been prepared because they knew the contents of the script before any of it happened. That's the power of understanding God's Word. If you can determine what it's talking about, you will have an enhanced perspective of the past, a better grasp of the present and a much clearer sense of the future.

Then Jesus said to them, "You foolish people! You find it so hard to believe all that the prophets wrote in the Scriptures. Wasn't it clearly predicted that the Messiah would have to suffer all these things before entering his glory?" Then Jesus took them through the writings of Moses and all the prophets, explaining from all the Scriptures the things concerning himself. - **Luke 24:25-27 (NLT)**

The scriptures prophesied the exact timing of the resurrection of Jesus. He was scheduled to die for the sins of all mankind, but He would rise from the dead after three days. With that level of detail, if people had truly believed God's Word they could have set a countdown clock for exactly three days. Their faith would not have been shaken and they would never have scattered if they trusted what the prophets said about the life of Jesus. Even as they watched Him die on the cross, it was only a matter of time before He rose again. In fact, the time was exactly three days. Obviously, since hindsight is 20-20, it was much easier for them to understand after the fact. So, after the resurrection, Jesus took His time to explain what happened and showed them how they missed it in the scriptures.

Practical Application of The Word's Timing

> *Surely the Lord God will do nothing, but he revealeth his secret unto his servants the prophets.* - **Amos 3:7(KJV)**

Before God does something, He tells His prophets. One way He does so is by directing them to applicable scriptures that reveal His plan. For example, in 2017, God directed me to the account of Joseph's rise to power in Egypt recorded in Genesis 41. Joseph interpreted Pharaoh's dream revealing that seven years of plenty were coming to Egypt followed by seven lean years. He then created and executed a plan to help Egypt conserve their resources during the good times. This enabled them to not just survive but thrive during the hard times.

After reading those scriptures, The Lord told me what would happen in the US. In 2017, we were amid the longest economic recovery ever recorded. God said those were the years of plenty and they would run out by 2025 for the latest. He then gave me a specific plan to execute in preparation for the lean years that were sure to follow. I shared what He revealed with as many people as would listen using all the platforms or outlets (blogs, books, workshops, videos, etc.) afforded to me at the time. Then everything changed in 2020. With the COVID-19 pandemic, trade wars, oil price wars and other factors creating the perfect storm, an economic downturn began earlier than expected in the US. I will share more details on this later in the book.

As we bring this chapter to a close, again, here are five ways God reveals His timing to people.

1. **The Word of God (complete)**
2. Prayer
3. Signs
4. Dreams and Visions
5. Prophecy

In the next chapter, we will look at how prayer can help reveal God's timing.

12 SECRETS OF TIME THROUGH PRAYER

Fools base their thoughts on foolish assumptions, so their conclusions will be wicked madness; they chatter on and on. No one really knows what is going to happen; no one can predict the future. - **Ecclesiastes 10:13-14(NLT)**

The future is God's secret. I once heard a preacher say, *"The man who knows the future owns the future and those who find out after it happens must pay him a premium for it."* There's no business like the future business. People exchange their hard-earned cash for fortune-tellers, palm readers, tarot cards, horoscopes, and others to tell them what to expect for their lives. Stock market analysts, traders, investors, and speculators make financial decisions based on their understanding of how market trends would impact the future. Wise parents steer their children's education and early career decisions so that they are properly positioned for success in the future. Children who are taught the principles of delayed gratification make sacrifices today for future enjoyment. Christians sow into God's Kingdom while on earth for eternal rewards.

The truth is that the future is a mystery. Nobody but God knows what will happen next year, month, week, day, hour, minute or second. We just trust that God knows what He is doing and live with anticipation of what will happen next. The most any human being can do in their natural ability is to use observable patterns and trends from the past, connect them with signs in the present and project future outcomes. Sometimes, that approach works and sometimes it doesn't. We can also use the principle of sowing and reaping to shape our futures. Yet, there is still no way to guarantee the outcome. While we can control what we sow, we cannot completely control the environment in which we sow and how it will affect our seed. Fortunately, there's an effective way to access God's secrets of the future and even directly impact it.

Daniel Prayed and God Answered

*I went on praying and confessing my sin and the sin of my people, pleading with the Lord my God for Jerusalem, his holy mountain. As I was praying, Gabriel, whom I had seen in the earlier vision, came swiftly to me at the time of the evening sacrifice. He explained to me, "Daniel, I have come here to give you insight and understanding. The moment you began praying, a command was given. And now I am here to tell you what it was, for you are very precious to God. Listen carefully so that you can understand the meaning of your vision. "A period of seventy sets of seven has been decreed for your people and your holy city to finish their rebellion, to put an end to their sin, to atone for their guilt, to bring in everlasting righteousness, to confirm the prophetic vision, and to anoint the Most Holy Place. Now listen and understand! Seven sets of seven plus sixty-two sets of seven will pass from the time the command is given to rebuild Jerusalem until a ruler—the Anointed One—comes. Jerusalem will be rebuilt with streets and strong defenses, despite the perilous times. "After this period of sixty-two sets of seven, the Anointed One will be killed, appearing to have accomplished nothing, and a ruler will arise whose armies will destroy the city and the Temple. The end will come with a flood, and war and its miseries are decreed from that time to the very end. The ruler will make a treaty with the people for a period of one set of seven, but after half this time, he will put an end to the sacrifices and offerings. And as a climax to all his terrible deeds, he will set up a sacrilegious object that causes desecration, until the fate decreed for this defiler is finally poured out on him." - *Daniel 9:20-27 (NLT)**

The prophet Jeremiah revealed the baseline of God's timing for the captivity of Judah in the books that Daniel was able to read many years after they were written. That provided a big picture understanding to Daniel of the season he was in at the time and what he should expect to see happen next. For many of us that would have been more than enough information to get us going. We would have run with that information and done whatever we saw fit. However, Daniel was different. He didn't want to be presumptuous, so he sought God's face for a deeper understanding of what he read. God heard and responded by sending the angel Gabriel with the answer plus much more.

Upon arrival, Gabriel stated upfront that he was there to give Daniel insight and understanding because of Daniel's prayer. He shared with Daniel how precious he was in the sight of God. Then the angel got down to the numbers. First, he didn't repeat what Daniel had already learned from reading Jeremiah's writings concerning the 70-year Jewish captivity in Babylon. He told Daniel what would happen far in the future that he would not be alive on earth to see. He foretold the rebuilding of the temple in Jerusalem, the coming of Jesus Christ, the destruction of that second Temple and the end of time. I tried to fit Gabriel's literal numbers into the historical record of Jewish history and could follow some, but not all of it. It would take some more detailed research to confirm everything within a modern context. Regardless, Daniel's prayer gave Him access to God's timing and that's what matters.

> *Thus says the Lord, The Holy One of Israel, and his Maker: "Ask Me of things to come concerning My sons; And concerning the work of My hands, you command Me.* - **Isaiah 45:11(NKJV)**

Do you want to know what God is doing? Ask Him. Is this your season to step out? Is this your season to step back? Is this your season to be still? Should you buy, sell, or hold? Should you move to another city or stay right where you are? He knows, so ask Him. That's one of the many benefits of prayer. In this chapter, we will study how prayer can be used to access the mystery of God's timing. When God knows something that we need to know, He allows us to communicate with Him through prayer to get access to it.

Let me tell you a personal story about God's timing revealed through prayer. I spent my first year of college starting in the Fall of 1998 studying Applied Physics at Morehouse College in Atlanta, GA. It was my first year living away from my parents and outside of my home country of Trinidad and Tobago. I lived on campus during the semester but had to find accommodations elsewhere during my first college summer break. Thankfully, my aunt and uncle also lived in Atlanta and opened their home to me. With no classes to take, no job and nothing really to do, I spent time at church, in The Word of God and in prayer in the basement of their home.

God knew that I greatly desired a summer job. He also understood the challenges I faced as a freshman and an international student. I also used my free time to attend my first ever Finance Convention at World Changers Church International in College Park, GA. Having no other commitments, I was able to attend every day and night session for the duration of the conference. I also purchased the tapes of every message that was preached and studied the notes like I was preparing for a final. With my faith concerning financial prosperity at an all-time high and my relationship with God getting stronger, I prayed for a miracle. God heard my prayer and executed His master plan for my success with precision timing. Here's a bit of what happened.

One of my daily pastimes during that summer was reading the free newspaper, *"Creative Loafing"*, especially the *"Classified Ads"* or *"Help Wanted"* sections. One day while reading, I saw an advertisement for tryouts for an all-male singing group in an Atlanta suburb. The Lord impressed upon my heart to respond, so I called the listed contact and set up an appointment for my tryout. I was excited because I thought I had found something to occupy my time, but I had no idea of the miracle God had set up for me through this experience. On the day of my tryout, I got dressed, completed some last-minute preparations, and boarded a bus to the train station.

I then rode the train to another station where I could catch another bus that would take me to my destination. I never made it. I reached as far as the bus depot in the final train station, where God had a much better plan for me. At the exact moment that I was walking to the area where I would wait for the bus, a gentleman was pacing up and down grumbling to himself. Even though he was acting like a crazy person which is typical in places like those I didn't believe he was crazy. He eventually sat next to me on the same bench. After a few minutes of awkward silence, we struck up a conversation that changed my entire summer and ultimately, my life.

He told me why he was so emotional and shared exactly what was on his heart. He told me that he was on his way home from work after a particularly challenging day during which one of his colleagues quit. Unbeknownst to me, he worked for a firm called Atlantic Engineering Associates on Auburn Avenue in downtown Atlanta. That summer they had a pressing deadline to finish mapping a portion of the City of Atlanta's sewer system. He was part of one of the field crews gathering manhole location information that would be entered into a Geographic Information System (GIS). He was also the nephew of the company's president.

I'm sure you could only imagine what happened next. I told him who I was, and we bonded over the next few minutes of conversation. I didn't even notice if the bus ever arrived because I completely abandoned my plans for the evening. My new friend called his uncle on the spot and told him he found an intern for the summer to take the guy's place on the team. I had an interview that Friday and started my new job the following week. That's the miracle of God's timing and why prayer can help you reveal it.

Interestingly, while I was a freshman Applied Physics student at Morehouse College I was also in the first year of the Dual Degree Engineering Program with the Georgia Institute of Technology. A little over a year later I transferred to the new school to pursue a degree in Civil Engineering with applicable work experience already on my resume. Not just that, when I interviewed for my first full-time job during my final year of graduate school, my freshman summer experience gave me an advantage over others competing for the same position. It happened to be in the same industry as the company interviewing me.

After several decades, I was blessed by God to build a career as a Civil/Structural Engineer in the Metro Atlanta area and across the US. Yet, none of it would have been possible without God's precision timing. What if I had ignored God's prompting to try out for the singing group? In hindsight, the decision made no sense. Even if I made it into the group, what was I going to do when school reopened in the fall? I am thankful that I put logic aside and simply obeyed God. When we pray, we never know how God will answer. We must trust that whatever He does will work out for our good in the end. Timing is everything and prayer is one avenue God uses to reveal His timing to His people. When I needed a job, He spoke to my heart at the perfect time to get up and do something about it. Had I delayed or moved ahead of His timing; nothing would have come of it. I heard from God and I was in the right place at the right time.

Trust in the Lord with all your heart, And lean not on your own understanding; In all your ways acknowledge Him, And He shall direct your paths. - **Proverbs 3:5-6(NKJV)**

When we're busy or dealing with urgent matters it's easy to forget to ask God for direction. It's easy to rely on experience, intelligence, relationships, research and anything else we can trust when we need quick solutions. However, God alone controls the future and He knows exactly how our present decisions affect our future. That's why it's wise to stop whatever we are doing and lean on His infinite wisdom. If you think His answer to your prayer is irrelevant to your situation, think again. As the saying goes, He's playing chess while you are playing checkers. While you're focused on what He's doing in one area, He's focused on where each move fits into His grand scheme for the entire board.

King David, at the height of his success as a military leader still took the time to ask God for wisdom before his greatest battles. Jesus, amid the most successful ministry to ever manifest on earth, took the time to get away to pray and receive instructions from His Heavenly Father. Prayer should be a lifestyle for every Christian. Even the simplest decisions in our lives require God's wisdom. We don't know if what seems to be the right answer now is really the wrong answer in the end. Some decisions make complete sense based on our limited perspective but when we see through God's eyes, they make no sense at all. Thankfully, God knows what we need to do. If we dare to pray, He will show us how and when to do what's right so that the results we achieve are favorable.

As we bring this chapter to a close, again, here are five ways God reveals His timing to people.

1. **The Word of God (complete)**
2. **Prayer (Complete)**
3. Signs
4. Dreams and Visions
5. Prophecy

In the next chapter, we will look at how signs can help reveal God's timing.

13 FOLLOW THE SIGNS

"Ask a sign for yourself from the Lord your God; ask it either in the depth or in the height above." - **Isaiah 7:11(NKJV)**

While driving to an event after church with my wife, Angel, The Lord spoke to me. I saw a sign on the expressway that said all lanes were blocked at an intersection up ahead due to a serious accident. Still, the flow of traffic looked normal at the time and my GPS directed me to continue as normal. Thus, I didn't attempt to get off at the next exit and kept going. Then I saw another sign saying the same thing again concerning all lanes being blocked due to an accident up ahead. I looked around and the traffic flow continued to be normal as far ahead as I could see. Additionally, my GPS did not change its directions.

While I approached the next exit, I had a decision to make. I could get off at the exit out of an abundance of caution and let the GPS guide me through backroads or I could keep going. The only risk would have been lost time if the trouble up ahead on the expressway was not that bad. I seriously considered continuing along the path of my GPS until God spoke. He said, *"Follow the signs."* The roads still looked clear and my GPS did not indicate any accident. Hence, there was no evidence of any traffic problems other than what we could read on the signs.

Thankfully, I'm not that much of a risk-taker so I got off at the next exit. Only then did my GPS update to show the major accident and subsequent traffic challenges. In addition, only after I got off the exit could I see the standstill traffic up ahead. I thanked God that I followed the signs and did not rely only on what I could see with my eyes or my GPS device. God used that situation to help me understand how to present this chapter since I was working on it at the time. God uses signs to help us make good decisions when we're confused or overwhelmed with uncertainty. However, we must follow them even when our natural senses don't support what they say.

> *Then the Pharisees and Sadducees came, and testing Him asked that He would show them a sign from heaven. He answered and said to them, "When it is evening you say, 'It will be fair weather, for the sky is red'; and in the morning, 'It will be foul weather today, for the sky is red and threatening.' Hypocrites! You know how to discern the face of the sky, but you cannot discern the signs of the times. A wicked and adulterous generation seeks after a sign, and no sign shall be given to it except the sign of the prophet Jonah." And He left them and departed.* - **Matthew 16:1-4(NKJV)**

The Pharisees and Sadducees were thorns in the side of Jesus for the duration of his three-year public ministry. They refused to simply let Him be and just had to take every opportunity to challenge Him. One such occasion that was particularly annoying was their request for a sign. The scripture says that they were testing Him which meant they really weren't looking for a sign, they were looking for an opportunity to get on His nerves. In response, Jesus scolded them for not recognizing that all the signs pointed to Him as the Messiah. He also gave what might appear to be mixed messages concerning the validity of pursuing signs.

On the one hand, He said that they were wrong for lacking discernment of the signs of the times. Yet, He followed that up by saying a wicked and adulterous generation seeks after a sign. So, which one is it? Are signs good or bad? The Pharisees and Sadducees, like others at the time, used signs in the sky to determine the weather. Jesus had no problem with that. He just used it as an example of how they were already familiar with the practice of working with signs to understand what was coming. He said what He said merely to prove that they had no excuse for missing the signs of His coming.

Why did He say that a wicked and adulterous generation seeks after a sign? Was that His way of saying that we should not pay attention to signs? If that's the case, why did He expect anyone to pay attention to the signs of His coming? Have we finally found a contradiction in the words of Jesus? No, we have not. The first thing we need to understand is that Jesus was responding to the intent of the Pharisees and Sadducees who asked Him for a sign. The scripture says that they were testing Him. They didn't believe that He was the Messiah and Jesus was responding to their unbelief more than their literal words.

He had no desire to prove Himself to them so He said they would get no sign from Him except one, His death and resurrection. Though it is true that He called the generation seeking a sign wicked and adulterous, His focus was on the intent of the seekers. They seek signs because they don't believe Him. They refuse to accept what He says so they want Him to prove Himself with signs over and over to justify that He is who He says He is. To Jesus, that attitude is wicked. Signs don't replace believing in what God says. Nevertheless, why would a Christian even pay attention to signs in the first place? Don't we already have the Bible and the Holy Ghost on the inside to lead and guide us?

> *However, when He, the Spirit of truth, has come, He will guide you into all truth; for He will not speak on His own authority, but whatever He hears He will speak; and He will tell you things to come.* - **John 16:13(NKJV)**

With the Holy Spirit already living inside of us we have access to the One who always knows where we need to go, what we need to do and how we need to do it. If we can hear His Voice and do what He says we should never have a need for signs. Right? That sounds very deep and spiritual so it must be right. However, that's wrong. Jesus spent considerable time describing in detail the signs of His coming. Why? He wants us to look out for them and discern the times by comparing what we see to what He said.

The Holy Spirit is our guide. He doesn't eliminate signs. He still uses signs and helps us to recognize the signs that He places in front of our eyes. He created each of us and knows exactly what signs would get our attention. Every day, there are signs along our path placed there by God and The Holy Ghost helps us navigate through them. Remember, it's one thing to see a sign but it's another to recognize what the sign represents for you and what God is trying to get you to see through it. Never get too deep to notice God's directions in the signs around you.

God Speaks Through Nature

> *But God shows his anger from heaven against all sinful, wicked people who suppress the truth by their wickedness. They know the truth about God because he has made it obvious to them. For ever since the world was created, people have seen the earth and sky. Through everything God made, they can clearly see his invisible qualities—his eternal power and divine nature. So they have no excuse for not knowing God.* - **Romans 1:18-20(NLT)**

People know there is a God. We might not all know who He is, believe in Him or His words, but we know He exists. It is true that God is invisible to all human sensory perception. It is also true that He exists outside of the realms of time and space. Yet, all we can see and perceive including our own existence came from Him. Therefore, the Apostle Paul revealed in Romans 1 that we can see God's invisible qualities through His visible creation. With that understanding, it's apparent that all people, including those who are not spiritually sensitive, can receive communication from God. That's right! Someone with no prophetic gift, no understanding of the scripture and no relationship with God has no excuse because God also speaks to people through nature.

Now before anyone gets carried away associating this with new age philosophies let me put this in context. I don't believe in Mother Nature nor do I believe in the sun, moon or star gods of ancient religions. That is not Biblical. God is not nature and nature is not God so you can roll up your yoga mat and pick back up your Bible. However, God can communicate with His people through nature. For instance, in Genesis 15:5, God used the stars to indirectly speak to Abraham. Then in Exodus 3, God spoke directly to Moses through a burning bush. Since communication is a two-way street, it's also possible to speak to nature and get a response. Joshua spoke to the sun and moon in Joshua 10:12-13 while Jesus spoke to the wind and sea in Mark 4:39.

I once visited a friend whose dog was quite sensitive to stormy weather. If a storm was in the forecast, long before the outside conditions began to change, the dog became uncontrollably anxious. So much so, that they were prescribed CBD capsules specially formulated to keep their dog calm. The sun could be shining outside, with perfectly calm conditions and the dog could be locked inside of the house in a dark room with no access to a window. Yet, without fail, it was able to sense any approaching storm even if it was still far on the horizon or hours away. It would then warn its owners like a watchman on the wall.

The scriptures provide precedence pertaining to animals being sensitive to the spirit realm and, in some cases, signaling God's timing. In Genesis 3, the devil inhabited a snake in the Garden of Eden. Jesus cast demons out of a man and into pigs in Matthew 8:32. The cock crew in Matthew 26:74 to confirm the prophetic word of Jesus to Peter that he would deny Jesus three times. In 1 Kings 17, God commanded ravens to feed Elijah with bread and meat while he hid by the Brook Cherith, sustaining his life during the famine. Yet, none of those is as riveting as the prophetic donkey in Numbers 22.

The Prophetic Donkey

Then the children of Israel moved, and camped in the plains of Moab on the

side of the Jordan across from Jericho. Now Balak the son of Zippor saw all
that Israel had done to the Amorites. And Moab was exceedingly afraid of the
people because they were many, and Moab was sick with dread because of the
children of Israel. So Moab said to the elders of Midian, "Now this company
will lick up everything around us, as an ox licks up the grass of the field."
And Balak the son of Zippor was king of the Moabites at that time… Then
God came to Balaam and said, "Who are these men with you?" So Balaam
said to God, "Balak the son of Zippor, king of Moab, has sent to me, saying,
'Look, a people has come out of Egypt, and they cover the face of the earth.
Come now, curse them for me; perhaps I shall be able to overpower them and
drive them out.' " And God said to Balaam, "You shall not go with them;
you shall not curse the people, for they are blessed." So Balaam rose in the
morning and said to the princes of Balak, "Go back to your land, for the Lord
has refused to give me permission to go with you." - **Numbers 22:1-4, 9-**
13(NKJV)

The Book of Numbers reads like a modern soap opera with a host of twists
and turns. Numbers 1-13 tells the story of the Israelites' escape from Egypt
and their 11-day journey to the Promised Land. During that time, God used
Moses to develop some structure in their lives in preparation for a future of
freedom. Numbers 14 then chronicles how the Children of Israel refused to
enter the Promised Land which destined most of them to a lifetime in the
wilderness. Still, The Lord was with them as they went on a rampage through
the wilderness crushing their enemies with the power of God. They built a
fearsome reputation as signs and wonders followed them everywhere they
went while nation after nation fell before them.

Balak, the king of Moab heard about them and knew he was next when
they set up camp in his area. He was so scared of the Israelites that he tried
to hire Balaam, a non-Israelite prophet to declare a curse on Israel. Why
Balaam? He was not an Israelite and Jude 11 describes Balaam as a prophet
for hire, who was willing to deceive people for money. Regardless, when
Balak's princes approached Balaam, he sought the face of God first before
responding, which was a good thing. God said no, so he said no which
typically should have ended it there.

And the princes of Moab rose and went to Balak, and said, "Balaam refuses
to come with us." Then Balak again sent princes, more numerous and more
honorable than they. And they came to Balaam and said to him, "Thus says
Balak the son of Zippor: 'Please let nothing hinder you from coming to me; for
I will certainly honor you greatly, and I will do whatever you say to me.
Therefore please come, curse this people for me.' " Then Balaam answered and
said to the servants of Balak, "Though Balak were to give me his house full of

silver and gold, I could not go beyond the word of the Lord my God, to do less or more. Now therefore, please, you also stay here tonight, that I may know what more the Lord will say to me." And God came to Balaam at night and said to him, "If the men come to call you, rise and go with them; but only the word which I speak to you—that you shall do." So Balaam rose in the morning, saddled his donkey, and went with the princes of Moab. -
Numbers 22:14-21(NKJV)

Balak was persistent and refused to take no for an answer. He must have known Balaam's reputation because he sweetened the deal to include compensation. What's fascinating about Balaam is that, regardless of his obvious character flaws, he had a genuine gift of hearing and speaking the Voice of God. I've heard debates concerning whether Balaam was a true prophet. Some say yes because what he said was from God which is the truth. Yet, that doesn't make him true, it makes him accurate. Perhaps, it would be better to call him an accurate prophet instead of a true prophet. Truth relates to his character and accuracy relates to the content of his prophecy. He only had one and not the other. That's a principle I learned from my father, a true and accurate prophet of God.

When Balak's princes approached Balaam for the second time, at first, he gave them the same answer, which was no. However, instead of leaving it there and closing the door behind him, he left the door open by saying he would approach God again. This time God gave him the "go ahead" which I thought was strange at first. Why would God tell Balaam no the first time then change His mind and tell him yes, the second time? Which was it? Yes, or no? The answer was still no! Yet, God knew it was in Balaam's heart to go with the men, so God allowed him to go with one condition. He could only say what God told him to say. That didn't mean God was happy about it. In fact, God was angry with Balaam for even wanting to go at all.

Then God's anger was aroused because he went, and the Angel of the Lord took His stand in the way as an adversary against him. And he was riding on his donkey, and his two servants were with him. Now the donkey saw the Angel of the Lord standing in the way with His drawn sword in His hand, and the donkey turned aside out of the way and went into the field. So Balaam struck the donkey to turn her back onto the road. Then the Angel of the Lord stood in a narrow path between the vineyards, with a wall on this side and a wall on that side. And when the donkey saw the Angel of the Lord, she pushed herself against the wall and crushed Balaam's foot against the wall; so he struck her again. Then the Angel of the Lord went further, and stood in a narrow place where there was no way to turn either to the right hand or to the left. And when the donkey saw the Angel of the Lord, she lay down under Balaam; so

144

Balaam's anger was aroused, and he struck the donkey with his staff. Then the Lord opened the mouth of the donkey, and she said to Balaam, "What have I done to you, that you have struck me these three times?" And Balaam said to the donkey, "Because you have abused me. I wish there were a sword in my hand, for now I would kill you!" So the donkey said to Balaam, "Am I not your donkey on which you have ridden, ever since I became yours, to this day? Was I ever disposed to do this to you?" And he said, "No." Then the Lord opened Balaam's eyes, and he saw the Angel of the Lord standing in the way with His drawn sword in His hand; and he bowed his head and fell flat on his face. And the Angel of the Lord said to him, "Why have you struck your donkey these three times? Behold, I have come out to stand against you, because your way is perverse before Me. The donkey saw Me and turned aside from Me these three times. If she had not turned aside from Me, surely I would also have killed you by now, and let her live." And Balaam said to the Angel of the Lord, "I have sinned, for I did not know You stood in the way against me. Now therefore, if it displeases You, I will turn back." Then the Angel of the Lord said to Balaam, "Go with the men, but only the word that I speak to you, that you shall speak." So Balaam went with the princes of Balak. -
Numbers 22:22-35(NKJV)

Prophets are the voice of God in the earth, not donkeys. When God uses a donkey to speak to a prophet, something must be totally wrong. Nevertheless, that was the case for Balaam, a man who could clearly hear God's Voice but found himself in a no-win situation. After repeated requests by King Balak's princes, God released Balaam to return with them to prophesy against Israel, or so they thought. Then, as soon as Balaam started on his journey, God was angry and put an angel in the way to stop him. That's when the prophetic donkey stole the show.

In this account of a talking animal, it is easy to see that it was not God's first preference to communicate to His own prophet in that manner. If Balaam's heart was in the right place, the donkey would not have spoken because there would have been no need. God had already spoken to Balaam once about not considering Balak's offer. If he listened not just to God's words but to God's heart, the first time, the situation would not have gotten that far. When prophets don't hear God's voice on the inside of their hearts, God will use whatever He can to get His message across.

They have forsaken the right way and gone astray, following the way of Balaam the son of Beor, who loved the wages of unrighteousness; but he was rebuked for his iniquity: a dumb donkey speaking with a man's voice restrained the madness of the prophet. - **2 Peter 2:15-16(NKJV)**

The Book of Numbers was, for the most part, historical in nature with its focus on the facts of what happened to Israel after escaping Egypt. Hence, it did not give much commentary on Balaam's character to accompany the account of his actions. However, in several other scriptures, when his name was mentioned, it was done with scorn. Peter reinforced the idea of Balaam as a prophet for hire in 2 Peter 2:15-16 and pulled no punches about his unhealthy relationship with money. He considered it madness for a prophet of God to be willing to say anything for the right price. Again, while it was fascinating that God spoke through a donkey, it was clearly not God's preferred mode of communication.

Though Balaam tried to prophesy against Israel, he could only bless them because God put the words in his mouth. Between Numbers 22 and 24, the scriptures recount four different occasions when Balaam declared blessings over Israel to the chagrin of Balak. It looked like a happy ending to the story because Balak's plan to derail Israel's progress was foiled and what was meant for evil God used for good. Unfortunately, the story doesn't end there. Like Balak, Balaam was persistent and found an even more sinister plan that worked like a charm against the Children of Israel. It's recorded in Numbers 25 directly following Balaam's final prophecy in Number 24 and though it appears to be unrelated it is not.

> Now Israel remained in Acacia Grove, and the people began to commit harlotry with the women of Moab. They invited the people to the sacrifices of their gods, and the people ate and bowed down to their gods. So Israel was joined to Baal of Peor, and the anger of the Lord was aroused against Israel. Then the Lord said to Moses, "Take all the leaders of the people and hang the offenders before the Lord, out in the sun, that the fierce anger of the Lord may turn away from Israel." So Moses said to the judges of Israel, "Every one of you kill his men who were joined to Baal of Peor." And indeed, one of the children of Israel came and presented to his brethren a Midianite woman in the sight of Moses and in the sight of all the congregation of the children of Israel, who were weeping at the door of the tabernacle of meeting. Now when Phinehas the son of Eleazar, the son of Aaron the priest, saw it, he rose from among the congregation and took a javelin in his hand; and he went after the man of Israel into the tent and thrust both of them through, the man of Israel, and the woman through her body. So the plague was stopped among the children of Israel. And those who died in the plague were twenty-four thousand. - **Numbers 25:1-4(NKJV)**

Balak, the king of Moab tried to attack Israel spiritually by hiring a rogue prophet to curse them, but his plan did not work. That was only Plan A. He still had Plan B and C ready to go. What sorcery could not do, women and food easily accomplished. Think about it a little. The Moabites didn't even think about attacking Israel with their armies because they were no match. However, they were able to indirectly cause the death of 24,000 Israelites without raising one spear, shooting one arrow, or swinging one sword. Their attempt to use witchcraft was also a complete miss on their part. Yet, they used their women and food to attack Israel with more effectiveness than any physical or spiritual weapon. How did they know Israel's weakness? One word; Balaam.

But I have a few things against you, because you have there those who hold the doctrine of Balaam, who taught Balak to put a stumbling block before the children of Israel, to eat things sacrificed to idols, and to commit sexual immorality. - **Revelation 2:14 (NKJV)**

Balaam earned his money. He may not have been able to curse Israel directly, but he knew how to defeat them. Therefore, God needed to use his donkey to speak the truth. Balaam's heart was wicked, and God knew it. He may have been incapable of cursing who God had blessed but that didn't stop him from finding another way to hurt them. Balaam had the honor of a direct line of communication with God. Still, his schemes cost the lives of 24,000 Israelites because Balak paid the right price. Nevertheless, in the end, the Israelites got their vengeance.

The sons of Israel also killed Balaam the son of Beor, the diviner (soothsayer), with the sword among [the rest of] their slain. - **Joshua 13:22(AMP)**

Balaam's reputation was so poor by the end of his life that he was described in The Book of Joshua as a diviner or a soothsayer and not a prophet. In fact, outside of the Book of Numbers, most of the other writers referred to him as a sorcerer. Perhaps, the talking donkey contributed to that reputation. At that moment, it was more of a true prophet than Balaam. Regardless, the day finally came when the Israelites got their hands on Balaam. They killed him and put him out of his misery for good. Well, maybe not for eternity, but for his time on the earth. After his inglorious ending, his memory lives on as the prophet who needed his donkey to prophesy for him to finally listen to God's Voice.

As we wrap up this case study, how can you apply the principles contained within it to your own life? God wants to speak to you, and He is willing to use any aspect of creation to get His message across. What has He been saying to you from inside your heart where He lives? Are you listening or is there so much noise that He must find an alternate channel of communication to reach you? For Balaam, it was a donkey. For Belshazzar in Daniel 5, it was God's hand breaking through the barrier of the natural realm to physically write an ominous warning on the wall. If you can't hear what God is saying to you on the inside, He'll find a way to say the same thing from the outside.

14 GOD IN THE STORM

He answered and said to them, "When it is evening you say, 'It will be fair weather, for the sky is red'; and in the morning, 'It will be foul weather today, for the sky is red and threatening.' Hypocrites! You know how to discern the face of the sky, but you cannot discern the signs of the times. - **Matthew 16:2-3(NKJV)**

God uses storms of different types to communicate with people. My wife and I have this inside joke which is not funny at all. Whenever something unusual or completely out of the ordinary happens in a situation we say there's a *"glitch in the Matrix"*. If you never saw the movie; The Matrix, let me explain. A *"glitch in the Matrix"* is a sign that something is wrong and it's your last warning sign before the situation takes a sudden turn for the worse. Anytime we notice a glitch, we immediately increase our level of alertness because we don't want to be complacent when God allows us to see warning signs.

Jonah was a prophet of God who was given the assignment to prophesy against Nineveh that he clearly understood. Instead of doing what God said, he went in the opposite direction and boarded a ship to Tarshish. Soon after, he encountered a *"glitch in the Matrix"* when an unusual wind hit the sea and they faced a storm like they never had before in their lives. God used the storm to speak to Jonah in a way that could not be denied. With every howling wind and violent wave, Jonah could hear God repeatedly saying to him; *"I said go to Nineveh"*. What we learn from Jonah's example is that God doesn't just speak in a storm, He speaks through storms.

The first thing you must do is define the cause of the storm. There are two general causes of storms: obedience and disobedience. If you don't know what type of storm you are in, you need to find out. Why? A different response is required for each storm. If you don't know that, you might suffer much more than you need to.

1) Storms of Disobedience

> *This is what the Lord says— your Redeemer, the Holy One of Israel: "I am the Lord your God, who teaches you what is good for you and leads you along the paths you should follow. Oh, that you had listened to my commands! Then you would have had peace flowing like a gentle river and righteousness rolling over you like waves in the sea. Your descendants would have been like the sands along the seashore— too many to count! There would have been no need for your destruction, or for cutting off your family name." -* **Isaiah 48:17-19(NLT)**

In this type of storm, God speaks to you directly and you choose to disobey. If you're in the middle of this type of storm and you expect to hear from God, you'll have to keep waiting. God's already spoken so there is nothing else for Him to say. If He says anything it will either be a reminder of what He has already said or something like; *"Repent!"* This is not the type of storm you want to go through. You want to get out as soon as possible.

John 16:8 says that The Holy Spirit will bring conviction of sin to the world. If you're a Christian, Romans 8:9 says The Holy Spirit lives in you. Therefore, He'll also bring conviction to your heart if you're in disobedience. Nonetheless, don't expect to hear anything profound in this storm. You already know what God has to say. Jonah is a great example.

Case Study #1 - Jonah

> *Now the word of the Lord came to Jonah the son of Amittai, saying, "Arise, go to Nineveh, that great city, and cry out against it; for their wickedness has come up before Me." But Jonah arose to flee to Tarshish from the presence of the Lord. He went down to Joppa, and found a ship going to Tarshish; so he paid the fare, and went down into it, to go with them to Tarshish from the presence of the Lord. But the Lord sent out a great wind on the sea, and there was a mighty tempest on the sea, so that the ship was about to be broken up. Then the mariners were afraid; and every man cried out to his god, and threw the cargo that was in the ship into the sea, to lighten the load. But Jonah had gone down into the lowest parts of the ship, had lain down, and was fast asleep. So the captain came to him, and said to him, "What do you mean, sleeper? Arise, call on your God; perhaps your God will consider us, so that we may not perish." And they said to one another, "Come, let us cast lots, that we may*

know for whose cause this trouble has come upon us." So they cast lots, and the lot fell on Jonah. Then they said to him, "Please tell us! For whose cause is this trouble upon us? What is your occupation? And where do you come from? What is your country? And of what people are you?" So he said to them, "I am a Hebrew; and I fear the Lord, the God of heaven, who made the sea and the dry land." Then the men were exceedingly afraid, and said to him, "Why have you done this?" For the men knew that he fled from the presence of the Lord, because he had told them. Then they said to him, "What shall we do to you that the sea may be calm for us?"—for the sea was growing more tempestuous. And he said to them, "Pick me up and throw me into the sea; then the sea will become calm for you. For I know that this great tempest is because of me." Nevertheless the men rowed hard to return to land, but they could not, for the sea continued to grow more tempestuous against them. Therefore they cried out to the Lord and said, "We pray, O Lord, please do not let us perish for this man's life, and do not charge us with innocent blood; for You, O Lord, have done as it pleased You." So they picked up Jonah and threw him into the sea, and the sea ceased from its raging. Then the men feared the Lord exceedingly, and offered a sacrifice to the Lord and took vows. Now the Lord had prepared a great fish to swallow Jonah. And Jonah was in the belly of the fish three days and three nights. - **Jonah 1:1-17(NKJV)**

Jonah heard from God and disobeyed so instead of speaking again using words, God spoke through a storm of disobedience. What did God say? *"Obey or pay with your life!"* Jonah heard Him loud and clear. Please note that there's only one way out of this type of storm; confession and repentance. Confession is admitting that you are wrong, while repentance is changing your actions. According to 1 John 1:9, if you confess your sins, God is faithful and just to forgive you.

There's nothing noble about a storm of disobedience and there's nothing to shout about. You don't praise through this storm until it stops. It won't stop until you stop disobeying God. Yet, pay close attention to Jonah 1:17, the last verse in the scripture passage quoted above. God had prepared a great fish ahead of time to swallow Jonah. Why is this important? Even though Jonah was disobedient and went in the wrong direction, God had a plan.

There hath no temptation taken you but such as is common to man: but God is faithful, who will not suffer you to be tempted above that ye are able; but will with the temptation also make a way to escape, that ye may be able to bear it. - **1 Corinthians 10:13(KJV)**

In a storm of disobedience, God creates a way of escape that you can access when you're ready to repent. He did it for Jonah, He'll do it for you.

Even though Jonah was out of The Will of God, the mercy of God was still extended to him. God always creates a way of escape out of storms of disobedience. You don't go through these storms expecting to learn valuable lessons, but you potentially still can. Still, you should look for a way to escape and get out as soon as you can.

Again, you can't assume you'll learn too much in this storm except; *"Don't disobey God!"* If God provides additional insight, that's great but that's not the best way to get it. These storms can be avoided, and you will still be able to live a full life without them. There's no need to go through hell on earth because you reject God's directions. Jesus never disobeyed His Father, so He never had to experience these types of storms in His own life. We should learn from His example.

2) Storms of Obedience

> *These things I have spoken unto you, that in me ye might have peace. In the world ye shall have tribulation: but be of good cheer; I have overcome the world.*
> - **John 16:33(KJV)**

This type of storm is inevitable. We live in a fallen world so you can expect to constantly run into storms of obedience. It's in these storms that your faith is tested. I heard someone wise once say; *"A faith that has not been tested cannot be trusted."* You can draw closer to God amid trials like these and hear from God clearly if you choose to tune in. Now, let me show you something fascinating in a very familiar scripture.

> *My brethren, count it all joy when ye fall into divers temptations; Knowing this, that the trying of your faith worketh patience. But let patience have her perfect work, that ye may be perfect and entire, wanting nothing. If any of you lack wisdom, let him ask of God, that giveth to all men liberally, and upbraideth not; and it shall be given him. But let him ask in faith, nothing wavering. For he that wavereth is like a wave of the sea driven with the wind and tossed. For let not that man think that he shall receive any thing of the Lord. A double minded man is unstable in all his ways.* - **James 1:2-8(KJV)**

Do you know that the verses in James 1:2-8 were meant to be read together? Most times, we pull out verses 2-4 and teach entire sermons on tribulation and temptations. We tell people that life is supposed to be hard, God never said it would be easy. We scream; *"Hallelujah! Praise God!"* However, there's a reason why verses 5-8 follow directly after.

In the middle of tribulations, you need to ask God for wisdom. When you can't see your way and your patience is being tested you have to say; *"Lord, I'm confused. I don't know what to do here. I need wisdom."* The Bible says that He will speak to you and give you wisdom. However, only on one condition. You must ask in faith.

> *And he saith unto them, Why are ye fearful, O ye of little faith? Then he arose, and rebuked the winds and the sea; and there was a great calm.* - **Matthew 8:26(KJV)**

Fear and faith can't exist together so you're either going to be in a state of fear in the middle of a storm or faith. If you're in a state of fear, you will receive nothing from The Lord because it will cancel out your faith. You won't get wisdom. You won't know what to do. You won't hear God. If you're fearful, expect to remain in the storm for a while. To make it simple, in the middle of a storm of obedience, ask God for wisdom to navigate the storm. You won't always get a quick exit like you would from a storm of disobedience, but you will get peace on the inside to ride it out if you must.

Case Study #2 - Jesus and His Disciples

> *Now when He got into a boat, His disciples followed Him. And suddenly a great tempest arose on the sea, so that the boat was covered with the waves. But He was asleep. Then His disciples came to Him and awoke Him, saying, "Lord, save us! We are perishing!" But He said to them, "Why are you fearful, O you of little faith?" Then He arose and rebuked the winds and the sea, and there was a great calm. So the men marveled, saying, "Who can this be, that even the winds and the sea obey Him?"* - **Matthew 8:23-27(KJV)**

> *And the same day, when the even was come, he saith unto them, Let us pass over unto the other side. And when they had sent away the multitude, they took him even as he was in the ship. And there were also with him other little ships. And there arose a great storm of wind, and the waves beat into the ship, so that it was now full. And he was in the hinder part of the ship, asleep on a pillow: and they awake him, and say unto him, Master, carest thou not that we perish? And he arose, and rebuked the wind, and said unto the sea, Peace, be still. And the wind ceased, and there was a great calm. And he said unto them, Why are ye so fearful? how is it that ye have no faith? And they feared exceedingly, and said one to another, What manner of man is this, that even the wind and the sea obey him?* - **Mark 4:35-41(KJV)**

The most important thing you can have in a storm is faith. What is faith? Complete trust in the invisible evidence provided by The Word of God confirmed by commensurate action (Hebrews 11:1, Romans 10:17 and James

2:17, 18). I compiled that definition in another one of my books, *Faith Science,* which is available at major online booksellers from anywhere in the world. The same power which was available to Jesus was available to His disciples. Yet, He had enough faith to calm the storms and they did not.

When you go through storms of obedience you must look for ways to build your faith. It's your faith that allows you to execute your authority. Every Christian has the same authority because it comes from Jesus, but we all don't operate with the same level of faith. Your faith comes by hearing and hearing by the Word of God. (Romans 10:17) The first step to your faith is your understanding, belief, and execution of the written Word of God. The Holy Ghost will bring the Word you need to remembrance when you need it. (John 14:26)

In the middle of a storm, God will speak to you. He will speak through scriptures. He will speak through your pastor. He will speak through other people. He will speak through signs. Whatever it takes, if you ask God for wisdom in a storm, He will speak. When you hear from God, you need faith in what you hear to execute your authority in the face of the storm. The name of Jesus gives you authority, but faith is what you need to execute and apply it.

3)   **Storms of Disobedience and Obedience Combined**

Sometimes, you may be caught in a special type of storm that may be a result of both disobedience and obedience. How is that possible? You may be in obedience while someone else may be in disobedience and because you are together you both go through the storm. For example, Jonah was in disobedience and all the other guys in the ship had to go through the storm because of him. Now, here's an example that clearly shows this type of storm.

Case Study #3 - Paul

> *We had lost a lot of time. The weather was becoming dangerous for sea travel because it was so late in the fall, and Paul spoke to the ship's officers about it. "Men," he said, "I believe there is trouble ahead if we go on—shipwreck, loss of cargo, and danger to our lives as well." But the officer in charge of the prisoners listened more to the ship's captain and the owner than to Paul. And since Fair Havens was an exposed harbor—a poor place to spend the winter— most of the crew wanted to go on to Phoenix, farther up the coast of Crete, and spend the winter there. Phoenix was a good harbor with only a southwest and northwest exposure. When a light wind began blowing from the south, the sailors thought they could make it. So they pulled up anchor and sailed close to*

the shore of Crete. But the weather changed abruptly, and a wind of typhoon strength (called a "northeaster") burst across the island and blew us out to sea. The sailors couldn't turn the ship into the wind, so they gave up and let it run before the gale. We sailed along the sheltered side of a small island named Cauda, where with great difficulty we hoisted aboard the lifeboat being towed behind us. Then the sailors bound ropes around the hull of the ship to strengthen it. They were afraid of being driven across to the sandbars of Syrtis off the African coast, so they lowered the sea anchor to slow the ship and were driven before the wind. The next day, as gale-force winds continued to batter the ship, the crew began throwing the cargo overboard. The following day they even took some of the ship's gear and threw it overboard. The terrible storm raged for many days, blotting out the sun and the stars, until at last all hope was gone. No one had eaten for a long time. Finally, Paul called the crew together and said, "Men, you should have listened to me in the first place and not left Crete. You would have avoided all this damage and loss. But take courage! None of you will lose your lives, even though the ship will go down. For last night an angel of the God to whom I belong and whom I serve stood beside me, and he said, 'Don't be afraid, Paul, for you will surely stand trial before Caesar! What's more, God in his goodness has granted safety to everyone sailing with you.' So take courage! For I believe God. It will be just as he said. But we will be shipwrecked on an island." - **Acts 27:9-26(NLT)**

The sailors didn't listen to Paul so they ended up in a storm of disobedience that could have been avoided. It was not Paul's fault that they were in that situation, but Paul was on the same ship facing the same storm. Though, even during the storm, God sent an angel to speak to Paul. It was this Word that saved them. Had Paul not been there they would have probably died. Paul was confident in the storm because He received a Word from The Lord. To everyone else's benefit, he was positioned to hear from God. He was doing God's Will, living in obedience and most importantly, he was in faith because he believed God. As a result, they all made it through the storm, and nobody died. Therefore, you must do the same.

Faith comes from God's Word. Meditate in God's Word and practice living by it daily so your faith will be ready for the storms of life. If you're already in a storm, ask for wisdom. God will answer. He gave you His Word. If you can't hear from Him yourself, spend time around people who hear from God, go to church, read books, just position yourself where you can hear from God. He'll speak through someone. If you have faith you will hear God. Also, if God gave you a Word before the storm that means He gave you The Word to take you through the storm. Let it anchor your soul. There's so much more I can say but I'll stop here. The Lord has spoken!

As we bring this chapter to a close, again, here are five ways God reveals His timing to people.

1. **The Word of God (Complete)**
2. **Prayer (Complete)**
3. **Signs (Complete)**
4. Dreams and Visions
5. Prophecy

In the next chapter, we will look at how dreams and visions help reveal God's timing.

15 DREAMS AND VISIONS

For God speaks again and again, though people do not recognize it. He speaks in dreams, in visions of the night, when deep sleep falls on people as they lie in their beds. He whispers in their ears and terrifies them with warnings. He makes them turn from doing wrong; he keeps them from pride. He protects them from the grave, from crossing over the river of death. - **Job 33:14-18(NLT)**

God is a Spirit and exists in a realm outside the confines of time and space. Everything that was, is and will be, exists right now in His eyes. He doesn't just see things in real-time as they take place, He sees all things that have taken place or will ever take place. Dreams and visions allow us to see like God. We step out of the natural realm of time and see into the spirit realm where time has no limiting power. Therefore, God uses dreams and visions to reveal His timing to us. By doing so, He enables us to prepare for situations that are yet to come. That gives us the advantage over our peers who don't have access to that type of inside information. Here's a perfect example from the scriptures.

Then Joseph said to Pharaoh, "The dreams of Pharaoh are one; God has shown Pharaoh what He is about to do: The seven good cows are seven years, and the seven good heads are seven years; the dreams are one. And the seven thin and ugly cows which came up after them are seven years, and the seven empty heads blighted by the east wind are seven years of famine. This is the thing which I have spoken to Pharaoh. God has shown Pharaoh what He is about to do. Indeed seven years of great plenty will come throughout all the land of Egypt; but after them seven years of famine will arise, and all the plenty will be forgotten in the land of Egypt; and the famine will deplete the land. So the plenty will not be known in the land because of the famine following, for it will

be very severe. And the dream was repeated to Pharaoh twice because the thing is established by God, and God will shortly bring it to pass. "Now therefore, let Pharaoh select a discerning and wise man, and set him over the land of Egypt. Let Pharaoh do this, and let him appoint officers over the land, to collect one-fifth of the produce of the land of Egypt in the seven plentiful years. And let them gather all the food of those good years that are coming, and store up grain under the authority of Pharaoh, and let them keep food in the cities. Then that food shall be as a reserve for the land for the seven years of famine which shall be in the land of Egypt, that the land may not perish during the famine."
- **Genesis 41:25-36(NKJV)**

Through the interpretation of Pharaoh's dream, God revealed to Joseph the exact timing of seven years of abundance and seven years of famine for Egypt and its neighbors. God also gave him the wisdom to prepare for the time of famine during the time of abundance. Then, once the time of famine came, God empowered Joseph to orchestrate one of the most effective wealth transfers in recorded history. In the process, he gathered all the money, livestock, land, and people of Egypt into the coffers of Pharaoh. Here's how everything played out.

Joseph was thirty years old when he stood before Pharaoh king of Egypt. And Joseph went out from the presence of Pharaoh, and went throughout all the land of Egypt. Now in the seven plentiful years the ground brought forth abundantly. So he gathered up all the food of the seven years which were in the land of Egypt, and laid up the food in the cities; he laid up in every city the food of the fields which surrounded them. Joseph gathered very much grain, as the sand of the sea, until he stopped counting, for it was immeasurable... Then the seven years of plenty which were in the land of Egypt ended, and the seven years of famine began to come, as Joseph had said. The famine was in all lands, but in all the land of Egypt there was bread. So when all the land of Egypt was famished, the people cried to Pharaoh for bread. Then Pharaoh said to all the Egyptians, "Go to Joseph; whatever he says to you, do." The famine was over all the face of the earth, and Joseph opened all the storehouses and sold to the Egyptians. And the famine became severe in the land of Egypt. So all countries came to Joseph in Egypt to buy grain, because the famine was severe in all lands. - **Genesis 41:46-49, 53-57(NKJV)**

Most accounts of the famine in Egypt taught in church settings begin and end in Genesis 41. Joseph interpreted the dream, was promoted to second in command in Egypt, gathered grain during the times of plenty and distributed it during the times of famine. Still, that is just a small part of the story. Joseph didn't give the grain away out of the kindness of his heart. He had stored so much grain that he became a grain magnate amid the famine. First, he sold grain to the people of Egypt then to people from other nations impacted by the famine.

With a monopoly on grain and considering the impact on prices by the law of supply and demand, we can only imagine the pricing structure created by Joseph. He could name his price and the people had no choice but to pay. This ensured the maximum payout for Pharaoh during that time. In fact, Joseph practically sold grain until there was no more money to pay for it and still, he had more grain available. So, he came up with a plan to return to the barter system accepting alternate forms of compensation until that option also ran out.

Now there was no bread in all the land; for the famine was very severe, so that the land of Egypt and the land of Canaan languished because of the famine. And Joseph gathered up all the money that was found in the land of Egypt and in the land of Canaan, for the grain which they bought; and Joseph brought the money into Pharaoh's house. So when the money failed in the land of Egypt and in the land of Canaan, all the Egyptians came to Joseph and said, "Give us bread, for why should we die in your presence? For the money has failed." Then Joseph said, "Give your livestock, and I will give you bread for your livestock, if the money is gone." So they brought their livestock to Joseph, and Joseph gave them bread in exchange for the horses, the flocks, the cattle of the herds, and for the donkeys. Thus he fed them with bread in exchange for all their livestock that year. When that year had ended, they came to him the next year and said to him, "We will not hide from my lord that our money is gone; my lord also has our herds of livestock. There is nothing left in the sight of my lord but our bodies and our lands. Why should we die before your eyes, both we and our land? Buy us and our land for bread, and we and our land will be servants of Pharaoh; give us seed, that we may live and not die, that the land may not be desolate." Then Joseph bought all the land of Egypt for Pharaoh; for every man of the Egyptians sold his field, because the famine was severe upon them. So the land became Pharaoh's. And as for the people, he moved them into the cities, from one end of the borders of Egypt to the other end. Only the land of the priests he did not buy; for the priests had rations allotted to them by Pharaoh, and they ate their rations which Pharaoh gave them; therefore they did not sell their lands. Then Joseph said to the people, "Indeed I have bought you and your land this day for Pharaoh. Look, here is seed for you, and you shall sow the land. And it shall come to pass in the harvest that you shall give one-fifth to Pharaoh. Four-fifths shall be your own, as seed for the field and for your food, for those of your households and as food for your little ones." So they said, "You have saved our lives; let us find favor in the sight of my lord, and we will be Pharaoh's servants." And Joseph made it a law over the land of Egypt to this day, that Pharaoh should have one-fifth, except for the land of the priests only, which did not become Pharaoh's. - **Genesis 47:13-26(NKJV)**

Through a series of steps, Joseph instituted a system of taxation in Egypt that still exists, though it has obviously increased in sophistication over time.

Step 1: Take all the money in exchange for food.
Step 2: Take all the livestock in exchange for food.
Step 3: Take all the land in exchange for food.
Step 4: Take all the people in exchange for food.
Step 5: Move all the people into cities owned by the Government.
Step 6: Provide the people rations to eat and seed to sow.
Step 7: Collect 20% tax from all their harvests.

In the end, Egypt became one of the world's first major superpowers flush with wealth and global influence. All of this took place because one man understood God's timing by interpreting some dreams.

But this is what was spoken by the prophet Joel: 'And it shall come to pass in the last days, says God, That I will pour out of My Spirit on all flesh; Your sons and your daughters shall prophesy, Your young men shall see visions, Your old men shall dream dreams. - **Acts 2:16-17(NKJV)**

One would think that over time our communication with God would become more and more sophisticated. By now, He should be able to move away from using dreams and visions to speak to people. On the contrary, as we go deeper into the last days, God intends to communicate with us in that way even more. It is my humble opinion that God uses this mode of communication because it's the most effective at avoiding distractions.

Think about it. You're either sleeping, unconscious or outside of your consciousness in some other way when you're dreaming or seeing a vision. That means you're not doing anything else. You're inaccessible to any natural distractions from anyone or anything outside of your own thoughts. I believe in dreams and visions because those are effective ways that God communicates with me. Here's some of my testimony.

My Testimony

And when they were departed, behold, the angel of the Lord appeareth to Joseph in a dream, saying, Arise, and take the young child and his mother, and flee into Egypt, and be thou there until I bring thee word: for Herod will seek the young child to destroy him. - **Matthew 2:13(KJV)**

Just after 5:00 AM on my birthday, Saturday, December 5th, 2015 I woke up suddenly and sat straight up on my bed. I just had the most vivid dream I ever experienced in my life. It felt like more than a dream. It was a real-life experience that simply hadn't happened yet. I was intimately familiar with the setting. I knew each of the people involved. I even felt the full range of emotions and understood exactly what God was showing me. After almost twelve challenging years of service, the time had come for me to leave my place of employment and move on to something better that God had reserved for me. I told my wife, Angel, what God revealed, and we instantly got to work on the exit plan.

Step one was building a curriculum vitae or resume. At the time, I was still working at my first job out of graduate school at Georgia Tech, so I had not updated or even looked at my resume for over a decade. It was out of date, at best, and obsolete, at worst. I had to take a copy of my wife's resume and update the content to match my qualifications and experience. That was our weekend assignment. I also called the leader of a respected engineering firm in my community to let him know that I was interested in talking more about an opportunity he brought to my attention a few months before.

Two days later, Monday, December 7th, I googled the words, *"Senior Structural Engineer jobs in Atlanta"* and found a plethora of openings including a few good ones that caught my eye. I applied to two of them that afternoon with a personal preference for just one. The next morning, Tuesday, December 8th, a recruiter called me to chat about my preferred position and on Thursday, December 10th I had my first phone interview. From that point on, the rest is history. I was offered the job and in February of 2016, I walked into my new season. What's even more interesting is that the position was open for five months and they had interviewed twelve other qualified candidates who just didn't match what they were looking for. By the time I showed up they must have been tired from the long process and ready to end their search. I named my price and was offered exactly that. My timing was perfect.

On the way out the door of my former job, I looked at each of my coworkers in the eye and thanked them for a great experience. Yet, leaving them behind was the best decision I could have ever made for my career which didn't have much further to go there. It would be an understatement to say that my career took off from that moment on. In many ways, I accomplished more in the next three years of my career than I did in the first twelve. Why? I heard the voice of God in a dream and responded accordingly. I know exactly what would have happened if I didn't do what God said. He showed it to me in the dream and it wasn't good. I didn't know when it would happen, but I felt the urgency that it was about to happen soon. God made a way of escape for me at the time in my career when I was the most vulnerable. Thank God for dreams and visions.

Then He said, "Hear now My words: If there is a prophet among you, I, the Lord, make Myself known to him in a vision; I speak to him in a dream. Not so with My servant Moses; He is faithful in all My house. I speak with him face to face, Even plainly, and not in dark sayings; And he sees the form of the Lord. Why then were you not afraid To speak against My servant Moses?" - **Numbers 12:6-8(NKJV)**

There was a season of my life when I was constantly dreaming. I remember having such vivid dreams that I had to write them down. Now I keep a daily appointment book right next to my bed for that purpose. I also ask the Lord for an interpretation just in case there is an important message I need to get that doesn't seem obvious in the dream. Do not despise dreams and visions. They were used throughout the scriptures by The Lord to convey to people some very important information. If He did it before, He will do it again because He does not change (Malachi 3:6).

Be not rash with thy mouth, and let not thine heart be hasty to utter any thing before God: for God is in heaven, and thou upon earth: therefore let thy words be few. For a dream cometh through the multitude of business; and a fool's voice is known by multitude of words. - **Ecclesiastes 5:2-3(KJV)**

Before we go too far to one extreme, we do need to seek some balance in the scriptures. After a long life of supernatural wisdom, success, favor, and accomplishments, Solomon made some bad decisions and learned some valuable lessons. Many of those life lessons are outlined in the Book of Ecclesiastes. According to the verse referenced above, some dreams mean nothing and are just a result of your own thoughts. Those dreams can be ignored. Though, there are other dreams which leave a great impact on your heart when you wake up. Pay close attention to those. God does communicate through dreams. He could be trying to tell you something that you can't hear during the hustle and bustle of your day. Thus, you don't want to go to either extreme.

In Genesis 20:1-7, God warned Abimelech in a dream not to touch Abraham's wife Sarah. In Genesis 31:9-13, God showed Jacob in a dream how to become rich off his scheming father-in-law Laban. In Genesis 37 God showed Joseph his future in dreams. However, in Genesis 41, it was Joseph's ability to interpret the dreams of others which caused his own dream to come to pass. In Matthew 1, God spoke to Joseph (Mary's husband) in a dream about the birth of Jesus. God also warned him in Matthew 2:19-21 through a dream to leave Egypt.

These are the last days which means that the time of dreams and visions is already here. Whether you believe it or not, that's what happens when God's Spirit is poured out. Dreams and visions are direct avenues into the spirit realm which make them excellent conduits for messages from God. Anybody can dream or see a vision. Still, not everyone can interpret what they see. Dreams and visions aren't always easy to understand using natural intelligence. The ability to interpret dreams comes only from The Lord. It made Joseph a very powerful man in Genesis 41 and saved Daniel and his three friends' lives in Daniel 2.

I know of books that provide tools to help people interpret dreams. They do so by attaching meanings to certain common images that people see during recurring dreams. I won't put my trust in them. Am I saying they are complete nonsense? I don't know. I do know that if you rely solely on one of those books, you should also check your horoscope, collect fortune cookies, and call a psychic while you're at it. You must choose for yourself, but I like to avoid anything that's "spiritual" that doesn't come from The Holy Spirit. Nonetheless, let's dig deeper into how people interpret dreams and visions.

As for these four young men, God gave them knowledge and skill in all literature and wisdom; and Daniel had understanding in all visions and dreams. - **Daniel 1:17(NKJV)**

There is a man in your kingdom who has within him the spirit of the holy gods. During Nebuchadnezzar's reign, this man was found to have insight, understanding, and wisdom like that of the gods. Your predecessor, the king— your predecessor King Nebuchadnezzar—made him chief over all the magicians, enchanters, astrologers, and fortune-tellers of Babylon. This man Daniel, whom the king named Belteshazzar, has exceptional ability and is filled with divine knowledge and understanding. He can interpret dreams, explain riddles, and solve difficult problems. Call for Daniel, and he will tell you what the writing means." - **Daniel 5:11-12(NLT)**

God has chosen to speak through dreams and visions in these last days so the ability to interpret them is priceless. God placed the gift within Daniel after he proved himself to be a man of integrity in Daniel 1. Do you know that God wants to give the same gift to you? In James 1:5-8, The Bible says that if you ask God in faith for wisdom, He will give it to you. It takes supernatural wisdom to interpret dreams. Thankfully, He promises to respond to every legitimate request for wisdom so go ahead and make one.

In Daniel's case, God placed the gift in Daniel in order to propel him to prominence in Babylon. God chose to speak to the heathen kings through dreams but only allowed the interpretation through His servant Daniel. In addition to his high level of integrity, Daniel's wisdom was an asset to the kingdom he lived in and the Kingdom of God. When a man walks in that type of wisdom, powerful people take notice.

"If there arises among you a prophet or a dreamer of dreams, and he gives you a sign or a wonder, and the sign or the wonder comes to pass, of which he spoke to you, saying, 'Let us go after other gods'—which you have not known—'and let us serve them,' you shall not listen to the words of that prophet or that dreamer of dreams, for the Lord your God is testing you to know whether you love the Lord your God with all your heart and with all your soul. You shall walk after the Lord your God and fear Him, and keep His commandments and obey His voice; you shall serve Him and hold fast to Him. But that prophet or that dreamer of dreams shall be put to death, because he has spoken in order to turn you away from the Lord your God, who brought you out of the land of Egypt and redeemed you from the house of bondage, to entice you from the way in which the Lord your God commanded you to walk. So you shall put away the evil from your midst. - **Deuteronomy 13:1-6(NKJV)**

Beloved, do not believe every spirit, but test the spirits, whether they are of God; because many false prophets have gone out into the world. - **1 John 4:1(NKJV)**

Be very careful of opportunists who conveniently interpret dreams using their human understanding for selfish reasons. If you pay some of them the right amount of money, they will tell you exactly what you want to hear. That's one reason why all prophecy and the interpretations of dreams and visions must be tested by The Holy Spirit living inside of you as well as the written Word of God. The Holy Spirit is the Spirit of Truth (John 16:13) who guides you into all truth and The Bible is your anchor so that you never drift outside of God's truth. (2 Timothy 2:15)

It's important to only rely on the Holy Ghost to interpret dreams because you don't want to be led astray. I'll give you an example. Several years ago, a young lady submitted an "Ask Donnell" question on my website, *TheCrackedDoor.com* asking me to interpret a dream she had concerning her friend. I asked The Lord for the answer and responded after probably a week.

Yes, it took that long for me to understand what God was saying. If I chose to make an educated guess, I would have completely screwed it up.

The interpretation from The Lord looked nothing like the dream because everything in the dream was deeply symbolic. I had no idea who the person was but a few years later I ran into the person at a church in NY. She thanked me for the accurate interpretation because it addressed a very specific situation her friend was dealing with at the time. She was blown away that God could speak to her so clearly in a dream and allow someone else with no knowledge of the situation to interpret it. That experience reinforced my belief that dreams can only be interpreted through the wisdom of God. If you guess or try to put things together through symbols and signs in the dream, you're at risk of getting it wrong and leading someone or yourself in the wrong direction.

> *The prophet that hath a dream, let him tell a dream; and he that hath my word, let him speak my word faithfully. What is the chaff to the wheat? saith the LORD.* - Jeremiah 23:28(KJV)

> *Surely the Lord GOD will do nothing, but he revealeth his secret unto his servants the prophets.* - **Amos 3:7(KJV)**

Now let's address something of vital importance. Sometimes, The Lord gives you a dream that contains a message to be broadcast. The wisdom of God will help you to know when to tell a dream and when to keep it quiet. If Joseph had known how much his brothers hated him, he probably would have kept his dreams to himself in Genesis 37. Regardless, all things worked together for his good because he loved The Lord and was called according to God's purpose. (Romans 8:28) Consequently, interpreting dreams and visions is not the only important ability you need to develop. You also need the wisdom to know what to do after.

> *Then the men got up from their meal and looked out toward Sodom. As they left, Abraham went with them to send them on their way. "Should I hide my plan from Abraham?" the Lord asked. "For Abraham will certainly become a great and mighty nation, and all the nations of the earth will be blessed through him. I have singled him out so that he will direct his sons and their families to keep the way of the Lord by doing what is right and just. Then I will do for Abraham all that I have promised." So the Lord told Abraham, "I have heard a great outcry from Sodom and Gomorrah, because their sin is so flagrant. I am going down to see if their actions are as wicked as I have heard. If not, I want to know."* - **Genesis 18:16-20(NLT)**

You might not know how to respond to dreams, especially ones that warn you of impending disaster, but I'll tell you right now. Pray! When God tells you something bad is going to happen, do something about it. Don't get scared and just wait around to see if it happens. Get on your face before God and pray that it doesn't happen. God won't show you something before it takes place unless He wants you to get involved.

That's what God did with Abraham. He told Abraham what was going to happen to Sodom and Gomorrah, but Abraham interceded on behalf of his family who lived there. Read Genesis 18:16-33 for the full story. Abraham's intercession was the only reason why Lot and his household were given an opportunity to escape the destruction. If God shows you something, He expects you to intercede. It's really that simple.

I've seen many disasters happen to people I love in dreams, but I ensured that by faith they never happened. If God showed them to me, He gave me the authority to do something about them in prayer. There is no time or space in the spirit so any glimpse into the spirit is a glimpse into eternity. Everything is clear and current in the dream even though what you see has not yet happened. Hence, if you don't want to see the negative outcome of a bad dream come to pass, respond in prayer and stop it.

Welcome to the last days. It's time for you to learn how to hear God through dreams and visions. Your first response to a dream or vision should always be prayer! Then, God will tell you what to do next.

As we bring this chapter to a close, again, here are five ways God reveals His timing to people.

1. **The Word of God (Complete)**
2. **Prayer (Complete)**
3. **Signs (Complete)**
4. **Dreams and Visions (Complete)**
5. Prophecy

In the next chapter, we will look at how prophecy can help reveal God's timing.

16 HOW PROPHECY REVEALS GOD'S TIMING

Do not despise prophecies. - **1 Thessalonians 5:20(NKJV)**

Never underestimate the power of a prophetic Word from God. Yet, if you are accustomed to prophecies at your local church, it's possible to become desensitized to the miracles they really are. Just the thought of God sharing His mind with a human being should be enough to keep us in awe. I believe that the expression of the gift of prophecy should not be limited to the typical church setting. It also should not be something rare. God has made this gift available to guide all His children through their daily lives.

Your ears shall hear a word behind you, saying, "This is the way, walk in it," Whenever you turn to the right hand Or whenever you turn to the left. - **Isaiah 30:21(NKJV)**

I was blessed to be ordained as a prophet in my early 20's. At the time, I didn't fully embrace the calling because I didn't really understand it. Yet, today, I tap into the Voice of God daily. I don't always tell other people what He says but I respond accordingly. I listen to God's Voice for daily direction. Life is confusing and I can't figure it all out on my own, so being told by God what to do is something I value greatly.

Surely the Lord God does nothing, Unless He reveals His secret to His servants the prophets. - **Amos 3:7(NKJV)**

Prophets are the eyes, ears, and mouth of the Body of Christ. God uses them to inform His people of what He is saying and to confirm what He has already said. He places them in our lives to enlighten us on exactly what He is doing and what He requires of us. Still, the onus is on us (pun intended) to recognize when the Lord is speaking through His prophetic voice. If we choose to do so, we position ourselves to always be in the right place at the right time which is a master key to success. I thank God for the prophetic voices He placed in my own life starting with my wife, parents, spiritual leadership, and siblings. He uses them to reinforce His Will in my life giving me peace and confidence to step out in faith based on His Word.

For instance, recognizing and responding to a prophetic word from my mother changed the direction of my career at an unexpected time. For three years, I was the Professional Structural Engineer for the fastest-growing US division of the second-largest multinational environmental services firm in the world. For the first time in my life, I genuinely loved my job. My boss, the Director of Engineering valued my expertise and gave me the space to be innovative. I worked with a great team of young engineers and traveled the country meeting clients, visiting project sites, and connecting with field staff. I also increased my professional network, attending and speaking at both local and national industry conferences.

Yet, with all my apparent success and personal satisfaction, my mother insisted that I keep my options open. It didn't cost me anything to maintain an updated resume in the online career databases, so I eventually did it. Thankfully, I listened, even though I didn't really think it was necessary. I had no plans to leave my job at the time because I was having too much fun. On top of that, the moment I updated my resume I knew that I would be inundated with calls from recruiters with job opportunities. Nevertheless, as I said before, I did it anyway and God provided me with the opportunity of a lifetime. In the end, what I thought was the voice of my mother was really the Voice of God. Once again, for me to accept the new position I named my price and they were willing to pay it. My life was never the same again.

Case Study: Israel in the Wilderness

These are the words which Moses spoke to all Israel on this side of the Jordan in the wilderness, in the plain opposite Suph, between Paran, Tophel, Laban, Hazeroth, and Dizahab. It is eleven days' journey from Horeb by way of Mount Seir to Kadesh Barnea. - **Deuteronomy 1:1-2(NKJV)**

At this stage of Bible history, the Children of Israel had only recently escaped four hundred years of bondage in Egypt. Next stop: the Promised Land... or so it seemed. Judging from the lifetime of prophetic words they received concerning God's promised redemption, it should have been simple enough. From the moment Moses delivered the Word of God to the Children of Israel, an eleven-day countdown began. If all went well, they would have been enjoying the Promised Land in less than two weeks. Unfortunately, as you should already know, all didn't go well and that's where we start this story.

> *"So we departed from Horeb, and went through all that great and terrible wilderness which you saw on the way to the mountains of the Amorites, as the Lord our God had commanded us. Then we came to Kadesh Barnea. And I said to you, 'You have come to the mountains of the Amorites, which the Lord our God is giving us. Look, the Lord your God has set the land before you; go up and possess it, as the Lord God of your fathers has spoken to you; do not fear or be discouraged.'* - **Deuteronomy 1:19-21(NKJV)**

After eleven days they arrived at the Promised Land and Moses told the people to go immediately and possess it per The Word of The Lord. He told them not to be afraid or discouraged. The Lord placed the land before them as an inheritance. They just had to possess it and do it quickly. Based on the scriptures, there is no doubt that it was God's intention for the Children of Israel to pass through the wilderness on their way from Egypt to their destination. However, what was not in God's plan was them staying there for an extended period. Alas, the Children of Israel missed the memo.

> *"Nevertheless you would not go up, but rebelled against the command of the Lord your God; and you complained in your tents, and said, 'Because the Lord hates us, He has brought us out of the land of Egypt to deliver us into the hand of the Amorites, to destroy us. Where can we go up? Our brethren have discouraged our hearts, saying, "The people are greater and taller than we; the cities are great and fortified up to heaven; moreover we have seen the sons of the Anakim there."' 'Then I said to you, 'Do not be terrified, or afraid of them. The Lord your God, who goes before you, He will fight for you, according to all He did for you in Egypt before your eyes, and in the wilderness where you saw how the Lord your God carried you, as a man carries his son, in all the way that you went until you came to this place.' Yet, for all that, you did not believe the Lord your God, who went in the way before you to search out a place for you to pitch your tents, to show you the way you should go, in the fire by night and in the cloud by day.* - **Deuteronomy 1:26-33(NKJV)**

The Children of Israel reached the entrance to their promise but could not take the necessary steps to receive it. As the saying goes, they were *"so close, yet so far."* Instead of possessing the land that God said was rightfully their own, they let fear rob them of God's promise. What's even worse is that they complained, and God considered that rebellion. They accused God of delivering them from Egypt just to deliver them into the hands of the Amorites. That's a serious accusation and if it was made about any of us, we would be justified if we were extremely offended. Yet, that's what they accused God of doing.

It didn't matter how much Moses told them of God's willingness to go before them and fight for them. They didn't care how much Moses reminded them of what God already did for them in Egypt and earlier in the wilderness. It's like they had selective amnesia and could not remember the pillar of fire that guided them by night nor the cloud that did the same during the day. They refused to believe in God's perfect love for them so they could not cast the fear out of their hearts. (1 John 4:18) Unfortunately, the clock kept ticking. After eleven days, the countdown was finished, and time was up for the Children of Israel. Based on the prophecy, they had one shot to get what was theirs and they blew it. End of story! Well, almost the end. Now, it was God's turn to respond.

> *"And the Lord heard the sound of your words, and was angry, and took an oath, saying, 'Surely not one of these men of this evil generation shall see that good land of which I swore to give to your fathers, except Caleb the son of Jephunneh; he shall see it, and to him and his children I am giving the land on which he walked, because he wholly followed the Lord.' The Lord was also angry with me for your sakes, saying, 'Even you shall not go in there. Joshua the son of Nun, who stands before you, he shall go in there. Encourage him, for he shall cause Israel to inherit it. -* **Deuteronomy 1:34-38(NKJV)**

Exodus 12:37 states that approximately 600,000 men of Israel left Egypt. So, considering that there were also women and children, that's a seven-figure total. Yet, God said that because of their refusal to obey His directions and possess the land just two of them; Joshua and Caleb, would enter the Promised Land while the rest would die in the wilderness. After the Children of Israel refused to obey God on His schedule, they were shocked that they would never see the Promised Land again. They assumed that they could always go at another time when it was more convenient for them. Nonetheless, they were dead wrong. (pun intended)

> *"Then you answered and said to me, 'We have sinned against the Lord; we will go up and fight, just as the Lord our God commanded us.' And when everyone of you had girded on his weapons of war, you were ready to go up into the mountain. "And the Lord said to me, 'Tell them, "Do not go up nor fight, for I am not among you; lest you be defeated before your enemies."' So I spoke to you; yet you would not listen, but rebelled against the command of the Lord, and presumptuously went up into the mountain. And the Amorites who dwelt in that mountain came out against you and chased you as bees do, and drove you back from Seir to Hormah. Then you returned and wept before the Lord, but the Lord would not listen to your voice nor give ear to you. -*

Deuteronomy 1:41-45(NKJV)

Once Moses explained the dire and permanent consequences of their actions or better yet, inaction, the Children of Israel had a change of heart. They were ready to go possess their promise. They picked up their weapons, put their fighting shoes on and charged up the mountain to fight for what was rightfully theirs. Nevertheless, there was one small change. The Lord was not with them anymore. Like Samson in Judges 16:20, they didn't realize the Spirit of The Lord had left them and they were on their own. Once God's presence left, their strength left with Him and they had no right to succeed in battle. As expected, they lost and had no excuse. When The Lord said go, the Children of Israel stayed. When The Lord said stay, the Children of Israel went. They just refused to obey God and paid dearly.

I pondered the direction of my life, and I turned to follow your laws. I will hurry, without delay, to obey your commands. - **Psalm 119:59-60(NLT)**

I don't know what God has told you to do today. If this is the time, He wants it done, do not delay obedience. God's Word works on His schedule, not your own. There have been times God spoke to me and I didn't move at the sound of His Word and there are other times that I moved immediately. Since hindsight is 20-20, I can confirm that I should have always moved immediately when I knew that was God's desire. You must know what God requires of you when you receive a prophetic Word. Even though He is personally not constrained by the limits of time, if you are alive on this earth, you are.

It is the Spirit who gives life; the flesh profits nothing. The words that I speak to you are spirit, and they are life. - **John 6:63(NKJV)**

When someone speaks a prophetic Word from the heart of God, those words are "spirit-words". They are life-giving. They revive you. Several years ago, my wife Angel and I were guests at the 11th-anniversary celebration of Christ United Church in Loganville, GA. It's one of the most prophetic churches in the area we lived at the time. The guest speaker was Apostle Ann Marie Alman of People of Destiny Ministries in Brooklyn, NY. After the message which was life-changing, she walked right up to us and began to prophesy. My goodness! What a Word from The Lord! She encouraged us concerning The Body Church and affirmed what God was doing in the ministry and personally for the two of us. Only The Lord knew how much we needed to hear that.

"The Lord God has given Me The tongue of the learned, That I should know

how to speak A word in season to him who is weary. He awakens Me morning by morning, He awakens My ear To hear as the learned. - **Isaiah 50:4(NKJV)**

In your lowest moments, when you feel tired and worn out from the challenges of life, a prophetic Word from The Lord changes everything. There are people on this earth who have been called by God to speak His Word of Life into others and you need them in your life. I grew up in a household of prophets and almost took it for granted because the Lord spoke to us all the time. We didn't fast and pray for 40 days and 40 nights to hear from The Lord. We just listened to God every day. If He had something to say, we would hear Him. Now I understand how valuable that is.

Let me encourage you. If you have a prophetic gift, there are weary people waiting to hear God's Voice and they need to hear it from you. There are people sitting next to you at work, school, or church hungry for a Word from God's heart. If God gives the Word to you, He expects you to deliver it. Do not be afraid. Be who God has called you to be. Don't stress yourself out about delivering The Word the right way now. Just say what you hear; no less and no more. Someone needs to hear it and that person needs to hear it from you. If that is not the case, God will choose to speak through someone else and not you. If He chooses you, it needs to come from you, just the way you will say it.

Pursue love, and desire spiritual gifts, but especially that you may prophesy... But if all prophesy, and an unbeliever or an uninformed person comes in, he is convinced by all, he is convicted by all. And thus the secrets of his heart are revealed; and so, falling down on his face, he will worship God and report that God is truly among you. - **1 Corinthians 14:1, 24-25(NKJV)**

Several years ago, I sat in a Wednesday night service and watched a young man walk in off the street. He said that he was going about his business looking for a church. He saw the church's sign, so he came in. The prophets in the house began speaking into his life with such precision that he was completely overwhelmed. He fell to his knees in tears and worshiped God. By the time they were finished, his life was changed forever. Now he's a vibrant part of the ministry. He got married about a year later and his wife is also a major part of the ministry. They had children and God continues to work wonders throughout their lives. That's the power of a prophetic Word from The Lord.

This is the third time I am coming to you. In the mouth of two or three witnesses shall every word be established. - **2 Corinthians 13:1(KJV)**

The bottom line is this. God is speaking but not everyone can hear Him for themselves. That's one reason why He raised up prophets. Another reason is for Him to confirm what He's saying to those who do hear His Voice. In other words, we all need prophets. Those of us who cannot hear from God need to know what He's saying and those of us who can hear from God need confirmation. If you are called to be a prophet, prophesy. If you need a Word from The Lord, find a place where God speaks through His prophets. Don't make decisions without hearing from God first and receiving confirmation.

> *So they rose early in the morning and went out into the Wilderness of Tekoa; and as they went out, Jehoshaphat stood and said, "Hear me, O Judah and you inhabitants of Jerusalem: Believe in the Lord your God, and you shall be established; believe His prophets, and you shall prosper."* - **2 Chronicles 20:20(NKJV)**

God has tied a dimension of our prosperity to our belief in His prophets. First, and foremost, we must believe the sure words of prophecy in the scriptures. (2 Peter 1:19-21) Then, we must believe in the prophetic gifts He has placed in His church. (1 Corinthians 12:27-31) With this, we complete our study of five ways God reveals His timing to people.

1. **The Word of God (Complete)**
2. **Prayer (Complete)**
3. **Signs (Complete)**
4. **Dreams and Visions (Complete)**
5. **Prophecy (Complete)**

17 WINDOWS OF OPPORTUNITY

I returned and saw under the sun that— The race is not to the swift, Nor the battle to the strong, Nor bread to the wise, Nor riches to men of understanding, Nor favor to men of skill; But time and chance happen to them all. - **Ecclesiastes 9:11(NKJV)**

The phrase *"window of opportunity"* is defined as *"the time during which there is a chance to do something"*. (Merriam-Webster, Incorporated)

What characterizes a window of opportunity?

1. Limited time between opening and closing
2. A unique chance to do something special

Time + Chance = Window of Opportunity

Talent, strength, wisdom, understanding, and skill are great to have but they only work when applied during windows of opportunity. While we don't all get the same talent, strength, wisdom, understanding, and skill, we all get windows of opportunity. Windows of opportunity upend the status quo. Slow people win races, weak people win battles, people of average intelligence get bread and acquire riches, and unskilled people receive favor. While the world calls this luck, the Bible calls this *"time and chance"* or *"windows of opportunity"*.

After this there was a feast of the Jews, and Jesus went up to Jerusalem. Now there is in Jerusalem by the Sheep Gate a pool, which is called in Hebrew, Bethesda, having five porches. In these lay a great multitude of sick people, blind, lame, paralyzed, waiting for the moving of the water. For an angel went down at a certain time into the pool and stirred up the water; then whoever stepped in first, after the stirring of the water, was made well of whatever disease he had. - **John 5:1-4(NKJV)**

An angel troubled the water annually at *"kairós"*, but it did not benefit anybody except the one person who stepped into the water first. What qualified that person to receive healing? Nothing! The person did not have stronger faith or a better prayer life. The person simply took advantage of the window of opportunity. It didn't matter that *"kairós"* came every year for the sick, blind, lame and paralyzed people in the five porches. If they remained in the porches and never got in the water when the window of opportunity was open, they never got their healing. God did everything He was going to do by troubling the water. Their healing was in their hands.

Now a certain man was there who had an infirmity thirty-eight years. When Jesus saw him lying there, and knew that he already had been in that condition a long time, He said to him, "Do you want to be made well?" The sick man answered Him, "Sir, I have no man to put me into the pool when the water is stirred up; but while I am coming, another steps down before me." Jesus said to him, "Rise, take up your bed and walk." And immediately the man was made well, took up his bed, and walked. And that day was the Sabbath. - **John 5:5-9(NKJV)**

There was a multitude of sick people at the pool of Bethesda but for one man who had missed *"kairós"* as many as 38 times, Jesus presented a special window of opportunity. At first, the man didn't recognize that Jesus was the person who gave the angel the power to trouble the water. Had he known; he would not have made any excuses. He might have been clueless about what was going to happen, but Jesus healed him anyway.

How to Miss Windows of Opportunity

1.   Disregard

He who gathers during summer and takes advantage of his opportunities is a son who acts wisely, But he who sleeps during harvest and ignores the moment of opportunity is a son who acts shamefully. - **Proverbs 10:5(AMP)**

Windows of opportunity open for everyone. Those who recognize and take advantage of them while they are still open are wise. Those who can see the opportunities but ignore them (show disregard) are shameful. It's one thing to miss a window of opportunity because you didn't notice that it was open but something completely different to recognize its existence and simply ignore it. There's no real excuse for doing something like that so The Bible calls it a shameful act.

I remember the housing crisis that coincided with the Great Recession in the US starting around 2007. To stimulate the economy, the Federal Reserve cut its benchmark interest rate as low as possible. This led to a reduction in mortgage rates creating a window of opportunity for homeowners to refinance the loans on their homes. The signs were everywhere that the time to refinance had come but I resisted for several years until the mortgage rates began rising from record lows. It took a direct phone call from my bank offering the refinance for me to finally act.

It's not like I didn't know the opportunity was out there, I just chose to ignore it until someone personally contacted me. Now as I look back, that was one of the best financial decisions I have ever made. Instead of refinancing my home mortgage rate to receive a lower payment, I cut eight years off my loan. I went from a 30-year fixed mortgage that had 22 years remaining to a 15-year fixed mortgage with basically the same monthly payment. By the time you read this book, I probably would have already paid off the loan. That was a window of opportunity that I disregarded until God intervened by sending someone my way. I'm forever grateful for His mercy. Don't be like me and ignore your window of opportunity. When it opens, act immediately.

2.   Laziness

The lazy person buries his hand in the dish [losing opportunity after opportunity]; It wearies him to bring it back to his mouth. - **Proverbs 26:15(AMP)**

Laziness casts one into a deep sleep [unmindful of lost opportunity], And the idle person will suffer hunger. - **Proverbs 19:15(AMP)**

Lazy people don't respond when windows of opportunity open in their lives. That's why even if they have natural talent, strength, education or intelligence, they never reach their full potential. They miss opportunity after opportunity and wonder why nothing good happens for them. Sometimes, lazy people with exceptional natural gifts are fortunate enough to ride those natural gifts as far as they can go. Still, even if they achieve a certain level of success, it's never at the level it really should be.

It takes effort to respond to opportunities. For instance, if you're looking for a new job, it could be tiring to search online, fill out applications, follow-up with recruiters and complete interviews. If you want to write a book, it's not easy to discipline yourself for years in some cases to go through this painstaking process of putting your thoughts on "paper". If you want to step out of your comfort zone and start your own business or ministry, it's even more demanding than working for or serving under someone else. Hence, even though windows of opportunity open for lazy people, they also close to them if they don't respond in time.

> *"Then the servant with the one bag of silver came and said, 'Master, I knew you were a harsh man, harvesting crops you didn't plant and gathering crops you didn't cultivate. I was afraid I would lose your money, so I hid it in the earth. Look, here is your money back.' "But the master replied, 'You wicked and lazy servant! If you knew I harvested crops I didn't plant and gathered crops I didn't cultivate, why didn't you deposit my money in the bank? At least I could have gotten some interest on it.' "Then he ordered, 'Take the money from this servant, and give it to the one with the ten bags of silver. To those who use well what they are given, even more will be given, and they will have an abundance. But from those who do nothing, even what little they have will be taken away.* - **Matthew 25:24-29(NLT)**

In the Parable of the Talents, the "one-talent" man returned his talent to his master intact with the excuse that he was afraid to lose the money. Yet, what the servant called fear, the master called laziness and wickedness. It's not that he was afraid to lose his master's money. He was too lazy to figure out how to make money for his master and he didn't even want to try. The master saw right through the excuses and diagnosed laziness. If you're sitting on your talents today, is it really because you are afraid to fail or are you just lazy? Are you still putting things off until a more convenient time knowing that a time that's truly convenient never comes? Don't let laziness stop you from taking advantage of your window of opportunity while it is still open.

3.   Impatience

> *And we desire that each one of you show the same diligence to the full assurance of hope until the end, that you do not become sluggish, but imitate those who through faith and patience inherit the promises.* - **Hebrews 6:11-12(NKJV)**

> *Do not, therefore, fling away your [fearless] confidence, for it has a glorious and great reward. For you have need of patient endurance [to bear up under difficult circumstances without compromising], so that when you have carried out the will of God, you may receive and enjoy to the full what is promised.* - **Hebrews 10:35-36(AMP)**

After you've done what you're supposed to do, you must be patient until God opens your window of opportunity. It's just as bad to act before your window of opportunity is open as it is to act after it's closed. Wait for your window to open, then move through it. Eagerness to act is a good thing when it's done at the right time. Never lose your eagerness, just temper it until God opens your window.

There are many times that I looked back at the way we started The Body Church and questioned if we moved too early. We made so many mistakes that we only recognize in hindsight. I could list them all right now, but it won't make a difference. We're in it and that's what matters. Despite it all, we committed to trusting God to bring us through.

Moses killed an Egyptian to deliver a Hebrew slave in Exodus 2 before it was God's time to set them free. Instead of triggering a series of events that quickly led to freedom for the Jews, Moses had to run for his life to the wilderness. It took forty years after that incident before God met him in the wilderness and sent him back to Egypt to finish what he started. Impatience will cause you to attempt to move the Hand of God before He wants to move it. That's not a good decision.

The promises of God are inherited through faith and patience, not faith alone. You must believe God's promises and wait for His timing to receive what He has for you. Don't lose your confidence while waiting for God to move because it comes with a reward. Regardless of the difficulties, you are facing, endure them all with patience. After you've done God's Will you can be assured that at the right time you will receive God's promises. Just don't get ahead of Him.

4.　　Fear

About three o'clock in the morning Jesus came toward them, walking on the water. When the disciples saw him walking on the water, they were terrified. In their fear, they cried out, "It's a ghost!" But Jesus spoke to them at once. "Don't be afraid," he said. "Take courage. I am here!" Then Peter called to him, "Lord, if it's really you, tell me to come to you, walking on the water. "Yes, come," Jesus said. So Peter went over the side of the boat and walked on the water toward Jesus. But when he saw the strong wind and the waves, he was terrified and began to sink. "Save me, Lord!" he shouted. Jesus immediately reached out and grabbed him. "You have so little faith," Jesus said. "Why did you doubt me?" When they climbed back into the boat, the wind stopped. - **Matthew 14:25-32(NLT)**

Fear has the power to close a window of opportunity that only God could have opened. Jesus opened the window of opportunity for Peter to walk on water with the word, "come." At first, Peter embraced the invitation and walked on water to meet Jesus but the instant he let fear into his heart, the window closed. Thankfully, when he cried for help, Jesus was right there to reopen it. Jesus was disappointed in Peter and commented on his lack of faith. Though, I want to focus on the question Jesus asked, *"Why did you doubt me?"*

That's the question He is asking you today. Why do you doubt Him? Why is it that you could know that God has opened a door for you, but you won't respond because you doubt Him? You doubt that He would do exactly what He said. You doubt that you have what it takes to do what He said you can do. Like Peter, You doubt that God's power can keep you afloat when the wind blows, and the waves crash around you. You doubt that He can continue the miracle in your life that He already started. His question to you is, "Why?"

I admit that it's scary to leave your comfort zone and do something you've never done before. The first time I quit a job was the most unnerving experience ever. I had never done anything like that before. If I had let fear stop me from following God's Voice, my career and probably my life would have fallen apart. I thank God for His perfect love which cast out all the fear. Listen to me. You can do anything God says you can do. You can win any battle God says you can win. If He opened the window of opportunity for you, don't let fear close it.

Case Study: The Children of Israel

These are the words that Moses spoke to all the people of Israel while they were in the wilderness east of the Jordan River. They were camped in the Jordan Valley near Suph, between Paran on one side and Tophel, Laban, Hazeroth, and Di-zahab on the other. Normally it takes only eleven days to travel from Mount Sinai to Kadesh-barnea, going by way of Mount Seir. But forty years after the Israelites left Egypt, on the first day of the eleventh month, Moses addressed the people of Israel, telling them everything the Lord had commanded him to say... "When we were at Mount Sinai, the Lord our God said to us, 'You have stayed at this mountain long enough. It is time to break camp and move on. Go to the hill country of the Amorites and to all the neighboring regions—the Jordan Valley, the hill country, the western foothills, the Negev, and the coastal plain. Go to the land of the Canaanites and to Lebanon, and all the way to the great Euphrates River. Look, I am giving all this land to you! Go in and occupy it, for it is the land the Lord swore to give to your ancestors Abraham, Isaac, and Jacob, and to all their descendants.'" - **Deuteronomy 1:1-3, 6-8(NLT)**

The moment that God told the Children of Israel to break camp at Mount Sinai, their window of opportunity to occupy the Promised Land at *Kadesh-barnea* opened.

"Then, just as the Lord our God commanded us, we left Mount Sinai and traveled through the great and terrifying wilderness, as you yourselves remember, and headed toward the hill country of the Amorites. When we arrived at Kadesh-barnea, I said to you, 'You have now reached the hill country of the Amorites that the Lord our God is giving us. Look! He has placed the land in front of you. Go and occupy it as the Lord, the God of your ancestors, has promised you. Don't be afraid! Don't be discouraged!' "But you all came to me and said, 'First, let's send out scouts to explore the land for us. They will advise us on the best route to take and which towns we should enter.' "This seemed like a good idea to me, so I chose twelve scouts, one from each of your tribes. They headed for the hill country and came to the valley of Eshcol and explored it. They picked some of its fruit and brought it back to us. And they reported, 'The land the Lord our God has given us is indeed a good land.' - **Deuteronomy 1:19-25(NLT)**

Eleven days after the window of opportunity was opened for the Children of Israel to enter the Promised Land, they arrived at *Kadesh-barnea*. While Moses said do not be afraid, go and occupy the land, the people said, not yet, send scouts.

"But you rebelled against the command of the Lord your God and refused to go in. You complained in your tents and said, 'The Lord must hate us. That's why he has brought us here from Egypt—to hand us over to the Amorites to be slaughtered. Where can we go? Our brothers have demoralized us with their report. They tell us, "The people of the land are taller and more powerful than we are, and their towns are large, with walls rising high into the sky! We even saw giants there—the descendants of Anak!"' "But I said to you, 'Don't be shocked or afraid of them! The Lord your God is going ahead of you. He will fight for you, just as you saw him do in Egypt. And you saw how the Lord your God cared for you all along the way as you traveled through the wilderness, just as a father cares for his child. Now he has brought you to this place.' "But even after all he did, you refused to trust the Lord your God, who goes before you looking for the best places to camp, guiding you with a pillar of fire by night and a pillar of cloud by day. - **Deuteronomy 1:26-33(NLT)**

The scouts added forty days to the process making it a total of fifty-one days since their window of opportunity was opened. The moment the scouts returned, they had one day left in the window. Unfortunately, the bad report from the scouts caused fear in their hearts and they missed their window on the last day.

"When the Lord heard your complaining, he became very angry. So he solemnly swore, 'Not one of you from this wicked generation will live to see the good land I swore to give your ancestors, except Caleb son of Jephunneh. He will see this land because he has followed the Lord completely. I will give to him and his descendants some of the very land he explored during his scouting mission.' "And the Lord was also angry with me because of you. He said to me, 'Moses, not even you will enter the Promised Land! Instead, your assistant, Joshua son of Nun, will lead the people into the land. Encourage him, for he will lead Israel as they take possession of it. I will give the land to your little ones—your innocent children. You were afraid they would be captured, but they will be the ones who occupy it. As for you, turn around now and go on back through the wilderness toward the Red Sea. - **Deuteronomy 1:34-40(NLT)**

The window of opportunity to leave the mountain where they were camped and enter the Promised Land was open for a total of fifty-one days. When they didn't enter in time, the window closed for everyone. It reopened forty years later for only Joshua, Caleb, and the next generation.

"Then you confessed, 'We have sinned against the Lord! We will go into the land and fight for it, as the Lord our God has commanded us.' So your men strapped on their weapons, thinking it would be easy to attack the hill country. "But the Lord told me to tell you, 'Do not attack, for I am not with you. If you go ahead on your own, you will be crushed by your enemies.' "This is what I told you, but you would not listen. Instead, you again rebelled against the Lord's command and arrogantly went into the hill country to fight. But the Amorites who lived there came out against you like a swarm of bees. They chased and battered you all the way from Seir to Hormah. Then you returned and wept before the Lord, but he refused to listen. So you stayed there at Kadesh for a long time. - **Deuteronomy 1:41-46(NLT)**

On the 52nd day, the Children of Israel didn't realize the window of opportunity was closed. When it was open, they had the supernatural power of God behind them to defeat the Amorites. Once the window was closed, they had no chance. Same Amorites, same Children of Israel, different outcome. What changed? They missed their window of opportunity and nothing good happens when you miss your window of opportunity. God gave them a chance to do something special and they didn't take it.

Be Wise: Recognize and Maximize Opportunities

Therefore see that you walk carefully [living life with honor, purpose, and courage; shunning those who tolerate and enable evil], not as the unwise, but as wise [sensible, intelligent, discerning people], making the very most of your time [on earth, recognizing and taking advantage of each opportunity and using it with wisdom and diligence], because the days are [filled with] evil. Therefore do not be foolish and thoughtless, but understand and firmly grasp what the will of the Lord is. - **Ephesians 5:15-17(AMP)**

How do you make the most of your time on earth? Recognize and take advantage of windows of opportunity. Use them with wisdom and diligence. They will give you the success that your talent, strength, wisdom, skill, or education never could. My life story is based on multiple decisions to walk through windows of opportunity. I know that I have overachieved in many areas of my life just because I was in the right place at the right time.

There are skilled, talented, qualified, anointed, and faithful people who deserve to be successful much more than I do but that's not how life works. You don't always get what you deserve, you get windows of opportunity. If you take advantage of them while they are open you get the benefits that come with them. If you don't take advantage of them, you miss out on the benefits.

This book you hold in your hand is a result of one such window of opportunity. God gave me a message on time to share during The Cracked Door Conference at the beginning of 2019. At the end of the conference, my father prophesied that it would be the topic of my next book. The moment he spoke those words, God opened the window and released His grace upon me to write. I put my head down and rode that anointing for over a year until I completed this assignment. I'm sure there are others who understand this topic much better than I do and could have written a much better book. Yet, this is the book you are reading right now.

Welcome to real life where the people who win are the ones who walk through windows of opportunity and the people who lose are the ones who don't. As we bring this chapter to a close, think carefully about the windows of opportunity that are open for you right now. Are you going to let them close without doing something? Are you going to miss your chance to let God's grace on your life make something happen that never should under natural circumstances? I hope not. Let these words spur you to action. Be an overachiever, make the most of your windows of opportunity.

Don't let the excitement of youth cause you to forget your Creator. Honor him in your youth before you grow old and say, "Life is not pleasant anymore." Remember him before the light of the sun, moon, and stars is dim to your old eyes, and rain clouds continually darken your sky. Remember him before your legs—the guards of your house—start to tremble; and before your shoulders— the strong men—stoop. Remember him before your teeth—your few remaining servants—stop grinding; and before your eyes—the women looking through the windows—see dimly. **Remember him before the door to life's opportunities is closed and the sound of work fades. Now you rise at the first chirping of the birds, but then all their sounds will grow faint.** *Remember him before you become fearful of falling and worry about danger in the streets; before your hair turns white like an almond tree in bloom, and you drag along without energy like a dying grasshopper, and the caperberry no longer inspires sexual desire. Remember him before you near the grave, your everlasting home, when the mourners will weep at your funeral. Yes, remember your Creator now while you are young, before the silver cord of life snaps and the golden bowl is broken. Don't wait until the water jar is smashed at the spring and the pulley is broken at the well. For then the dust will return to the earth, and the spirit will return to God who gave it. "Everything is meaningless," says the Teacher, "completely meaningless." Keep this in mind: The Teacher was considered wise, and he taught the people everything he knew. He listened carefully to many proverbs, studying and classifying them. The Teacher sought to find just the right words to express truths clearly. The words of the wise are like cattle prods—painful but helpful. Their collected sayings are like a nail-studded stick with which a shepherd drives the sheep. But, my child, let me give you some further advice: Be careful, for writing books is endless, and much study wears you out. That's the whole story. Here now is my final conclusion: Fear God and obey his commands, for this is everyone's duty. God will judge us for everything we do, including every secret thing, whether good or bad.* - **Ecclesiastes 12:1-14(NLT) (Emphasis mine)**

The Lord spoke to me through this scripture and it is my prayer that He is speaking to you right now also. In Psalm 103:14-16, Isaiah 40:6-8 and 1 Peter 1:23-25, the scriptures agree that life is like grass or a flower that fades. It is here today and gone tomorrow. King Solomon reminds us in Ecclesiastes 12 that we can't waste time. The doors of opportunity in life will not remain open forever. While you still have your health, physical strength, and you are in your right mind, remember your Creator. Fear The Lord, obey His commands, and carry out His purpose for your life before the windows and doors of opportunity close for the final time.

18 EMBRACE THE PROCESS

And I am certain that God, who began the good work within you, will continue his work until it is finally finished on the day when Christ Jesus returns. -
Philippians 1:6(NLT)

When God starts something, He will continue it until He's finished. What does that mean? His good work in your life is not something instantaneous but a process. Embrace the process! Even though God has the power to do anything He wants in an instant He chooses to work through processes that take varying periods of time. For instance, you may receive a Word from God today concerning His plans for your life. That doesn't mean it will happen instantly nor will its manifestation be independent of your actions. Attached to God's promise is a process. If you go through the process successfully, you will get to see the promise at the end of it.

For 4000 years there were prophecies about Jesus and what He would accomplish on the cross. Yet, when He came to earth, He had to decide to go to the cross for any of it to happen. How do we know that? We can read the account in Matthew 26:36-46 of Jesus making the tough decision in the Garden of Gethsemane. He had to accept God's process of redemption even though He momentarily didn't want to go through it. God's process for Jesus included taking the sin of all humanity on His shoulders and dying on the cross. Nothing else would work to break the curse of sin and death that was initiated when Adam and Eve sinned in the Garden of Eden. Jesus embraced the process and now we're free from sin. If He didn't accept the experience of the cross, the time of redemption would never come.

For ye have need of patience, that, after ye have done the will of God, ye might receive the promise. - **Hebrews 10:36(KJV)**

Many people receive a promise from God, then sit around waiting for it to happen. What they don't realize is that they only receive the promise after they have done the Will of God. Obedience, not chronological time, is the controlling factor. Only after obedience is complete, does chronological time become the controlling factor. You can't wait for the promise to manifest before you do God's Will. The countdown clock to the promise doesn't start until after your obedience. Consequently, it's important to evaluate the true circumstances behind any delay in the manifestation of a promise from the Lord. While you might be waiting on God to deliver on His promise, He might be waiting on you to do His Will.

Where are you in the process right now? Perhaps, you are waiting for a Word from The Lord. Maybe you've passed that stage. Perhaps, you already received The Word but have done nothing with it, yet you are waiting for it to come to pass. Maybe you are even further along. Perhaps, you have already carried out God's instructions that are attached to His Word. If that's the case, you are in a good place because now that you've done your part, God's on the clock. Just be patient. When He makes a promise and you go through the process, He delivers on His promise at His appointed time.

If you're single and God promised you a spouse, there's a process. If you're unemployed and God promised you a job, there's a process. If you're poor and God promised you wealth, there's a process. If you're sick and God promised your health, there's a process. When God makes a promise, that's the beginning of His good work in your life. He will continue to work through the process until it is complete. Only then, can the promise of God you received by faith become tangible. As a result, whatever it is that God requires of you, just do it. Don't delay or block God's promise by delaying or withholding your obedience.

Here's a simple example. When the Children of Israel were on the brink of entering the Promised Land for the first time in Numbers 13, they didn't follow God's instructions. They were afraid of the giants that stood before them. They forfeited the promise and God waited for all of them to die before their children were given another chance. God's promise came with a process and they didn't embrace it because of fear. We should all learn from their example and do better. What's the process attached to your promise? Embrace the process and you'll get the promise.

When Impossible is your Only Option

He answered him and said, "O faithless generation, how long shall I be with you? How long shall I bear with you? Bring him to Me." Then they brought him to Him. And when he saw Him, immediately the spirit convulsed him, and he fell on the ground and wallowed, foaming at the mouth. So He asked his father, "How long has this been happening to him?" And he said, "From childhood. And often he has thrown him both into the fire and into the water to destroy him. But if You can do anything, have compassion on us and help us." Jesus said to him, "If you can believe, all things are possible to him who believes." Immediately the father of the child cried out and said with tears, "Lord, I believe; help my unbelief!" - **Mark 9:19-24(NKJV)**

This is a fascinating encounter between a father with a demon-possessed son and Jesus. The man had a simple request of Jesus. He asked Jesus to help if He could do something about the situation. Think about that. His question to Jesus was twofold. First, he questioned whether Jesus had the capability to do something about his situation. Second, he questioned whether Jesus had the compassion or willingness to do something. That's serious. He didn't know whether Jesus could or would help.

As expected, Jesus delivered a profound response by issuing a conditional statement of His own; *"If you can believe, all things are possible to him who believes."* Then, with tears in his eyes, the man responded that he believed but needed help with his unbelief. Jesus then delivered the young man from the grip of the devil. The bottom line of this entire passage can be seen in that short conversation between the man and Jesus. The man questioned Jesus' ability and desire to perform a miracle, so Jesus questioned the man's ability to believe. Why? There would be no miracle until there was belief. Now think about your situation. Do you question God's ability and/or desire to help in your situation? If so, He questions your belief.

But Jesus looked at them and said to them, "With men this is impossible, but with God all things are possible." - **Matthew 19:26(NKJV)**

Do you believe in miracles? That's a trick question. Miracles don't exist in a vacuum. They exist within God. The real question is, *"Do you believe in God?"* If your answer is yes, then you should expect miracles because nothing is impossible with God. It's your belief in God that allows you to patiently embrace the process that God puts you through to attain His promises. Faith is the fuel that carries you to the end of your timeline of experiences.

Are you faced with something impossible in your life? Maybe there's a bill due soon and you just don't have the money. Maybe you're dealing with a sickness that has no cure. Maybe your relationship is over, or it seems like what you have is beyond repair. Maybe your application for employment or admission to school got rejected and time is up for you to make another move. While human wisdom says it's impossible, God's wisdom says nothing is impossible.

> *Jesus said to him, "If you can believe, all things are possible to him who believes." -* **Mark 9:23(NKJV)**

Every miracle has at least two parts; one for us and one for God. We get the easy part, which is always to believe, and God's part is to do everything else. This type of belief is not merely a passive acceptance of what God has done in the past, can do in the future or is doing for someone else. It is an active belief in what He can and will do for you right now. It's only when you believe in God's current ability and willingness to intervene on your behalf that you're willing to do what God says to activate His miraculous power. Even though you can't make miracles happen, you can make yourself ready through your faith in God.

> *How then shall they call on Him in whom they have not believed? And how shall they believe in Him of whom they have not heard? And how shall they hear without a preacher? And how shall they preach unless they are sent? As it is written: "How beautiful are the feet of those who preach the gospel of peace, Who bring glad tidings of good things!" But they have not all obeyed the gospel. For Isaiah says, "Lord, who has believed our report?" So then faith comes by hearing, and hearing by the word of God. -* **Romans 10:14-17(NKJV)**

Your miracle depends on your belief, your belief depends on what you hear and what you hear depends on the preacher you listen to. Accordingly, if you need a miracle, carefully consider the words you allow to enter your ears. You can't believe for something you never heard is possible nor can you believe for what you've been taught is impossible, even for God. To change the fruit of unbelief in your life, change the seeds (words) being sown into your heart.

Faith comes by hearing and hearing by the Word of God. Sometimes, impossible is your only option. That's when you need your faith to be at its strongest. Be sure to feed your faith with God's Word ahead of time so when you need it, you can believe for the impossible. God's ability to perform miracles has not diminished since the days of the patriarchs and Apostles in The Bible. What He did for them He can also do for you. You must believe in Him the way they did.

When the Process takes too Long

To everything there is a season, A time for every purpose under heaven: A time to be born, And a time to die; A time to plant, And a time to pluck what is planted; A time to kill, And a time to heal; A time to break down, And a time to build up; A time to weep, And a time to laugh; A time to mourn, And a time to dance; A time to cast away stones, And a time to gather stones; A time to embrace, And a time to refrain from embracing; A time to gain, And a time to lose; A time to keep, And a time to throw away; A time to tear, And a time to sew; A time to keep silence, And a time to speak; A time to love, And a time to hate; A time of war, And a time of peace. - **Ecclesiastes 3:1-8(NKJV)**

The most common thread that is woven throughout this book is that time is a created entity. Let's recap a few of the common thoughts. In Genesis 1:1, the scripture says that God created the heavens and the earth in the beginning. Hence, time began with creation. Since the beginning of creation, the clock has kept on ticking as chronological time continues to exist. Before time began, God existed in eternity and after time ends, we will join Him. Nevertheless, until the end of time, we must continue to live within the constraints of time.

We can't slow chronological time down. We can't speed it up. We can't make it do anything we want. Chronological time is out of our hands. On the other hand, the only thing we can control is what we do with the time we have been given by God. In our timeline of experiences, we can choose to successfully complete what God has placed before us at our own pace. There are 24 hours in each day for every single person on the earth; good or bad. When one person seems to have more time than another it's not a measure of actual time but a measure of time-management. Time, as we know it, is a non-renewable resource and we can choose how we want to invest it based on the returns we desire.

Declaring the end from the beginning, and from ancient times the things that are not yet done, saying, My counsel shall stand, and I will do all my pleasure: - **Isaiah 46:10(KJV)**

From the vantage point of eternity, God makes declarations. He speaks of things to come like they are already in existence. Hence, His eternal nature cannot be contained within the confines of time. For instance, many of the prophecies in The Old Testament span long periods of time even though they were written in the present tense. What might have started as The Word of The Lord to their current generation, in some cases, quickly turned into prophetic declarations for consideration only in future generations.

Until the time that his word came: the word of the Lord tried him. - **Psalms 105:19(KJV)**

If you live long enough, you'll know that everything has a process. Seeds go through a process before they can produce seeds of their own. Water goes through a process from the river to the tap. Ideas go through a process from incubation to implementation. In the same way, God's Word goes through a process from the point you first hear it to the point that it comes to pass in your life. Do you ever feel like the process is taking too long? Do you ever feel like you've been waiting forever for a change and it seems like nothing's changing or the changes taking place are happening much too slowly? You're not alone.

One night Joseph had a dream, and when he told his brothers about it, they hated him more than ever. "Listen to this dream," he said. "We were out in the field, tying up bundles of grain. Suddenly my bundle stood up, and your bundles all gathered around and bowed low before mine!" His brothers responded, "So you think you will be our king, do you? Do you actually think you will reign over us?" And they hated him all the more because of his dreams and the way he talked about them. Soon Joseph had another dream, and again he told his brothers about it. "Listen, I have had another dream," he said. "The sun, moon, and eleven stars bowed low before me!" This time he told the dream to his father as well as to his brothers, but his father scolded him. "What kind of dream is that?" he asked. "Will your mother and I and your brothers actually come and bow to the ground before you?" But while his brothers were jealous of Joseph, his father wondered what the dreams meant. - **Genesis 37:5-11(NLT)**

I had a dream about Joseph one night and through it, God reminded me to trust the process. Well, not really the process per se but trust Him and His Word while I go through the process. Joseph had a dream from an early age in which God showed him a bright future. Yet, from that day on, his life took a turn for the worst. He was a victim of human trafficking at the hands of his brothers. He then became a slave in Egypt and eventually got thrown into prison. The progression of his life appeared to be going further and further away from the palace before he had a sudden change of fortune. Through Joseph's dream, God spoke the end from the beginning, but He didn't speak the process.

And let us not be weary in well doing: for in due season we shall reap, if we faint not. - **Galatians 6:9(KJV)**

Don't grow weary of the process until you see it all the way through.

190

Whatever God has promised will come to pass on His schedule of experiences. You can't make Him move any faster so being impatient doesn't help. Abraham and Sarah grew weary of the process while waiting for God to bless them with a son, so they rushed the process and ended up with Ishmael. That's what happens when people get tired of waiting on God. It's true that many times the process takes much too long for our liking, but we must trust God to see us through. If you don't get tired of doing what's right, you will reap the harvest God has promised. Certain promises are not simply on a chronological timeline, but a timeline of experiences. Go through the experiences and get the promises.

19 REDEEMING YOUR TIME

I form the light and create darkness, I make peace and create calamity; I, the Lord, do all these things.' - **Isaiah 45:7(NKJV)**

At first glance, this may be a difficult scripture to digest for some of us. How could the good God we serve form both light and darkness or create both peace and calamity? Shouldn't God only be associated with good? If you read Isaiah 45:1-13, God considered Cyrus, a king who did not know Him, as His anointed. Cyrus was handpicked by God to carry out God's purpose on behalf of His people. It's a scripture full of apparent contradictions that are not easy to reconcile. Yet, that was God's intention. He's sovereign and He answers to no one, so He occasionally reminds us of that. If I were to choose a scripture that aligns with what some of us typically believe, it would be more like this one.

> *Every good gift and every perfect gift is from above, and comes down from the Father of lights, with whom there is no variation or shadow of turning.* - **James 1:17(NKJV)**

Everything that's good comes from God. That's more like it. Scriptures like these make me happy and if they existed in a vacuum, life would be simple and clear-cut. Still, we know that this is not the case. Sometimes, good things happen to bad people and bad things happen to good people. Still, God is in the middle of it all. There is no easy explanation for why that happens on this side of eternity. For instance, it's been thousands of years since Job experienced disaster and redemption. He had everything, then he lost everything, then God gave him double what he had before. All the while, God knew what He was doing. It was God who agreed to remove the hedge of protection from around Job.

I don't know why God did that and neither did Job, his family nor his friends. Perhaps, if you read the Book of Job, you might be able to figure it out. If you do, share it with me because I would love to know. That's just one major example of God's sovereignty in action. He does what He wants to do when He wants to do it because He can. In the same way, God is the master of time. He created it and controls it. Both the good and the bad times serve His purpose. Nothing is wasted in God's hands, especially time.

"Every commandment which I command you today you must be careful to observe, that you may live and multiply, and go in and possess the land of which the Lord swore to your fathers. And you shall remember that the Lord your God led you all the way these forty years in the wilderness, to humble you and test you, to know what was in your heart, whether you would keep His commandments or not. So He humbled you, allowed you to hunger, and fed you with manna which you did not know nor did your fathers know, that He might make you know that man shall not live by bread alone; but man lives by every word that proceeds from the mouth of the Lord. Your garments did not wear out on you, nor did your foot swell these forty years. You should know in your heart that as a man chastens his son, so the Lord your God chastens you. - **Deuteronomy 8:1-5(NKJV)**

God was behind everything the Children of Israel went through in the wilderness. For 40 years, He humbled, tested, and allowed them to hunger but He also preserved, empowered, and fed them. He didn't cause them to miss their opportunity to enter the Promised Land the first time around. Yet, once they refused to enter, He determined their path through the wilderness for the next 40 years.

It never occurs to them to say, 'How can we honor our God with our lives, The God who gives rain in both spring and autumn and maintains the rhythm of the seasons, Who sets aside time each year for harvest and keeps everything running smoothly for us?' - **Jeremiah 5:24(MSG)**

God operates in times and seasons. He expects us to honor that. When things go according to His schedule, He keeps everything running smoothly for us. According to Ecclesiastes 3:1-8, there's a time for all the seasons of our lives. Since God put a rhythm to life, things should happen to match that rhythm. When we stay in God's Will we remain in sync with His rhythm. Also, in Ecclesiastes 3:11, we learn that life is beautiful when lived according to God's timing. With God, it doesn't only matter what you do, how you do it or even who you do it with, but it also matters when. Above all, based on Psalm 31:15 we may feel like we have autonomy over our own time but at any moment, God can remind us of who is really in control.

You have decided the length of our lives. You know how many months we will live, and we are not given a minute longer. - **Job 14:5(NLT)**

We all get 60 seconds in a minute, 60 minutes in an hour and 24 hours in a day but we don't all get the same number of days. As we've established throughout this book, time is a non-renewable resource. If you lose it, you can't find it. If something or someone takes it, they can't give it back. Once it's gone, it's gone forever.

So teach us to number our days, That we may gain a heart of wisdom. - **Psalm 90:12(NKJV)**

Because we don't know how many days we will live on this earth we should treat each day as a gift from God and make the most of it. We should live intentionally so that at the end of our days we will have no regrets. Yet, that doesn't always happen. What if we mess up and lose valuable time? What if we miss opportunities to maximize our time due to circumstances outside of our control? What happens then? Even though God is a God of second chances, can He give us a second chance at the lost time in our lives; the one thing we can never have back?

"But Jesus looked at them and said to them, "With men this is impossible, but with God all things are possible." - **Matthew 19:26(NKJV)**

See then that you walk circumspectly, not as fools but as wise, redeeming the time, because the days are evil. Therefore do not be unwise, but understand what the will of the Lord is. - **Ephesians 5:15-17(NKJV)**

The Greek word for "redeem" used in this scripture is *"exagorazō"* which, in this context, according to Strong's Concordance means, *"to buy up, to buy up for one's self, for one's use; to make wise and sacred use of every opportunity for doing good, so that zeal and well doing are as it were the purchase money by which we make the time our own".* (Strong, The New Strong's Exhaustive Concordance of the Bible, 2003) Time is such a valuable gift that God expects us to make wise and sacred use of it. We must live with urgency and do our very best to maximize the time we have on this earth for God's glory.

The steps of a good man are ordered by the Lord, And He delights in his way. Though he fall, he shall not be utterly cast down; For the Lord upholds him with His hand. - **Psalm 37:23-24(NKJV)**

We sometimes stumble in our walk with God. When that happens, we lose valuable time. Even worse, we sometimes miss God by no fault of our own. Thankfully, God finds a way to redeem our time. He supernaturally buys back the time that was lost and restores it to us. Here's an example of how God redeemed Caleb's time.

Case Study: Caleb

Then the children of Judah came to Joshua in Gilgal. And Caleb the son of Jephunneh the Kenizzite said to him: "You know the word which the Lord said to Moses the man of God concerning you and me in Kadesh Barnea. I was forty years old when Moses the servant of the Lord sent me from Kadesh Barnea to spy out the land, and I brought back word to him as it was in my heart. Nevertheless my brethren who went up with me made the heart of the people melt, but I wholly followed the Lord my God. So Moses swore on that day, saying, 'Surely the land where your foot has trodden shall be your inheritance and your children's forever, because you have wholly followed the Lord my God.' And now, behold, the Lord has kept me alive, as He said, these forty-five years, ever since the Lord spoke this word to Moses while Israel wandered in the wilderness; and now, here I am this day, eighty-five years old. As yet I am as strong this day as on the day that Moses sent me; just as my strength was then, so now is my strength for war, both for going out and for coming in. Now therefore, give me this mountain of which the Lord spoke in that day; for you heard in that day how the Anakim were there, and that the cities were great and fortified. It may be that the Lord will be with me, and I shall be able to drive them out as the Lord said." And Joshua blessed him, and gave Hebron to Caleb the son of Jephunneh as an inheritance. Hebron therefore became the inheritance of Caleb the son of Jephunneh the Kenizzite to this day, because he wholly followed the Lord God of Israel. - **Joshua 14:6-14(NKJV)**

Caleb lost over forty years of his life wandering through the wilderness because others refused to obey God and take the Promised Land. Still, God redeemed his time by giving him the land he originally spied as his inheritance. To do so, God extended his life, provided supernatural health, and preserved his strength for four decades. He can do the same for you. Do you feel like you wasted years of your life? Perhaps, you made some bad decisions or experienced personal tragedies like sickness, unsuccessful relationships, dead-end jobs, scams, addiction or failed educational pursuits. Do you think your time is lost forever? God has a Word for you! What's impossible for humans is possible with God.

"Do not fear, for you will not be ashamed; Neither be disgraced, for you will not be put to shame; For you will forget the shame of your youth, And will not

remember the reproach of your widowhood anymore. For your Maker is your husband, The Lord of hosts is His name; And your Redeemer is the Holy One of Israel; He is called the God of the whole earth. For the Lord has called you Like a woman forsaken and grieved in spirit, Like a youthful wife when you were refused," Says your God. "For a mere moment I have forsaken you, But with great mercies I will gather you. With a little wrath I hid My face from you for a moment; But with everlasting kindness I will have mercy on you," Says the Lord, your Redeemer. - **Isaiah 54:4-8(NKJV)**

God is your redeemer. He paid the price for your life; the good, the bad and the ugly. Even if you mismanaged it or you're the victim of mismanagement, He acquired it. Now, He has taken responsibility for every aspect of your life. Here's how the Apostle Paul described it in 1 Corinthians 6:20(AMP); *"You were bought with a price [you were actually purchased with the precious blood of Jesus and made His own]. So then, honor and glorify God with your body."* God purchased your entire life with the Blood of Jesus. He purchased your good parts and "not so good" parts. He purchased your debt, your lost time, your problems, all of it, so He has assumed responsibility.

"So I will restore to you the years that the swarming locust has eaten, The crawling locust, The consuming locust, And the chewing locust, My great army which I sent among you. You shall eat in plenty and be satisfied, And praise the name of the Lord your God, Who has dealt wondrously with you; And My people shall never be put to shame. - **Joel 2:25-26(NKJV)**

God is ready to restore all that you lost. However, if you read the scripture carefully you will notice something interesting. It says that God will restore the years that the locusts have eaten. We know that locusts eat plants, crops, grass, leaves, fruits, vegetables, etc. so why didn't the scripture say that God would restore those things? Isn't that what locusts eat, so why would God choose to restore years? For farmers, when swarms of locusts devastate their crops, while it's obvious that they lost the monetary value of their crops, what's even worse is the time that they lost. They can't simply re-plant fully grown crops the next day. There is time built into the process that's non-negotiable and that's what they lose when locusts eat their crops. That's the true revelation in this scripture.

God understands what you really lose when you lose something of great value. You lose time. If you lose your house, what's more devastating than losing all the contents, is how long it will take you to replace them. When you lose a marriage after 10 years, it's not like you can just walk into a church the next Sunday, meet someone and get back all you lost. When you lose your life savings in a scam or a bad investment, it's not just about the money, it's about the lifetime it took to accumulate it. How are you supposed to get that back?

God wants to do the impossible. He wants to turn back the clock for your life and give you back what you thought was lost forever. He wants to do what cannot be done under natural circumstances. He wants to give you back your lost time. He wants to restore the years that the swarming, crawling, consuming, and chewing locusts have eaten. One way He does so is through acceleration.

How God Redeems Your Time

1. Supernatural Health and Strength in Old Age

I would have lost heart, unless I had believed That I would see the goodness of the Lord In the land of the living. - **Psalm 27:13(NKJV)**

As you grow older, the chances that you would be able to accomplish great things in life may seem to fade away. While that's not entirely true, people sometimes regret missed chances from their youth as the years roll by. They look back fondly at what could or should have been instead of looking forward to what will be. They lose their passion to go after what God has called them to do because they assume that they're getting too old. If you're like that, there's nothing to be ashamed of because you're simply being human. You're using your natural senses to discern the possibilities that exist. With the changes in your body, you can't help but feel like those possibilities are becoming less and less. Fortunately, God doesn't think like that and there's precedent for adopting His perspective in the scriptures.

And now, look, the Lord has let me live, just as He said, these forty-five years since the Lord spoke this word to Moses, when Israel wandered in the wilderness; and now, look at me, I am eighty-five years old today. I am still as strong today as I was the day Moses sent me; as my strength was then, so is my strength now, for war and for going out and coming in. So now, give me this hill country about which the Lord spoke that day, for you heard on that day that the [giant-like] Anakim were there, with great fortified cities; perhaps the Lord will be with me, and I shall drive them out just as the Lord said." So Joshua blessed him and gave Hebron to Caleb the son of Jephunneh as an inheritance. Therefore, Hebron became the inheritance of Caleb the son of Jephunneh the Kenizzite to this day, because he followed the Lord, the God of Israel, completely. - **Joshua 14:10-14(AMP)**

At eighty-five years old and forty-five years behind schedule, Caleb still had the fire in his belly to get the inheritance God promised. Fortunately, he also had the physical and mental strength to fight for it. By basically turning back the clock on Caleb's health, God enabled him to accomplish in his old age what he could not in his youth. Yes, he could never literally get forty-five years of his life back but that didn't mean that the time was completely lost.

God restored his inheritance which was the opportunity cost of his time in the wilderness. Most importantly, God gave him the health and strength to fully enjoy it while he was alive. The inheritance was set aside by God for Caleb, so God kept it safe until the time was right for him to receive it again. Once he received his inheritance from God, it was his to enjoy until the day of his death then pass down to his descendants as their inheritance from him. This is important because even though it's a blessing for God to restore to your children what you lost in your lifetime, it's even better for Him to restore it to you while you are alive. You can then pass it down to your children.

"Where is Sarah, your wife?" the visitors asked. "She's inside the tent," Abraham replied. Then one of them said, "I will return to you about this time next year, and your wife, Sarah, will have a son!" Sarah was listening to this conversation from the tent. Abraham and Sarah were both very old by this time, and Sarah was long past the age of having children. So she laughed silently to herself and said, "How could a worn-out woman like me enjoy such pleasure, especially when my master—my husband—is also so old?" Then the Lord said to Abraham, "Why did Sarah laugh? Why did she say, 'Can an old woman like me have a baby?' Is anything too hard for the Lord? I will return about this time next year, and Sarah will have a son." Sarah was afraid, so she denied it, saying, "I didn't laugh." But the Lord said, "No, you did laugh."
- **Genesis 18:9-15(NLT)**

The Lord kept his word and did for Sarah exactly what he had promised. She became pregnant, and she gave birth to a son for Abraham in his old age. This happened at just the time God had said it would. And Abraham named their son Isaac. Eight days after Isaac was born, Abraham circumcised him as God had commanded. Abraham was 100 years old when Isaac was born. And Sarah declared, "God has brought me laughter. All who hear about this will laugh with me. Who would have said to Abraham that Sarah would nurse a baby? Yet I have given Abraham a son in his old age!" - **Genesis 21:1-7(NLT)**

Sarah and Abraham were called by God to begin the lineage of God's chosen people. So, why are we surprised that God supernaturally provided them with a child? In that way, there would be no question that their child was special. The mere existence of the child was a miracle. Is anything too hard for The Lord? Does someone's age limit God's supernatural power? What can't God do because you are a bit older? The answers are no, no, and nothing. There's a pattern in scripture of God's Spirit resting on people who are older and in some cases, younger than expected just because He felt like it. If He determines that He is going to do something of note through you, it doesn't matter your age, He's going to do it.

2. Supernatural Acceleration

"Behold, the days are coming," says the Lord, "When the plowman shall overtake the reaper, And the treader of grapes him who sows seed; The mountains shall drip with sweet wine, And all the hills shall flow with it. - **Amos 9:13(NKJV)**

Supernatural acceleration is one of God's tried and true methods of redeeming your time. By compressing the schedule, He compensates for lost time and restores your life to where it would be if nothing had ever gone awry. What should take ten years, God will do in ten months. What should take a lifetime, God will do in a couple of years. When He's redeeming time on your behalf, He finds ways to remove chunks of time from natural processes. He removes obstacles and barriers that are typically in place to keep things in order just so that you can skip the line and get to the front.

That's the story of my engineering career. At one point I was stuck in a rut and my career was going nowhere. As the years kept rolling along, I was repeatedly passed over for promotions. My raises were meager, and the opportunities afforded to me for growth were minimal. I was hurt every time I thought about the best years of my career simply wasting away. Yet, what hurt me the most was watching my peers leave me behind in the dust. I saw coworkers with less experience than me bypass me and keep going higher and higher in the organization. I even distinctly remember lending my books to one of them to study for the professional exams that I had already passed. She passed the exam and got promoted past me.

Then one day, everything changed. Like a high-end sports car, my career went from "zero to sixty" in record time. Now, I'm no longer behind my peers. I also didn't just catch up to them. I have left them behind. After the redemption of my time, I look back fondly at what I thought were the "lost" years of my career and thank God for every one of them. I gained valuable experience in dealing with people. I gained perspective on the plight of the overlooked. I learned lessons during those years that I would have never learned elsewhere and those are the lessons that guide my decisions today. That was my wilderness experience and God used it to prepare me for what is now the Promised Land. For a better understanding of why God takes us through periods like these, let's look at the plight of the Israelites.

"Be careful to obey all the commands I am giving you today. Then you will live and multiply, and you will enter and occupy the land the Lord swore to give your ancestors. Remember how the Lord your God led you through the wilderness for these forty years, humbling you and testing you to prove your character, and to find out whether or not you would obey his commands. Yes, he humbled you by letting you go hungry and then feeding you with manna, a food previously unknown to you and your ancestors. He did it to teach you that people do not live by bread alone; rather, we live by every word that comes from the mouth of the Lord. For all these forty years your clothes didn't wear out, and your feet didn't blister or swell. Think about it: Just as a parent disciplines a child, the Lord your God disciplines you for your own good. -* **Deuteronomy 8:1-5(NLT)**

Wilderness seasons are designed by God to humble us, test us, prove our character, and determine if we will truly obey Him. What we may lack for that period, God provides daily. It's during those seasons that we learn to trust God for our provision and listen to His Voice intently. Thankfully, He preserves us and disciplines us until He brings us out. Once we're out, He does what only He can do. He restores our time. That's what He did for Joshua and Caleb because they remained faithful and that's what He will do for you if you do the same. Never consider a wilderness season as a period that was wasted or lost because of missed opportunities. Those are priceless times for character building. You will come out of them and when you do you will better than you went in.

When Job prayed for his friends, the Lord restored his fortunes. In fact, the Lord gave him twice as much as before! Then all his brothers, sisters, and former friends came and feasted with him in his home. And they consoled him and comforted him because of all the trials the Lord had brought against him. And each of them brought him a gift of money and a gold ring. So the Lord blessed Job in the second half of his life even more than in the beginning. For now he had 14,000 sheep, 6,000 camels, 1,000 teams of oxen, and 1,000 female donkeys. He also gave Job seven more sons and three more daughters. He named his first daughter Jemimah, the second Keziah, and the third Keren-happuch. In all the land no women were as lovely as the daughters of Job. And their father put them into his will along with their brothers. Job lived 140 years after that, living to see four generations of his children and grandchildren. Then he died, an old man who had lived a long, full life. - **Job 42:10-17(NLT)**

Job's life is a story of God's redemptive power. After taking him through what seemed like hell on earth God made up for the lost time. He gave Job double all his possessions. God gave him more money, assets, and children than he had before. He also gave him the health and strength to enjoy it all for another one hundred and forty years. If you want the perfect example of how God redeems someone's time, look at the life of Job. By some estimates, Job suffered for about a year but to him, we know it would have felt like a lifetime. In hindsight, what he went through for that short period pales in comparison to what God did for him after. Job didn't just receive rewards on earth, but He continues to receive rewards in heaven.

Are you willing to believe in God's redemptive power for your own situation? If so, God is going to accelerate some things in your life that seem impossible to accomplish now. He will do it so quickly that it will seem like a blur. It will look like you came out of nowhere, but you didn't. You and God know what happened. This is your time of redemption and restoration. This is your season to see God accomplish in a short time what should take years and years to take place. In the process, God will redeem your time by restoring all that was lost. Then, you can expect Him to restore your health and strength so you can enjoy the fullness of God's redemption in your old age. Of course, that's not all. When you successfully complete all God has for you on earth in this time, you will relish His rewards for you in eternity.

20 RECLAIMING MY TIME

We must quickly carry out the tasks assigned us by the one who sent us. The night is coming, and then no one can work. - **John 9:4(NLT)**

In July 2017, at a US House of Representatives Financial Services Committee meeting, Representative Maxine Waters (D-CA) popularized the phrase "reclaiming my time". She repeated it continuously after she posed a question to US Treasury Secretary Steve Mnuchin. He was appearing before the committee but refused to give her a straight answer. Instead, he kept going off-topic and wasting the limited time afforded to her to ask questions. By uttering the phrase, she let the committee chair know that she wanted all her time back. She would not allow Mr. Mnuchin to run out the clock while avoiding her questions. The time she had for questions was her own and if she was not getting genuine answers, that should not count against her allotted time. Hence, she reclaimed it.

As you can see in John 9:4, Jesus walked the earth with a sense of urgency and made full use of the 33 years afforded to Him by His Father. I feel a similar sense of urgency. Life is to be lived to the fullest and for me, that means doing meaningful activities with my time. With that, I have made the decision that I am reclaiming my time from anything or anyone who wastes it. For instance, if I don't want to be at an event, I'm simply not going. If I have something important to get finished, I'm not letting someone pull me in another direction. In the middle of meetings at work that are wasting my time, I'll excuse myself and go do something productive. If my phone rings and it's someone that will drain my emotional energy for no good reason, I won't answer it. I don't overstay my welcome in any situation. If I'm not welcome, I'm out. I am reclaiming my time. You should reclaim your time too. Let's dig a little deeper into this.

Five P's of Reclaiming your Time

1. **Purpose:** Have short-term, mid-term and long-term goals you're working toward.
2. **Pragmatism:** Be realistic about what you can do in the time available.
3. **Planning:** When appropriate, use lists, schedules, calendars, daily planners, etc.
4. **Prioritization:** Start with what you must do, then what you should do, then what you can do.
5. **Perseverance:** Don't let distractions stop you from finishing what you started.

Purpose

> *You can make many plans, but the Lord's purpose will prevail.* - **Proverbs 19:21(NLT)**

Why do you wake up in the morning? What motivates you to commit your time to anything? Hopefully, it's your purpose. I once learned in a sermon delivered by my brother, Deon, that you can't live solely based on the purpose for your life, you need the purpose for your year, month, week and day. Without that, you will struggle to focus your time daily. Moreover, your purpose can't be self-generated. It must come from God. Otherwise, you will frustrate yourself pursuing something that eventually will be meaningless because it took you away from what God wanted you to do. God has a purpose for your life so you must discover it and make it your own so that you will prevail.

I wrote an entire book on discovering your purpose called, "Well Done". You can pick it up from any online bookseller and read more. In this context, I want to emphasize that having clear goals allows you to reclaim your time. When you know what you're working on, you can merely choose activities that contribute to those goals and remove those that do not. I have simple goals for the ministry that I use to judge our corporate time and financial commitments. I have goals for my career that are very specific that cause me to prune my daily to-do list. I have goals for my physical body that enable me to discipline my workout schedule and dietary intake.

> *Where there is no vision [no revelation of God and His word], the people are unrestrained; But happy and blessed is he who keeps the law [of God].* -

Proverbs 29:18(AMP)

Vision brings restraint. It provides boundaries and allows you to operate at the highest level within a given set of constraints. It's the antithesis of the modern connotation of being a free spirit. It might seem like fun to just do whatever you feel like doing, whenever you feel like doing it, but the unintended consequence is that you waste precious time. According to the scripture, a free spirit is someone without a vision and the KJV uses the word perish to describe what happens to a person like that.

In every season of my life, I have a purpose that shapes my priorities. I set very short-term goals that fit into that purpose and go hard after them. As I accomplish those goals, I walk out God's purpose for my season. I also eliminate everything that gets in my way. Even if it's a good thing, if it doesn't fit the season, it's gone. It might be good but because it's not a good time for it, it's a distraction and it needs to go. My purpose allows me to reclaim my time. So, what's your vision for today? What do you want to accomplish by the time you lay your head to sleep tonight? What is your vision for this week? What should your testimony sound like on Sunday about the week? What's your vision for this season? When you discover what it is, you'll be able to discipline your life and reclaim your time.

Pragmatism

> *Because of the privilege and authority God has given me, I give each of you this warning: Don't think you are better than you really are. Be honest in your evaluation of yourselves, measuring yourselves by the faith God has given us.* -
> **Romans 12:3(NLT)**

There's no worse person that you can deceive than yourself. When you deceive yourself into believing that you are what you are not, you cannot win in life. Knowing your limits is an important step in reclaiming your time. As Apostle Paul said, don't think higher of yourself than you really are. That's a recipe for personal failure and in some cases, a public disaster. People who overestimate themselves end up in "no-win" situations they could have avoided. They take on challenges they are ill-prepared to face. They make promises they cannot keep. They pursue goals they will never achieve. They position themselves for disappointment.

There are only 24 hours in a day and on your best day, you probably have 12 of those hours available to be productive. Keeping that in mind, you must be realistic about what you can accomplish with your time. My wife Angel and I, remind each other continuously that nobody has everything, and nobody can do everything. We must be thankful for our God-given portion and be practical about what we can do with it. If you choose to join this journey of reclaiming your time, this is an important step. Be practical about what you can and cannot do! Be pragmatic about what you know and do not know! Be realistic about your time! Determine what you can accomplish with your time, then start thinking about what you're going to do with it.

I had to learn this important life lesson in late 2016 when for the first and only time in my life I approached the level of complete burnout. I was working full-time as a Professional Structural Engineer at the 2nd largest environmental resources firm in the world and the job included 40% travel across the US. I was studying for the California Professional Engineering Seismic and Surveying exams. I was an adjunct professor at a local university teaching Engineering Graphics to students who weren't all eager to learn.

I was teaching several classes in the School of The Bible including filling in for other instructors when needed. Apart from preaching on Sundays at The Body Church, I was leading monthly "Understanding the End Times" workshops which required significant research and preparation. On top of that, every Thursday we had Coffee Shop Conversations and one Friday per month we had Decatur Community Workshops at the church.

I thought nothing of it because that's how I always operated. My philosophy was that human limits are in the mind. If you keep pushing yourself, you will keep stretching and extending your capacity. I thought I could do it all until one day I woke up with my head spinning and it would not stop. I didn't have a headache. I wasn't just dizzy. I was mentally and emotionally exhausted. Here's how I got to that point. That week I had accepted the challenge to fill in for my mother on Tuesday night as a School of the Bible instructor. I was tasked with teaching a brand new book of The Bible that I had never taught before which meant extensive study in a short period of time.

I also had to prepare a Friday night workshop on the juxtaposition between Bible prophecy and historical records of the destruction of the 2nd Jewish Temple. I was also taking a review course with two 3-hr classes that week for the California Professional Civil Engineering exam. I then had to prepare a message to preach on Sunday. All the while, I kept working full-time as a Structural Engineer. I knew that I was getting a bit overwhelmed, but I thought I could push through. Unexpectedly, I hit my limit by Saturday, and it was drastic. My brain simply just stopped working properly and my thoughts went into a complete tailspin.

By a total miracle, I was able to accomplish everything that was before me. However, the Lord mercifully allowed me to see my fallibility without letting me fail. At the end of that week, I told my wife that every non-essential activity in my life was getting cut. Those included weekly church events other than services that we had to personally lead. Unless someone else was willing to take the lead, they were off the calendar. I then had to make some hard decisions about my personal life.

I didn't have enough time built into my schedule for rest and relaxation. I didn't have enough time to enjoy my wife. All I did was work, work, work and when I was not working, I was preparing for more work. If I was not working at my secular job, I was doing the work of the ministry. My wife would get tired just watching me work. So, in 2016, I took stock of my life and started reclaiming my time because I had to. I added a word to my vocabulary that could double as a complete sentence; "No!"

Planning

Good planning and hard work lead to prosperity, but hasty shortcuts lead to poverty. - **Proverbs 21:5(NLT)**

Once you have established your purpose and developed a sober perspective of what you can accomplish you're ready to start planning. Proper planning is one way you can reclaim your time. Have you ever had so much to do that you became totally flustered and could do nothing at all? That's when you must stop what you're doing, which is absolutely nothing and develop a plan. Lists, schedules, daily planners, calendars, and all other planning tools are your friends. While they require time for you to properly enter the data you need into them, the time is well spent. You save time in the long run by not spinning your wheels because you're overwhelmed.

For instance, my cell phone calendar is connected to my email calendar and I use it to capture my appointments. Once my appointments are accounted for, I look for gaps and set priorities for what I will do during those gaps. I use that for my weekly planning. Daily, I determine either the night before or early in the morning what I intend to do with the gaps in my schedule for the day. That's when I make the final decision on what I need to get done for the day and in what order.

Sometimes, I have so many things going on that I must do even more planning. I have a small notebook that I use to create daily lists that I use to track my accomplishments in real-time. When I have too many responsibilities to manage in each timeframe, I use the list to guide me through the day outside of the appointments that are already on my calendar. Nevertheless, that's just a glimpse at some practical ways to apply short-term planning. Let's step back a bit to talk about planning in general. People without plans end up spinning their wheels even if they have clear goals. It's the plan that outlines the steps to accomplishing those goals. There's also another benefit to planning that's spiritual in nature.

> *A man's mind plans his way [as he journeys through life], But the Lord directs his steps and establishes them.* - **Proverbs 16:9(AMP)**

God gives you a purpose that sets the course for your life. Once you embrace His purpose, it's your responsibility to create a layout of your plans for accomplishing that purpose. Once you have some plans laid out, God will guide and establish your steps through the plans to the successful fulfillment of your purpose. If you think you're too busy to plan, you're too busy. Take time out of your schedule for planning purposes so that the Lord has something to work with. He initiates the course of your life with your purpose, you structure your life with your plan, and He empowers your steps to carry it all out to completion. As Apostle Paul stated in Philippians 1:6AMP); *"I am convinced and confident of this very thing, that He who has begun a good work in you will [continue to] perfect and complete it until the day of Christ Jesus [the time of His return]."*

Prioritization

> *Turn my eyes away from vanity [all those worldly, meaningless things that distract—let Your priorities be mine], And restore me [with renewed energy] in Your ways.* - **Psalm 119:37(AMP)**

Once your priorities are aligned with God's priorities you should commit to living by them. Plans without priorities lead to inefficiencies. If you don't prioritize you may end up "majoring in minors and minoring in majors". In other words, you may invest an inordinate amount of time working on something that is not really that important while neglecting to complete a crucial task. I have learned to prioritize my life in the following order: what I must do, what I should do and what I can do.

Deciding what I must do at any given time is driven by a combination of the activity's importance and the deadline. As much as I can, I live by the philosophy; "under-promise and over-deliver". I use that approach extensively when it comes to setting deadlines. That way, I can prioritize my activities by importance instead of continually chasing deadlines.

I also let my priorities, which are the things that I must do, override my schedule. Let me explain what I mean. If something is a priority and must be completed, I choose to clear everything else from my calendar to the best of my ability until it's done. I cancel my meetings. I delay other submittals. I push appointments further down my calendar so that I'm not engaging in activities outside of the order of priority. It's not easy sometimes to do so but it's essential. If something that must be done is competing against something that should be done, the latter will get done later (pun intended). In addition, if something that can be done is competing against what must be done or should be done, the truth is that if my schedule is packed, the former may never get done and I'm okay with that. That's how you live with priorities. Yet, there's more.

I have learned that while time-management, which is really managing what you do with your time is important, energy management is even more important. When you're reclaiming your time, you should also be reclaiming your energy. When you manage what you do with your time without managing your energy you may put aside time for important activities, but you may not have the level of energy needed to be successful at performing them. Hence, I try to effectively manage my energy. That means, even if there are activities that don't take much time, they need to be priorities if they take much of my energy.

For instance, I avoid negative people because even with minimal time they can sap my energy. I also avoid useless arguments and fights over things of little value. I accept that it's okay not to care about certain things. If it doesn't matter, I don't care about it. Just like I've added the word "no" to my vocabulary, walking away has been added to my list of frequently used actions. There's nothing wrong with walking away from a situation that doesn't deserve the level of energy it demands.

You don't need to live a lopsided life where you're giving energy and attention to things that don't matter while you lack energy for the things that do. Since I started reclaiming my time, I took cognizance of the importance of my energy. You should too. If a situation is not worth your time or your energy, cut it out of your life. Reclaim your time and reclaim your energy.

Perseverance

Therefore, since we are surrounded by so great a cloud of witnesses [who by faith have testified to the truth of God's absolute faithfulness], stripping off every unnecessary weight and the sin which so easily and cleverly entangles us, let us run with endurance and active persistence the race that is set before us, [looking away from all that will distract us and] focusing our eyes on Jesus, who is the Author and Perfecter of faith [the first incentive for our belief and the One who brings our faith to maturity], who for the joy [of accomplishing the goal] set before Him endured the cross, disregarding the shame, and sat down at the right hand of the throne of God [revealing His deity, His authority, and the completion of His work]. - **Hebrews 12:1-2(AMP)**

Life is full of distractions. It doesn't matter what you do, there seems to always be circumstances and people in our lives trying to take our focus away from what is important. Above all else, when these distractions arise you must reclaim your time. Saying no, walking away, avoiding traps, or ignoring those who try to take your attention away from your priorities are just a few ways you can reclaim your time.

Still, some distractions are unavoidable. In those cases, you need the perseverance to keep moving in the right direction despite the challenges. You also need the ability to recognize the distractions in your life. If you don't realize something is a distraction you might embrace it instead of rejecting it and make things worse for yourself. As I alluded to earlier, even good things could be distractions when they're not priorities.

Jesus had perseverance. He did what needed to be done regardless of what was going on around Him. The same could be said of Apostle Paul who modeled his life after Jesus and encouraged us all to do the same in Hebrews 12:1-2. After laying out the Hall of Faith in Hebrews 11, he started Hebrews 12 with a challenge to the Body of Christ. While all those faithful saints who went before us, look down from heaven as witnesses, we must finish the race of life that God set before us with a singular focus on Jesus Christ. Along the way, we will have short-term, mid-term and long-term goals we need to accomplish to get there.

I call distractions time-stealers. They show up at the most inconvenient times to steal our time. Like an NFL running back or rugby player, we must put our heads down, square our shoulders and push forward through everything that tries to stop us. Don't let distractions steal your time for good, reclaim it before it's too late. When you fix your eyes on Jesus and commit to complete what He wants you to do, don't stop until you're finished. There will always be something else you could be doing with your time. There will always be important things left to do. When you finish what's most important, you can move on to what's next. Don't falter or stumble, persevere until you see with your own eyes the results of what you've been working toward. Take control of the time you have. Reclaim it!

21 THIS IS YOUR TIME

"After a long absence, the master of those three servants came back and settled up with them. The one given five thousand dollars showed him how he had doubled his investment. His master commended him: 'Good work! You did your job well. From now on be my partner.' "The servant with the two thousand showed how he also had doubled his master's investment. His master commended him: 'Good work! You did your job well. From now on be my partner.' "The servant given one thousand said, Master, I know you have high standards and hate careless ways, that you demand the best and make no allowances for error. I was afraid I might disappoint you, so I found a good hiding place and secured your money. Here it is, safe and sound down to the last cent.' "The master was furious. 'That's a terrible way to live! It's criminal to live cautiously like that! If you knew I was after the best, why did you do less than the least? The least you could have done would have been to invest the sum with the bankers, where at least I would have gotten a little interest. "'Take the thousand and give it to the one who risked the most. And get rid of this "play-it-safe" who won't go out on a limb. Throw him out into utter darkness.' - **Matthew 25:19-30(MSG)**

I finished writing this book in 2020, the year when the world reeled from the sudden death of NBA superstar, Kobe Bryant alongside his daughter and several others. Also, one of the young men originally from our church in Trinidad was killed in a car chase while serving as a sheriff's deputy in Georgia, US. Then, in a startling twist, the global COVID-19 (Coronavirus) pandemic gripped the earth claiming over 100,000 lives. On top of that, while working from home under quarantine, I received news that the CEO of the company I work for died suddenly. With each death, God reminded me of the frailty of human life and the urgency we should ascribe to each day. Since tomorrow is not promised to anyone, we must choose to make the most of today.

There's something special about the beginning of each new year and in the case of 2020 and beyond, each new decade. I don't know about you, but I believe so. Many of us have been waiting a long time for certain opportunities to be made available to us. God has also been waiting for the right time to present us with these opportunities. Now is that time! It's time for God to do what He promised and it's time for us to respond to whatever God does. As we approach the conclusion of this book, I want to bring your attention back to what matters the most. Time is short, so do something special with it.

The big question is, *"What will you do when God opens the door and gives you the opportunity you've dreamed of?"* It is easy to say you will take advantage of it without hesitation but what if it comes with major risks? What if it requires you to leave your comfort zone and risk what you already have in your hands to get what God has for you? When the Children of Israel were first presented with the opportunity to enter the Promised Land, they didn't. The writer of Numbers 13 and 14 documented how their fear of the giants in the land was too much for them to bear. So, they stayed in the wilderness where they felt *"safe"* until they died. What about you? Do you feel *"safe"* where you are? Are you really?

The Parable of The Kingdom in Matthew 25 lays the principles out in a simple illustration so that we can easily understand how God operates. He gives us the resources, tools, and opportunities we need to be successful then He gives us the time to do something productive with them. When He believes we've had enough time He holds us accountable for our actions. If we are profitable and can demonstrate fruitfulness He lavishes us with rewards. If we are unprofitable and have the audacity to make excuses for our incompetence He responds in kind. What response will God give to you at the end of this year?

The servant who received five thousand dollars doubled his money, which is the same return on a percentage basis gained by the servant who received two thousand dollars. Have you ever doubled an investment? Do you know it's almost impossible to do so without taking a big risk? In some cases, you may potentially lose all your investment. I once doubled a financial investment in the stock market, and it was a very stressful experience because the value kept decreasing before eventually skyrocketing up. As the value of the company dipped, I raised the amount of my investment because I knew a turnaround was coming. While I poured money in, it looked like I could lose big, but I was confident in the viability of the company. Then one day the catalyst I was waiting for finally came and the stock doubled.

To be honest, I could have saved myself the stress and put the money under my mattress. That would guarantee that I could not lose. However, it also guaranteed that I could not win. In God's eyes, that is worse than taking a chance and losing everything. At least, you tried. Believe me, I know what it's like to play not to lose, instead of playing to win. That's what the first part of my career looked like. I took no chances. I let other people decide the trajectory of my career and hoped they would take care of me. That didn't happen.

If I can teach you anything from my experience, it's this. If you don't take a chance on yourself, other people will determine your future in a manner that benefits them the most and not you. If you don't believe in yourself enough to take a chance on you, why would anyone else? Even God who alone fully understands the extent of your potential expects you to take a chance before He can do the miracle He knows you need. If you don't do something, nothing happens.

In 1 Kings 17, the widow in Zarephath had to risk everything by making a cake for the prophet Elijah first. If the plan didn't work, they would all have died but if it worked, they would all live. She went for it and thousands of years later we still tell her story. In 2 Kings 4, the widow of the prophet first had to gather the vessels by faith and then the miracle of the perpetual flow of oil began. The Word of God through the prophet Elisha had the power to make the oil last forever but the widow determined how long it lasted. The more vessels she collected the more oil she could get.

When Jesus told Peter to come on the water in Matthew 14:29, it was Peter who had to step out of the boat and start walking on the water. An angel didn't pick Peter up and put him there. Once he took the first step out of the boat, the power of The Word, *"Come"* was enough to change the molecular structure of the water under his feet so he could walk on it. In fact, since we're on the topic of water, long before Peter was even born, Noah was instructed to build an ark in Genesis 6 without any sign of rain. As you should know, Noah risked his reputation in obedience to God and it worked out in his favor.

Now there were set there six waterpots of stone, according to the manner of purification of the Jews, containing twenty or thirty gallons apiece. Jesus said to them, "Fill the waterpots with water." And they filled them up to the brim. And He said to them, "Draw some out now, and take it to the master of the feast." And they took it. When the master of the feast had tasted the water that was made wine, and did not know where it came from (but the servants who had drawn the water knew), the master of the feast called the bridegroom. And he said to him, "Every man at the beginning sets out the good wine, and when the guests have well drunk, then the inferior. You have kept the good wine until now!" - **John 2:6-10(NKJV)**

The miracle of turning water into wine didn't take place until the water was poured out and taken to the governor of the feast. By the time the governor grabbed the cup of water and put it to his lips, it was wine. Now, who in their right mind would hand the governor a cup of water to taste when he's expecting wine? Jesus never said anything about changing the water to wine. He simply said, scoop out the water and give it to the governor to taste. The servants risked their reputation listening to Jesus, but they did, and it worked out.

Now faith is the substance of things hoped for, the evidence of things not seen... But without faith it is impossible to please him: for he that cometh to God must believe that he is, and that he is a rewarder of them that diligently seek him. - **Hebrews 11:1, 6(KJV)**

So then faith cometh by hearing, and hearing by the word of God. - **Romans 10:17(KJV)**

For as the body without the spirit is dead, so faith without works is dead also. - **James 2:26(KJV)**

(For we walk by faith, not by sight:) - **2 Corinthians 5:7(KJV)**

The essence of walking by faith is risk-taking. The essence of risk-taking is that there are no natural guarantees. Some outcomes may be more probable than others, but no single outcome is absolute. If you take a chance on yourself one possible outcome is that you might fail. My advice is that you go ahead and think through that possibility. What will you do if things don't work out? You don't have to believe it will happen, but you do have to accept that it can happen and be okay with it. Otherwise, you will never have the confidence to even try in the first place.

Esther said in Esther 4:16, *"... and if I perish, I perish."* She needed to reassure herself that she had no choice but to take the chance of meeting with the king. The risk was high, but the reward was higher. If she had to pay the ultimate price, so be it. The truth is that even if she didn't take the risk, she would probably have died anyway. Haman had a plan to kill all the Jews and she was one of them. She could take the risk and probably die, or she could not take the risk and still die. She made the right choice.

> *If that is the case, our God whom we serve is able to deliver us from the burning fiery furnace, and He will deliver us from your hand, O king. But if not, let it be known to you, O king, that we do not serve your gods, nor will we worship the gold image which you have set up."* - **Daniel 3:17-18(NKJV)**

Shadrach, Meshach, and Abednego said in Daniel 3:17 that God would save them from the fiery furnace, then followed that up in Daniel 3:18 by saying that even if He didn't, they still would not worship the golden image. Were they contradicting themselves? No! They were being realistic. They knew that they could die in the fire even if they didn't believe that they would. Yet, accepting the risk gave them the courage to take the step of faith. God would save them but that's not why they were doing it. They were doing it because it was what they were supposed to do and if God didn't save them, they would do it anyway. With that mindset, they were unstoppable.

What's my point? A person who accepts the cost of possible failure and determines it is not high enough to justify losing the benefit of possible success cannot fail. This is especially true for a Christian who has received a Word from God. Our faith is in God's Word and we know it is dead if we don't do something with it. If you have a Word from God and refuse to take a risk to carry it out because the cost of failure is too high you won't see the Word come to pass. On top of that, don't forget that there's an eternal cost for disobedience that is unaccounted for in a typical earthly risk analysis.

Like Esther who knew that she would die anyway, we need to remember to consider all potential outcomes, including eternal ones. In the Parable of the Kingdom when the master held his servants accountable for his investments, the one who didn't take a chance still paid a high price. He may have saved himself from losing his master's money but instead, he lost his master's trust and that was worse. Then after losing his master's trust, he still lost his master's money because his master took it back and gave it to someone else. What are you afraid of more? Losing God's investment in your life or losing God's trust? When you don't step out on faith, you lose both.

> *Farmers who wait for perfect weather never plant. If they watch every cloud, they never harvest. Just as you cannot understand the path of the wind or the mystery of a tiny baby growing in its mother's womb, so you cannot understand the activity of God, who does all things. Plant your seed in the morning and keep busy all afternoon, for you don't know if profit will come from one activity or another—or maybe both.* - **Ecclesiastes 11:4-6 (NLT)**

Take a chance on yourself. If that's too much of a risk, take a chance on God's Word. Don't watch the weather. Don't watch every cloud. Go outside and sow the seeds of your destiny. You cannot understand the activity of God. You don't know how He will do what He has promised. Yet, your faith in His Word is the assurance that He will do it. Don't deny the possibility of failure, accept it and determine that it's not worth missing out on God's best for you. Never forget that the only guaranteed failure takes place if you never try. Take a chance on yourself. Better yet, take a chance on God and His Word because He took a chance on you!

22 UNDERSTANDING THE SIGNS OF THE END

So they asked Him, saying, "Teacher, but when will these things be? And what sign will there be when these things are about to take place?" And He said: "Take heed that you not be deceived. For many will come in My name, saying, 'I am He,' and, 'The time has drawn near.' Therefore do not go after them. But when you hear of wars and commotions, do not be terrified; for these things must come to pass first, but the end will not come immediately." Then He said to them, "Nation will rise against nation, and kingdom against kingdom. And there will be great earthquakes in various places, and famines and pestilences; and there will be fearful sights and great signs from heaven. -
Luke 21:7-11(NKJV)

Eschatology, the study of the end times, is essentially the art and science of discerning signs. From Genesis to Revelation, the scriptures list signs of the first and second comings of Jesus, the destruction and rebuilding of the Jewish Temple, the first and "second" Resurrections, the spirit and person of the Antichrist and so much more. As we bring this study of time to a close, I feel strongly by the inspiration of the Holy Ghost that a short discourse on the end times would be beneficial.

All we need to know about what The Lord has done throughout history, what He is doing right now and what He will do until the end of time is located somewhere in the 66 books of the Bible. The challenge to all of us is to not just find what the scripture says about the end times but understand where it fits in the trajectory of all human history. Let's take a closer look at how Jesus used the signs of the times to prepare the hearts of His disciples for the challenges ahead.

Then Jesus went out and departed from the temple, and His disciples came up

217

to show Him the buildings of the temple. And Jesus said to them, "Do you not see all these things? Assuredly, I say to you, not one stone shall be left here upon another, that shall not be thrown down." Now as He sat on the Mount of Olives, the disciples came to Him privately, saying, "Tell us, when will these things be? And what will be the sign of Your coming, and of the end of the age?" - **Matthew 24:1-3(NKJV)**

Jesus was asked a direct three-part question by His disciples that was recorded in Matthew 24:3, Mark 13:4 and Luke 21:7. Though there are signs of the end listed throughout scripture, His responses in these passages form the foundation of our study. As we explore the available information, we will discover that the signs of the end outlined by Jesus ranged from the days of the early church, through our time today, to His triumphant return at the end of time. Therefore, we must distinguish the signs which applied back then from those which apply now and those still to come. We also must identify the repeated signs.

Step #1 - Analyze the Question

Traditionally, many interpret the signs in Matthew 24, Mark 13, and Luke 21 to refer only to the return of Jesus Christ and the end of the age. Hence, they try to fit every single sign into a modern or future context instead of also accepting the historical context. Still, we don't have to force things to make sense when we have the right context. If you read the conversation between Jesus and His disciples, you will notice something. He was asked for signs concerning the following three distinct events.

1) The destruction of the temple
2) The 2nd coming of Jesus
3) The end of the age

Step #2 – Group the Signs

To answer the three-part question before Him, Jesus listed a variety of signs. Certain things are obvious in those signs. They extend for thousands of years. They are all related to one another and some are repeated. They culminate with significant events, e.g. the destruction of Jerusalem and the return of Jesus. They are not all relevant to the return of Jesus.

There are five groups of signs that can be summarized as follows.

A. Beginning of sorrows. (Matthew 24:1-8, Mark 13:2-8 and Luke 21:5-11)

B. Persecution of the early church. (Matthew 24:9-13, Mark 13:9-13 and Luke 21:12-19)
C. Destruction of Jerusalem in 70 AD. (Luke 21:20-24)
D. The Great Tribulation. (Matthew 24:14-28, Mark 13:14-23, Daniel 11:36-45, Revelation 11:1-14, Revelation 13)
E. Return of Christ and the end of the age. (Matthew 24:29-44, Mark 13:24-36 and Luke 21:25-36)

Groups A to C point to the destruction of the temple. Groups D and E point to the 2nd coming of Jesus Christ and the end of the age. If we don't group the signs and determine which ones apply to each significant event mentioned by Jesus we will either get confused or we will start forcing things to make sense that really don't. It's a shame that some people try to manufacture connections between Bible prophecy and current events when the connections are not there.

Perhaps, that's why predictions of the exact dates of the return of Jesus keep popping up in each generation. Then once each date comes and nothing happens the proponents of those prophecies make excuses for why they were wrong. Let us now take a detailed look at the first three groups of signs: the beginning of sorrows, persecution of the early church and the destruction of Jerusalem. We will stick to the scriptures pertaining to these signs and juxtapose Biblical records with historical facts. The last two groups of signs have been set aside for your self-directed study using the scriptures provided.

Beginning of Sorrows

And Jesus answered and said to them: "Take heed that no one deceives you. For many will come in My name, saying, 'I am the Christ,' and will deceive many. And you will hear of wars and rumors of wars. See that you are not troubled; for all these things must come to pass, but the end is not yet. For nation will rise against nation, and kingdom against kingdom. And there will be famines, pestilences, and earthquakes in various places. All these are the beginning of sorrows. - **Matthew 24:4-8(NKJV)**

And Jesus, answering them, began to say: "Take heed that no one deceives you. For many will come in My name, saying, 'I am He,' and will deceive many. But when you hear of wars and rumors of wars, do not be troubled; for such things must happen, but the end is not yet. For nation will rise against nation, and kingdom against kingdom. And there will be earthquakes in various places, and there will be famines and troubles. These are the beginnings of sorrows. - **Mark 13:5-8(NKJV)**

219

Jesus did what He could to distinguish the first group of signs from those of the end times. For instance, He specifically stated that when these things happen, the end is not yet. In other words, these are not the signs of the end, but signs of the beginning. After studying these scriptures and measuring the historical record against the signs contained within them, I believe the beginnings of sorrows took place during the lifetime of the disciples.

When someone uses this group of signs from these specific scriptures to explain the end of time, it is a misinterpretation of the exact intentions of Jesus. While these signs may be repeated at the end of time, as evidenced by other scripture references, Jesus spoke of an earlier period of human history. He told His disciples that when they see the following signs, they will be experiencing the beginning of sorrows.

1) Mass deception by false Christs
2) Wars and rumors of wars
3) Natural disasters – earthquakes in different places, famines, pestilences

Mass Deception by False Christs

Now, brethren, concerning the coming of our Lord Jesus Christ and our gathering together to Him, we ask you, not to be soon shaken in mind or troubled, either by spirit or by word or by letter, as if from us, as though the day of Christ had come. Let no one deceive you by any means; for that Day will not come unless the falling away comes first, and the man of sin is revealed, the son of perdition, who opposes and exalts himself above all that is called God or that is worshiped, so that he sits as God in the temple of God, showing himself that he is God. Do you not remember that when I was still with you I told you these things? - **2 Thessalonians 2:1-5(NKJV)**

But there were also false prophets among the people, even as there will be false teachers among you, who will secretly bring in destructive heresies, even denying the Lord who bought them, and bring on themselves swift destruction. And many will follow their destructive ways, because of whom the way of truth will be blasphemed. By covetousness they will exploit you with deceptive words; for a long time their judgment has not been idle, and their destruction does not slumber. - **2 Peter 2:1-3(NKJV)**

Soon after the beginning of the early church, deceivers entered and started spreading false doctrines. One such doctrine was concerning the second coming of Christ. Some had spread the rumor that Jesus had already returned, and it confused the saints. Apostle Paul had to make it clear that Jesus had not yet returned and explained why that was impossible. Jesus will return after a specific sequence of events including the falling away, the unveiling of the antichrist and the abomination of desolation.

Since these events are prerequisites, Jesus could not have already returned. It's the same logic we need to use today. We can't say that Jesus will return today if we can't say that the prerequisites of his return have been met. It was that simple for the Apostle Paul so it should be that simple for us. Apostle Peter confirmed the mass deception that took place in the early church in 2 Peter 2:1-3. This was prophesied by Jesus as the beginning of sorrows and it took place just like He said, merely a few years after his ascension to heaven. However, this is just one sign, let's look at a few others.

Wars and Rumors of Wars

Jesus walked the earth for 30 years before commencing 3 years of public ministry (approximately 30-33 AD). During that time, He prophesied that wars and rumors of wars would be the signs that signal the beginning of sorrows. For the fulfillment of the prophecy to make any logical sense, the frequency and/ or intensity of wars should have drastically increased at that time in such a way that it would have been obvious. Here are the wars that took place during the lifetime of Jesus in the vicinity where He and His disciples lived. (Cartwright, 2013)

- *27 BC - 19 BC - Cantabrian Wars: Roman conquest of the Iberian Peninsula.*
- *9 AD - Battle of the Teutoburg Forest: The Rhine River is established as the boundary between the Latin and German speaking worlds, following the defeat of the Roman army, under the command of Varus.*
- *16 AD - Battle of the Weser River: Germanicus leads 12,000 men across the Rhine to attack the Chatti.*

That's a grand total of two wars during the lifetime of Jesus and one, several decades before His birth. Compared to what we're used to, that's a relatively peaceful season of sorts. Hence, the disciples would have noticed the change in the environment at the first sign of a major war. While Jesus lived in a time when major wars were few and far between, here is the list of wars directly after His death and resurrection. (Cartwright, 2013)

- *43 AD - Claudius commences the Roman conquest of Britain.*
- *54 AD - 60 AD - Roman general Corbulo successfully campaigns in Armenia.*
- *58 AD - 63 AD - Roman-Parthian War.*
- *60 AD - 61 AD - Boudicca's Revolt in Britain.*

- *70 AD - The city of Jerusalem is besieged and captured by Rome; the Second Temple destroyed.*
- *75 AD - 77 AD - Romans defeat the last of the Northern tribes; Roman conquest of Britain complete.*
- *101 AD - 106 AD - Trajan conquers Dacia.*

After Jesus prophesied of wars, it only took ten years for the Roman conquest of Britain to begin in 43 AD. Then, if you notice closely, the conquest continued for 34 years and culminated in the defeat of the last Northern tribes in 77 AD. That's 34 years of continuous war after a mere 2 major battles during the lifetime of Jesus. In the eyes of the disciples who lived to see these events, that was the fulfillment of the prophetic declaration of wars and rumors of wars. The twelve disciples may not all have lived through the end of that prophetic season but the seventy disciples (Luke 10) and many others most likely did. Most importantly, the siege of Jerusalem and the destruction of the Second Temple in 70 AD would have been significant events in the lives of the disciples.

Natural Disasters – Earthquakes in Different Places

> *And Jesus cried out again with a loud voice, and yielded up His spirit. Then, behold, the veil of the temple was torn in two from top to bottom; and the earth quaked, and the rocks were split, and the graves were opened; and many bodies of the saints who had fallen asleep were raised; and coming out of the graves after His resurrection, they went into the holy city and appeared to many. So when the centurion and those with him, who were guarding Jesus, saw the earthquake and the things that had happened, they feared greatly, saying, "Truly this was the Son of God!"* - **Matthew 27:50-54(NKJV)**

Do you know that the earthquake which took place at the death of Jesus is not just recorded in the Bible but can be substantiated by other historical documents? An online tool provided by The National Centers for Environmental Information/NOAA – National Oceanic and Atmospheric Administration allows the public to search their Significant Earthquake Database from 2150 BC to present. Believe it or not, the database shows an earthquake in Israel: Palestine in 33 AD, the exact year Jesus died. (NOAA: National Oceanic and Atmospheric Administration)

Here's the list of earthquakes during the lifetime of Jesus; (NOAA: National Oceanic and Atmospheric Administration)

- *10 AD - Turkmenistan: Nisa*

- *11 AD - Turkey*
- *17 AD - Turkey: Izmir, Efes, Aydin, Manisa, Alasehir, Sart*
- *23 AD - Greece*
- *25 AD - Pakistan*
- *27 AD – South Korea: Kwangju*
- *29 AD - Turkey: Iznik, Izmit*
- *33 AD - Israel: Palestine*

From the look of it, earthquakes were quite frequent in the Middle East, Europe, and Asia at the time. Now, here's the list of significant earthquakes directly following the death and resurrection of Jesus. Let's see if there was a spike of any significance. (NOAA: National Oceanic and Atmospheric Administration)

- *37 AD - Turkey: Antakya (Antioch)*
- *46 AD - China: Henan Province: Nanyang*
- *50 AD - Afghanistan: Aikhanum*
- *52 AD - Greece: Philippi, Drama, Kavala*
- *52 AD - Turkey: Antakya (Antioch)*
- *55 AD - Greece: Crete*
- *57 AD - Albania: Durres*
- *60 AD - Turkey: Laodecia, Hierapolis, Colossae, [Pamukkale]*
- *62 AD - Greece: Crete*
- *63 AD - Italy: Pompei*
- *76 AD - Cyprus: Paphos, Salamis*
- *79 AD - Italy: Naples (Napoli)*
- *89 AD - South Korea: Kwangju*
- *93 AD - Turkey: Hellespont*
- *100 AD – South Korea: Kyongju*

After the earthquake that occurred at the crucifixion of Jesus in 33 AD, there was only one of significance until 46 AD. From that point, there were consistent earthquakes at least every 2 to 3 years until AD 63. After that period, there was a thirteen-year lull until AD 76. Again, if the disciples looked at earthquakes as a sign of the beginning of sorrows, the period between AD 46 and just before AD 70 would have qualified. Why use AD 70 as a milestone? That's the year Jerusalem was soundly defeated by the Romans and the beloved 2nd Jewish Temple was destroyed. With mass deception, wars and earthquakes happening simultaneously, three of the five signs signifying the beginnings of sorrows were in place. What about famines and pestilences?

Natural Disasters – Famines

> *And in these days prophets came from Jerusalem to Antioch. Then one of them, named Agabus, stood up and showed by the Spirit that there was going to be a great famine throughout all the world, which also happened in the days of Claudius Caesar. Then the disciples, each according to his ability, determined to send relief to the brethren dwelling in Judea. This they also did, and sent it to the elders by the hands of Barnabas and Saul.* - **Acts 11:27-30(NKJV)**

There was a major famine prophesied in the Book of Acts which is easy to miss if you don't carefully search for it. Since the scripture says that it happened in the days of Claudius Caesar, we can conduct a parallel search through the historical record to substantiate its occurrence as well as narrow down the date range. Why do that? With such an approach, we can juxtapose the timing of the famine alongside the other signs of the beginnings of sorrows outlined by Jesus. If the timing is comparable, we have further support that the disciples and early church witnessed the beginnings of sorrows. Here's a direct quote from the renowned Roman historian Josephus.

> *Now her coming was of very great advantage to the people of Jerusalem; for whereas a famine did oppress them at that time, and many people died for want of what was necessary to procure food withal, queen Helena sent some of her servants to Alexandria with money to buy a great quantity of corn, and others of them to Cyprus, to bring a cargo of dried figs. And as soon as they were come back, and had brought those provisions, which was done very quickly, she distributed food to those that were in want of it, and left a most excellent memorial behind her of this benefaction, which she bestowed on our whole nation. And when her son Izates was informed of this famine, he sent great sums of money to the principal men in Jerusalem. However, what favors this queen and king conferred upon our city Jerusalem shall be further related hereafter.* - **Flavius Josephus. Antiquities of the Jews 20.2.5-49** (Josephus, Antiquities of the Jews, 1895)

> *Then came Tiberius Alexander as successor to Fadus; he was the son of Alexander the alabarch of Alexandria, which Alexander was a principal person among all his contemporaries, both for his family and wealth: he was also more eminent for his piety than this his son Alexander, for he did not continue in the religion of his country. Under these procurators that great famine happened in Judea, in which queen Helena bought corn in Egypt at a great expense, and distributed it to those that were in want, as I have related already.* - **Flavius Josephus. Antiquities of the Jews 20.5.2-101**

(Josephus, Antiquities of the Jews)

The historical record of this famine is further substantiated by the Anglo-Saxon Chronicle which records the details as follows.

A.D. 46. This year Claudius, the second of the Roman emperors who invaded Britain, took the greater part of the island into his power, and added the Orkneys to rite dominion of the Romans.

This was in the fourth year of his reign. And in the same year (12) happened the great famine in Syria which Luke mentions in the book called "The Acts of the Apostles". After Claudius Nero succeeded to the empire, who almost lost the island Britain through his incapacity.

A.D. 47. This was in the fourth year of his reign, and in this same year was the great famine in Syria which Luke speaks of in the book called "Actus Apostolorum".

(12) An. 48, Flor. See the account of this famine in King Alfred's "Orosius".
(Great, AD 890)

With this historical evidence, we can safely confirm that around 13 years after the death and resurrection of Jesus, the disciples experienced a major famine that was so significant it received international attention. At the same time, mass deception was rampant in the church accompanied by an increased frequency of wars and earthquakes. What's interesting to note is that the intensity increased and seemed to crescendo around AD 70.

That year, a significant event took place which sealed the transition from the beginning of sorrows to the next step in Jesus' prophecy. There was one more sign that Jesus mentioned would signal the beginning of sorrows and that's pestilences (plagues, epidemics, pandemics, disease outbreaks, etc.). However, I could not find evidence of these taking place until AD 70 as the prophetic sequence outlined by Jesus transitioned into the next phase. We will study this some more in the next chapter.

23 DISCERNING THE TIME OF PERSECUTION

Then Jesus went out and departed from the temple, and His disciples came up to show Him the buildings of the temple. And Jesus said to them, "Do you not see all these things? Assuredly, I say to you, not one stone shall be left here upon another, that shall not be thrown down." Now as He sat on the Mount of Olives, the disciples came to Him privately, saying, "Tell us, when will these things be? And what will be the sign of Your coming, and of the end of the age?" - **Matthew 24:1-3(NKJV)**

In the previous chapter, you should have noticed the level of detailed research it takes to match some of the historical data with the signs of the times in the scriptures. Just so we don't lose focus, let's recap a bit. As I noted earlier, if you read the conversation between Jesus and His disciples in Matthew 24:1-3 you will notice something. He was asked for signs concerning the following three distinct events.

1) The destruction of the temple
2) The 2nd coming of Jesus
3) The end of the age

To answer the three-part question before Him, Jesus listed the following signs in five distinct groups with groups A to C answering the first question and D to E answering the last two.

A. Beginning of sorrows. (Matthew 24:1-8, Mark 13:2-8 and Luke 21:5-11)
B. Persecution of the early church. (Matthew 24:9-13, Mark 13:9-13 and Luke 21:12-19)
C. Destruction of Jerusalem in 70 AD. (Luke 21:20-24)

D. The Great Tribulation (Matthew 24:14-28, Mark 13:14-23, Daniel 11:36-45, Revelation 11:1-14, Revelation 13)

E. Return of Christ and the end of the age. (Matthew 24:29-44, Mark 13:24-36 and Luke 21:25-36)

Now that we've established the signs pertaining to the beginning of sorrows let's shift our focus to the persecution of the early church leading up to the destruction of Jerusalem and the beloved temple. As I mentioned in the previous chapter, we'll only address the first three groups in this book. If you have an interest in studying the last two, feel free to use the scriptural references listed as a good place to get started.

Persecution of the Early Church

"Then they will deliver you up to tribulation and kill you, and you will be hated by all nations for My name's sake. And then many will be offended, will betray one another, and will hate one another. Then many false prophets will rise up and deceive many. And because lawlessness will abound, the love of many will grow cold. But he who endures to the end shall be saved. - **Matthew 24:9-13(NKJV)**

"But watch out for yourselves, for they will deliver you up to councils, and you will be beaten in the synagogues. You will be brought before rulers and kings for My sake, for a testimony to them. And the gospel must first be preached to all the nations. But when they arrest you and deliver you up, do not worry beforehand, or premeditate what you will speak. But whatever is given you in that hour, speak that; for it is not you who speak, but the Holy Spirit. Now brother will betray brother to death, and a father his child; and children will rise up against parents and cause them to be put to death. And you will be hated by all for My name's sake. But he who endures to the end shall be saved. - **Mark 13:9-13(NKJV)**

But before all these things, they will lay their hands on you and persecute you, delivering you up to the synagogues and prisons. You will be brought before kings and rulers for My name's sake. But it will turn out for you as an occasion for testimony. Therefore settle it in your hearts not to meditate beforehand on what you will answer; for I will give you a mouth and wisdom which all your adversaries will not be able to contradict or resist. You will be betrayed even by parents and brothers, relatives and friends; and they will put some of you to death. And you will be hated by all for My name's sake. But not a hair of your head shall be lost. By your patience possess your souls. - **Luke 21:12-19(NKJV)**

As referenced above in each of the synoptic gospels (Matthew, Mark, and Luke), Jesus prophesied to His followers that they would experience persecution. The significance of this declaration is that even though the persecution of the church continued throughout history and will not end until His triumphant return, these prophetic words quoted above were directed to His generation. Within a year of the death and resurrection of Jesus, in AD 34, the persecution started with the stoning of Stephen (Acts 7:54-60). Yet, that was an isolated incident until AD 44 when Herod escalated the persecution by taking the life of Apostle James then arresting Apostle Peter.

> *About that time King Herod Agrippa began to persecute some believers in the church. He had the apostle James (John's brother) killed with a sword. When Herod saw how much this pleased the Jewish people, he also arrested Peter. (This took place during the Passover celebration.) Then he imprisoned him, placing him under the guard of four squads of four soldiers each. Herod intended to bring Peter out for public trial after the Passover. But while Peter was in prison, the church prayed very earnestly for him.* - **Acts 12:1-5(NLT)**

One of the most inspiring teachings on prayer comes out of Acts 12. In it, the power of prayer was demonstrated at an unprecedented level by the early church. After Herod killed James, he got carried away by the adulation of the Jewish people and chose to arrest Peter. The church was having none of it and broke out into mass intercession for Peter. A large group gathered at the home of Mary, the mother of John Mark, for what could easily be described as the most effective prayer meeting ever. Before they could finish praying, God miraculously answered their prayers. He sent an angel to free Peter from prison and personally escort him out.

On top of that, Peter showed up safe and sound to the same prayer meeting to greet them. It was such a surprise visit to them that at first, they didn't believe it was really him and would not open the door. Thank God for a persistent young lady who knew that the answer to their prayer was outside knocking while they continued praying. Now, let's get to the facts. Here's a concise timeline of the persecution that the early church experienced. It started soon after their triumphant launch in the Upper Room right up to the destruction of Jerusalem.

- *A.D. 34. This year was St. Paul converted, and St. Stephen Stoned.*
- *A.D. 44. This year the blessed Peter the apostle settled an episcopal see at Rome; and James, the brother of John, was slain by Herod.*
- *A.D. 50. This year Paul was sent bound to Rome.*
- *A.D. 62. This year James, the brother of Christ, suffered.*

- *A.D. 63. This year Mark the evangelist departed this life.*
- *A.D. 69. This year Peter and Paul suffered.*
- *A.D. 70. This year Vespasian undertook the empire.*
- *A.D. 71. This year Titus, son of Vespasian, slew in Jerusalem eleven hundred thousand Jews.*

(Great, AD 890)

For over three decades, church persecution was mostly directed to the leadership. One by one, the Apostles and other clergy were harassed, arrested, or even killed for their roles in promoting the gospel of Jesus Christ. Their first oppressors were their own Jewish brothers and sisters who perceived early Christianity as a Jewish sect that had lost its way. Yet, what was originally perceived as a threat against Jewish religious traditions in the AD 30's grew into the personal obsession of Roman leadership in the AD 50's and 60's. This eventually culminated in one of the worst displays of human depravity in history when Jerusalem was burned under the direction of Emperor Nero.

Here's a quick look at the historical record.

The first persecution of the Church took place in the year 67, under Nero, the sixth emperor of Rome. This monarch reigned for the space of five years, with tolerable credit to himself, but then gave way to the greatest extravagancy of temper, and to the most atrocious barbarities. Among other diabolical whims, he ordered that the city of Rome should be set on fire, which order was executed by his officers, guards, and servants. While the imperial city was in flames, he went up to the tower of Macaenas, played upon his harp, sung the song of the burning of Troy, and openly declared that 'he wished the ruin of all things before his death.' Besides the noble pile, called the Circus, many other palaces and houses were consumed; several thousands perished in the flames, were smothered in the smoke, or buried beneath the ruins.

This dreadful conflagration continued nine days; when Nero, finding that his conduct was greatly blamed, and a severe odium cast upon him, determined to lay the whole upon the Christians, at once to excuse himself, and have an opportunity of glutting his sight with new cruelties. This was the occasion of the first persecution; and the barbarities exercised on the Christians were such as even excited the commiseration of the Romans themselves. Nero even refined upon cruelty, and contrived all manner of punishments for the Christians that the most infernal imagination could design. In particular, he had some sewed up in skins of wild beasts, and then worried by dogs until they expired; and others dressed in shirts made stiff with wax, fixed to axletrees, and set on fire in his gardens, in order to illuminate them. This persecution was general throughout the whole Roman Empire; but it rather increased than diminished the spirit of Christianity. In the course of it, St. Paul and St. Peter were martyred.

To their names may be added, Erastus, chamberlain of Corinth; Aristarchus, the Macedonian, and Trophimus, an Ephesians, converted by St. Paul, and fellow-laborer with him, Joseph, commonly called Barsabas, and Ananias, bishop of Damascus; each of the Seventy. - **The First Persecution, Under Nero, A.D. 67; Fox's Book of Martyrs; Edited by William Byron Forbush** (Fox)

Before we move on, take note that Erastus, Aristarchus, Trophimus, Joseph, and Ananias were from the 70 disciples sent out by Jesus in Luke 10. Their names were not mentioned anywhere in the scripture, but they did make history. Nevertheless, by AD 67, there should have been no question in the minds of Jesus' disciples that the prophetic signs signaling the destruction of the temple were taking place. They must have known that they were decades into the beginning of sorrows after witnessing most of the following signs taking place and, in some cases, intensifying.

1) Mass deception by false Christs
2) Wars and rumors of wars
3) Natural disasters – earthquakes in different places, famines, pestilences

As I stated previously, the historical evidence is quite exhaustive for every one of these signs except pestilences. However, all of that changed as time closed in on the destruction of Jerusalem and their beloved temple. At that time, they experienced the worst pestilences of their lifetime. This effectively closed the loop on the first two elements of the prophetic sequence and transitioned to the third and most significant element of their time.

Destruction of Jerusalem in 70 AD. (Luke 21:20-24)

"But when you see Jerusalem surrounded by armies, then know that its desolation is near. Then let those who are in Judea flee to the mountains, let those who are in the midst of her depart, and let not those who are in the country enter her. For these are the days of vengeance, that all things which are written may be fulfilled. But woe to those who are pregnant and to those who are nursing babies in those days! For there will be great distress in the land and wrath upon this people. And they will fall by the edge of the sword, and be led away captive into all nations. And Jerusalem will be trampled by Gentiles until the times of the Gentiles are fulfilled. - **Luke 21:20-24(NKJV)**

For a moment, put yourself in the place of the disciples as they listened to Jesus prophesy about the destruction of Jerusalem. Mere moments earlier, they asked him directly what the signs of the temple's destruction would be. Since they were under Roman rule and understood that the first temple was similarly destroyed by Babylon hundreds of years earlier, nothing Jesus said was far-fetched. In the three years of His public ministry, He didn't just prepare his followers for His own death, He prepared them for the end of life as they knew it.

Many popular, modern, Bible prophets interpret Luke 21:20-24 in the context of the final days before the return of Jesus and that's understandable. Yet, the disciples saw it come to pass in their lifetime. Like several prophecies in the Bible, the prophecy transcends generations and epochs of time. For instance, what started as a prophetic word against the King of *Tyre* in Ezekiel 28 transitioned in verse 11 into a prophetic word against Satan.

It was so seamless that the shift could have easily been missed. In the same way, Jesus first prophesied about a time that His disciples would see with their own eyes then switched to the end of time all within the same prophecy. Though He may not have explicitly drawn the line, we need to do so at the risk of misinterpretation. That's where historical records come in.

In 69 CE, Vespasian returned to Rome to serve as emperor, but first he appointed his son, Titus, to carry on in his stead. In 70 CE, Titus came towards Jerusalem with an army of 80,000 soldiers... The Roman soldiers attacked the weakest side of Jerusalem, the north side, first. They pounded the wall surrounding the New City with their battering rams and threw stones into the city with their catapults... When Titus saw he could not conquer them by force, he decided to starve the Jews into submission. He built a stone wall around the city and sealed all the exits, allowing only Romans with passes to pass through.

A terrible hunger now ravaged the overcrowded city. Soon the last stores of food dwindled down. Rich people gave all their wealth for a bit of food. Even leather was cooked and eaten. At first the Zealots had not been affected by hunger because they took other people's food, but eventually they too became desperately hungry, eating their horses and even their horses' dung and saddles.

In Josephus's account (The Jewish Wars, 5:10): "The roofs were filled with women and small children expiring from hunger, and the corpses of old men were piled in the streets. Youths swollen with hunger wandered like shadows in the marketplace until they collapsed. No one mourned the dead, because hunger had deadened all feeling. Those who fell to the ground turned their eyes for the last time to the Holy Temple and beheld the defenders still fighting and holding out." The best of friends would snatch food from each other. The Talmud recounts the sorry tale of a woman who killed and consumed her own baby, recalling the verse in Leviticus 26:29, "You will eat the flesh of your sons, and the flesh of your daughters you will eat."

The streets were soon filled with corpses, and, as it was hot summer weather, terrible epidemics broke out. Hundreds of people were found dead every morning. In their despair, many of the Jews tried to leave the enclosure of Jerusalem under the cover of night to seek something edible in the fields. They were easily captured, and Titus had them crucified in plain view of the city's defenders on the wall. In one night, Josephus tells us, five thousand Jews were discovered searching for food and were all crucified. - **Rabbi Yochanan ben Zakkai's Request and Starvation, The Destruction of the Second Holy Temple, A Historical Overview** (Chabad.org)

By AD 70 all the signs of the beginning of sorrows had been fulfilled. The Roman army had surrounded Jerusalem forcing starvation, death, and terrible epidemics to break out in Jerusalem. Records of these events can be found in the Talmud, The Jewish Wars by Josephus, and the Anglo-Saxon Chronicle among other sources. The disciples asked Jesus when the temple would be destroyed, and He gave them detailed signs that in hindsight could not have been any clearer. Here's the culmination of the first part of Jesus' prophecy. This is how the second temple was destroyed.

According to Josephus, Titus did not want the Temple to be burnt, apparently because a standing (but vanquished) Temple would reflect more on Rome's glory. It was a Roman soldier acting on his own initiative who, hoisted on the shoulders of another soldier, threw a firebrand into the Temple. Titus tried to put a stop to the fire, but in the chaos, his soldiers did not hear him. (Other historians contradict this account of Titus's enlightened perspective and report that Titus ordered the Temple destroyed.)

In either case, before long, the Temple was engulfed in flames. The Jews frantically tried to stop the fire, but were unsuccessful. In despair, many Jews threw themselves into the flames. The Roman soldiers rushed into the melee. Romans and Jews were crowded together, and their dead bodies fell on top of each other. The sound of screaming filled the air and the floor of the Temple was covered with bodies, with blood streaming down the steps.

The Romans brought idols into the Temple and offered sacrifices to it. They took the golden vessels of the Temple and killed everyone they found. Before the fire consumed the Temple completely, Titus entered the Holy of Holies and performed the most despicable acts. The still-surviving Jews in the Upper City could only watch as the Temple burned down to the foundations. It burnt well into the next day.

When the flames finally died down, left standing was the retaining wall on the western side of the Temple Mount. This is the Western Wall that still stands in Jerusalem today, where Jews over the centuries have gathered to pray. - **The Destruction of the Temple, The Destruction of the Second Holy Temple, A Historical Overview** (Chabad.org)

For any disciple who lived to see the destruction of the Temple, there was no doubt that they were witnessing the fulfillment of the prophetic words of Jesus. They were nowhere close to the 2nd coming of Jesus, but they should have known the distinction. As they watched the temple burn to the ground, the chapter pertaining to the beginning of sorrows and the destruction of the temple closed for good. Yet, some modern Christians can't seem to let it go. They believe that there's just no way that this prophecy could already be fulfilled. It must happen during the end times, so they take it upon themselves to find creative ways to fit these signs into our generation. To do so is unnecessary because, as shown below, there are enough scriptural references that concentrate exclusively on the end times.

1) **Beginning of sorrows. (Matt 24:1-8, Mark 13:2-8 and Luke 21:5-11)**
2) **Persecution of the early church. (Matt 24:9-13, Mark 13:9-13 and Luke 21:12-19)**
3) **Destruction of Jerusalem in 70 AD. (Luke 21:20-24)**
4) The Great Tribulation (Matthew 24:14-28, Mark 13:14-23, Daniel 11:36-45, Revelation 11:1-14, Revelation 13)
5) Return of Christ and the end of the age. (Matthew 24:29-44, Mark 13:24-36 and Luke 21:25-36)

Now that we have studied the first three groups of signs that have already come to pass you should understand the level of effort it takes to fully understand the signs of things to come. Nevertheless, it's a journey worth taking because what God says will happen before the end of time, will happen exactly the way He said it. At your own pace, look at the scriptures laid out above and take the first step toward understanding the Great Tribulation, the return of Jesus Christ and the end of the age. As I've said repeatedly in this book, time has a beginning and a finite end. Only God understands it all but thankfully, He revealed what we need to know and understand in the scriptures.

24 FINANCIAL END TIMES

"This will happen just as I have described it, for God has revealed to Pharaoh in advance what he is about to do. The next seven years will be a period of great prosperity throughout the land of Egypt. But afterward there will be seven years of famine so great that all the prosperity will be forgotten in Egypt. Famine will destroy the land. This famine will be so severe that even the memory of the good years will be erased. As for having two similar dreams, it means that these events have been decreed by God, and he will soon make them happen. "Therefore, Pharaoh should find an intelligent and wise man and put him in charge of the entire land of Egypt. Then Pharaoh should appoint supervisors over the land and let them collect one-fifth of all the crops during the seven good years. Have them gather all the food produced in the good years that are just ahead and bring it to Pharaoh's storehouses. Store it away, and guard it so there will be food in the cities. That way there will be enough to eat when the seven years of famine come to the land of Egypt. Otherwise this famine will destroy the land." - **Genesis 41:28-36(NLT)**

An economic downturn came to The United States of America in 2020. I had known in my heart for a few years that it was coming but every day The Holy Ghost kept reminding me. I was not the only person who knew it. God strategically sent others to confirm what He already said to me. It is time for us to increase the sense of urgency we have for the prophetic Word of God. That way, when He speaks to us about things to come, we will take Him seriously and act accordingly.

When God first spoke to me about this, He said that we have 8 years for the bottom to fall out on this booming economy. That was in 2017. Unfortunately, that was the max time available to get ready and was the best-case scenario. What does that mean? The deadline for it to take place would be 2025 but there was no guarantee that it would take that long. I don't know when you will be reading this but it's an example of how God speaks. If God is gracious enough to allow us to make it that far without an economic crash we can only be grateful. He also warned that the predicted crash would be worse than The Great Depression of the 1930s and the Great Recession of the early 2000s.

For two weeks in 2017, I watched my investment accounts plummet. Each day, as the stock market indices showed red I searched frantically for answers from the experts I typically listened to. They all said the same thing. The correction (10% reduction) was due to the markets being overheated so there was no need to panic. The good times were still rolling, and stocks remained the hottest investments in town. They advised us to not sell our investments and lock in losses but just ride it out. From all indications, they were right. Even though volatility was high, the market crept back up slowly.

However, God spoke to my heart during that market correction reminding me of how sudden an economic crash can take place. There are no final warning signs. It just starts dropping and keeps dropping. Then economic pundits do their best to explain what happened after the fact. I learned during the correction in 2017 that many of them did not know what was coming. They were experts in hindsight which is 20-20 for everyone. Hindsight does not help you after an economic crash starts. It only helps if you survived the previous crash and are preparing for the next one.

As I write this book, we are now coming to the end of the years of plenty. After the rough times of The Great Recession, it's been party time again in the US. President Trump signed the "largest tax cut in history" into law and followed that up with a trillion-dollar spending bill that received bipartisan support. Even some of the "deficit hawks" who usually oppose deficit spending and growing national debt were unusually quiet. Several financial regulations put in place in response to The Great Recession have been under threat because they are no longer convenient.

Until the COVID-19 pandemic, jobs, jobs, jobs were everywhere and *"hardworking Americans"* were *"going back to work."* Several major corporations were offering one-time bonuses to their workforce. Cranes littered the skylines of major cities like Atlanta as construction projects were in full swing. If we discount the correction in 2017, the stock market had been on a tear for several years. The real estate market was sizzling again, and people were willing to overpay for properties because of increasing demand. The car industry was back. Black Friday shopping was at its highest in the last few

Thanksgiving holidays. People were in the mood to spend, spend, spend. The Recession was over. It was time for a celebration!

By some estimations, we were over 8 years into a cycle of economic prosperity, and it was yet to peak. Many people were understandably cautious during the first few years but as the boom continued not so much. So you know what happened next. The perfect storm of a US trade war with China, an oil price war between Saudi Arabia and Russia, a global COVID-19 pandemic and a stock market in freefall brought the boom to a crashing end.

> *As predicted, for seven years the land produced bumper crops. During those years, Joseph gathered all the crops grown in Egypt and stored the grain from the surrounding fields in the cities. He piled up huge amounts of grain like sand on the seashore. Finally, he stopped keeping records because there was too much to measure... At last the seven years of bumper crops throughout the land of Egypt came to an end. Then the seven years of famine began, just as Joseph had predicted. The famine also struck all the surrounding countries, but throughout Egypt there was plenty of food. Eventually, however, the famine spread throughout the land of Egypt as well. And when the people cried out to Pharaoh for food, he told them, "Go to Joseph, and do whatever he tells you."*
> **- Genesis 41:47-49, 53-55(NLT)**

If you have not taken the time to read my last book, *"The Fish with the Coin in Its Mouth"*, do so. It will help you navigate economic crashes and believe me; you need to prepare. I do not expect this to be on the cover of Charisma magazine or broadcast across the world on TBN or The Word Network. I also do not expect this to be the hottest topic on the preaching circuit but mark my words. An economic crash was declared by God to come by 2025 and if we did not get ready it was destined to crush us. However, if we did get ready, we would benefit from the greatest wealth transfer of our generation.

> *"Do not lay up for yourselves treasures on earth, where moth and rust destroy and where thieves break in and steal; but lay up for yourselves treasures in heaven, where neither moth nor rust destroys and where thieves do not break in and steal. For where your treasure is, there your heart will be also.* **- Matthew 6:19-21(NKJV)**

Preparation for the Next Recession

1. **Pray:** I wish I could tell you the exact date of the next crash, but I cannot. Only The Holy Ghost knows. He has a detailed plan for each of us to make it successfully through what is coming. Only those of

us who hear from Him will know it. If you do not usually pray, start now!

2. **Make as much money as possible:** In a booming economy, opportunities are available to start and grow a business, invest in the stock market, get a much higher paying job, etc. Do not hesitate! The window is open during good times and will close. If God has given you an idea, when the economy is doing well, the time is now!

3. **Save as much money as possible:** The people with cash thrive in an economic recession. It is not the time for frivolous spending. Joseph advised Pharaoh to save 20% during the years of plenty. Do that! In the worst-case scenario, you may need to survive for 4 or 5 years without substantial income or an increase in income, at best.

4. **Get out of debt:** Interest rates are relatively low during the first few years of economic recovery, so debt is cheap. Do not take the bait. If you can get' out of debt, do it. When the economy crashes and your income is threatened, the last thing you need to worry about is bills you could have avoided that are disproportionate to your income.

5. **Consider recession-proof investments:** Nothing's really recession-proof but some investments do better in a recession than others. For instance, start doing research on US Government bonds. They worked well during the Great Recession so consider shifting some investments there soon. You can also invest in residential and commercial rental properties.

6. **Stack your heavenly account:** Economic crashes will only affect your earthly resources. What you have placed in God's hands will be safe. Be sure to consistently give your tithes and offerings. You will need to tap that account when things get rough.

7. **Consider recession-proof industries:** If you work or do business in an industry that depends on discretionary consumer spending or luxuries, start thinking about your next gig. When the economy crashes, consumers focus on essentials like shelter, utilities, transportation, and food.

"Maybe you missed an opportunity during the economic downturn of 2008. In my community, I saw investors buy homes for half-price. Fortunately, if you live long enough it will happen again. The state of the global economy rotates

cyclically between periods of boom and bust. Sometimes, it will be up and other times it will be down. What you do during the good times determines what you can do during the hard times." - **The Fish with the Coin in Its Mouth**

Find Your Prophetic Voice

And they rose early in the morning, and went forth into the wilderness of Tekoa: and as they went forth, Jehoshaphat stood and said, Hear me, O Judah, and ye inhabitants of Jerusalem; Believe in the Lord your God, so shall ye be established; believe his prophets, so shall ye prosper. - **2 Chronicles 20:20(KJV)**

The Lord woke me up one morning with a Word that started with the question; *"Who is the prophetic voice in your life?"* Think about it for a moment. If The Lord wants to speak to you right now through someone else, who is the person in your life that He can use? Your answer to that question is directly connected to your potential for prosperity. In this season, God is speaking through prophetic voices in the earth as I have never seen or heard before. That is a good thing but who is really listening? I know every Christian should be able to hear from God, but the scripture says in 1 Corinthians 13:9(NKJV), *"For we know in part and we prophesy in part."* That means that no single person hears everything that God says, so we all need other prophetic voices to get the full picture.

Many of us have experienced a time of unprecedented opportunities. I shared more details on that earlier. As I stated, the time of plenty was upon us for almost a decade. It was destined to be followed by lean times for a few years. Even if we are late, we always need to be prepared. One of the most important steps in our preparation is connecting ourselves with the prophetic voices of our generation. Doing so is a matter of maximizing opportunities right now but will be a matter of survival at some point.

So it was, as the multitude pressed about Him to hear the word of God, that He stood by the Lake of Gennesaret, and saw two boats standing by the lake; but the fishermen had gone from them and were washing their nets. Then He got into one of the boats, which was Simon's, and asked him to put out a little from the land. And He sat down and taught the multitudes from the boat. When He had stopped speaking, He said to Simon, "Launch out into the deep and let down your nets for a catch." But Simon answered and said to Him, "Master, we have toiled all night and caught nothing; nevertheless at Your word I will let down the net." And when they had done this, they caught a great number of fish, and their net was breaking. So they signaled to their partners in the other boat to come and help them. And they came and filled both the boats, so that they began to sink. When Simon Peter saw it, he fell down at Jesus' knees, saying, "Depart from me, for I am a sinful man, O Lord!" - **Luke 5:1-8(NKJV)**

This is an example of the power of a prophetic voice. Simon and his partners were professional fishermen. They knew the best times to fish, where to find the best fish and how to catch the fish they wanted. Yet, with all their knowledge and skill they spent an entire night fishing but caught absolutely nothing. Let us put it in context. How can a commercial fisherman with a large net dragging along the ocean floor for an entire night catch nothing? Maybe they did not catch the type of fish they were looking for, but nothing at all? That must have been frustrating, but it was part of God's plan.

Jesus showed up while they were washing their nets and preparing to leave. He borrowed Simon's boat to teach the multitudes. Then, He gave a simple, prophetic instruction that changed Simon's life. Jesus said, *"Launch out into the deep and let down your nets for a catch."* We do not need to imagine the first thought that popped into Peter's mind. He said, *"Master, we have toiled all night and caught nothing; nevertheless at Your word I will let down the net."* Fortunately, he was smart enough to check himself and make the right choice to obey. Not only did his decision bless his life, but it also prospered his friends.

Simon Peter's instantaneous change of fortune had nothing to do with his fishing skills, the type of fish nor the weather. It had all to do with the prophetic word he received from Jesus and his decision to obey. Jesus showed up right on time and presented Simon with a Word that changed his frustrating situation into something amazing. Again, I ask you the question, *"Who is the prophetic voice in your life?"*

A certain woman of the wives of the sons of the prophets cried out to Elisha, saying, "Your servant my husband is dead, and you know that your servant feared the Lord. And the creditor is coming to take my two sons to be his slaves." So Elisha said to her, "What shall I do for you? Tell me, what do you have in the house?" And she said, "Your maidservant has nothing in the house but a jar of oil." Then he said, "Go, borrow vessels from everywhere, from all your neighbors—empty vessels; do not gather just a few. And when you have come in, you shall shut the door behind you and your sons; then pour it into all those vessels, and set aside the full ones." So she went from him and shut the door behind her and her sons, who brought the vessels to her; and she poured it out. Now it came to pass, when the vessels were full, that she said to her son, "Bring me another vessel." And he said to her, "There is not another vessel." So the oil ceased. Then she came and told the man of God. And he said, "Go, sell the oil and pay your debt; and you and your sons live on the rest." - **2 Kings 4:1-7(NKJV)**

Why did this widow have the money to pay off her debts? It had nothing to do with her business acumen, specialized skills, or the power of persuasion. If she had made the decision on her own to borrow all those vessels she would merely have had a house full of empty pots. The reason why she was successful also had nothing to do with her unfortunate situation. God did not do a miracle for her because He felt sorry for her. We can safely assume that she was not the only widow in the community in a bad financial situation. Still, they did not all experience the same miracle even if they needed it. What made her special? She was the widow of a prophet who served Elisha. She had access to the prophetic voice of Elisha when she needed it. In addition, she did exactly what he instructed her to do. Now the results speak for themselves.

So He humbled you, allowed you to hunger, and fed you with manna which you did not know nor did your fathers know, that He might make you know that man shall not live by bread alone; but man lives by every word that proceeds from the mouth of the Lord. - **Deuteronomy 8:3(NKJV)**

I know we are deep into the 21st century and the concept of prophecy is not widely accepted. That does not make a difference to me nor should it to you either. The Word of God is The Word of God and the gift of prophecy is the Word of God. Yes, you can read The Bible and get the Word of God but where exactly in those 66 books are the specific instructions for your current situation? That is where prophecy comes in. You do not just need every written Word of God in the Bible; you need to know which one applies to you now. One more time I ask, *"Who is the prophetic voice in your life?"*

Then the word of the Lord came to him, saying, "Arise, go to Zarephath, which belongs to Sidon, and dwell there. See, I have commanded a widow there to provide for you." So he arose and went to Zarephath. And when he came to the gate of the city, indeed a widow was there gathering sticks. And he called to her and said, "Please bring me a little water in a cup, that I may drink." And as she was going to get it, he called to her and said, "Please bring me a morsel of bread in your hand." So she said, "As the Lord your God lives, I do not have bread, only a handful of flour in a bin, and a little oil in a jar; and see, I am gathering a couple of sticks that I may go in and prepare it for myself and my son, that we may eat it, and die." And Elijah said to her, "Do not fear; go and do as you have said, but make me a small cake from it first, and bring it to me; and afterward make some for yourself and your son. For thus says the Lord God of Israel: 'The bin of flour shall not be used up, nor

shall the jar of oil run dry, until the day the Lord sends rain on the earth.'"
So she went away and did according to the word of Elijah; and she and he and
her household ate for many days. - **1 Kings 17:8-15(NKJV)**

If the prophet Elijah did not show up, the widow and her son were surely going to die. God sent Elijah in her direction right on time not just to save himself but to save her and her son. Even though it was God's providence that saved her life, she passed the test of faith that Elijah presented to her. When asked by the prophet to sacrifice the little water, flour, and oil she had remaining for her family, she obeyed. Her obedience justified her selection by God for survival as outlined in the following scripture.

But I tell you truly, many widows were in Israel in the days of Elijah, when the heaven was shut up three years and six months, and there was a great famine throughout all the land; but to none of them was Elijah sent except to Zarephath, in the region of Sidon, to a woman who was a widow. And many lepers were in Israel in the time of Elisha the prophet, and none of them was cleansed except Naaman the Syrian." - **Luke 4:25-27(NKJV)**

Why did God select the widow at Zarephath for salvation from famine and why should God select you for salvation from the next recession? She was obedient. Are you facing a season of famine in any area of your life? Do you have a feeling of desperation in your current situation? Today, the prophetic voice in your life will direct you to opportunities you may not be aware of but tomorrow the prophetic voice may save your life. There is a connection between prophecy and prosperity. It is time for you to benefit from it.

Be the person who listens to God's Voice through His prophets during these financial end times. Be positioned to thrive while people struggle all around you. Tough times are times of separation. The difficulty of the circumstances will bring out the best or worst in people. Let the challenging times ahead bring out your very best. Be prepared for what is coming by paying attention to all that The Lord is revealing to you. God is merciful enough to warn us of things to come, let us value His words and heed His warning.

25 GODLY CONTENTMENT

But godliness actually is a source of great gain when accompanied by contentment [that contentment which comes from a sense of inner confidence based on the sufficiency of God]. For we have brought nothing into the world, so [it is clear that] we cannot take anything out of it, either. But if we have food and clothing, with these we will be content. But those who [are not financially ethical and] crave to get rich [with a compulsive, greedy longing for wealth] fall into temptation and a trap and into many foolish and harmful desires that plunge people into ruin and destruction [leading to personal misery]. For the love of money [that is, the greedy desire for it and the willingness to gain it unethically] is a root of all sorts of evil, and some by longing for it have wandered away from the faith and pierced themselves [through and through] with many sorrows. But as for you, O man of God, flee from these things; aim at and pursue righteousness [true goodness, moral conformity to the character of God], godliness [the fear of God], faith, love, steadfastness, and gentleness. Fight the good fight of the faith [in the conflict with evil]; take hold of the eternal life to which you were called, and [for which] you made the good confession [of faith] in the presence of many witnesses. - **1 Timothy 6:6-12(AMP)**

After reading this book about time you may feel a bit retrospective. Certainly, that is how I feel. After some internal reflection, here are my closing thoughts. Nobody has everything! That is one of the principles my wife Angel and I live by. It keeps us grounded and helps to curb our expectations out of life. Here is what I mean by that statement. There is no person on this earth whose life is perfect. Regardless of how things appear, looks can be deceiving. While some may appear to have it all, they do not. Two years before I wrote this book, the number of high profile suicides spiked, drawing international attention. Why would rich, successful people like Kate Spade and Anthony Bourdain who seemed to have it all want to end their own lives?

The glamorous existence of the rich and famous appears to be the stuff of dreams but what we see in the media is not entirely real. It is rehearsed, scripted, air-brushed, edited, auto-tuned and perfected for human consumption. What looks like a dream life on the outside might be a nightmare to the one living it. We do not want to live other people's lives. Yes, we think we want the stuff they have but we do not want their problems. We might want their pleasures, but we do not want their pain. We might want their money, but we don't want their problems.

That perspective started for me when I was disappointed in the lack of support I received for a venture I had started. While complaining about how hard it was to keep going without help, Angel told me something profound that never left me. She said, *"Be thankful for what people do for you, don't be disappointed about what they don't do."* It might sound simple now but at that time, it was like the heavens opened and God Himself shined a light on me. My focus was in the wrong place. I was fixated on what I didn't have instead of what I did have. Once my perspective changed, I was content.

Content people have the right perspective on life. They don't major in minors and minor in majors. They understand what is important and focus their energy on the things that will last forever. There is so much we can complain about daily, yet, at the same time there is so much we can be thankful for. Each day, we have a choice to make. Do we focus on the things to complain about or do we focus on the things to be thankful for? Let's now dig into the scriptures for some answers.

The Path to Contentment

1) Be satisfied with God!

But godliness actually is a source of great gain when accompanied by contentment [that contentment which comes from a sense of inner confidence based on the sufficiency of God]. - **1 Timothy 6:6(AMP)**

God is enough. At least, He should be for those who know Him. Apart from the simple fact that He is the eternal Creator of all things and owns it all, He's also the ultimate giver. Apostle James said in James 1:17(NKJV); *"Every good gift and every perfect gift is from above, and comes down from the Father of lights, with whom there is no variation or shadow of turning."* If there's any good that we can get out of life, it must come from God. Hence, if we have God we have everything that's good. That's the first step to being content.

When we started The Body Church it was a struggle to see it grow. Committed and faithful people are hard to come by when you're a small church in a Decatur, GA office park. Yet, every time we show up for our services The Lord was and continues to be there. His presence is a constant reminder that we are approved by Him. It's also a test of our hearts. God asked me several times whether I was satisfied with Him. Was He enough or was I missing out if all I got was Him? If I had to choose, would I prefer a large crowd or His presence? Those were some very insightful questions at the time. They spoke to the condition of my heart.

After these things the word of the Lord came to Abram in a vision, saying, "Do not be afraid, Abram. I am your shield, your exceedingly great reward."
- **Genesis 15:1(NKJV)**

God introduced Himself to Abram as his grand prize. Think about it. How would you feel if God says to you that He is your exceedingly great reward? That's it! He's the best you can get. Not money, not fame, not worldly success, not anything else but The Lord Himself. Would you be satisfied, or would you need more? Is God enough or does He need to come with something else for you to be satisfied? According to Apostle Paul in 1 Timothy 6:6, that's the first step to contentment. You can't be content with your life if you can't be content with God.

2) Focus on what really matters!

For we have brought nothing into the world, so [it is clear that] we cannot take anything out of it, either. - **1 Timothy 6:7(AMP)**

One day, each of us will leave this earth in one of two ways: death or The Resurrection. When we do so, we will have to leave everything behind that has no eternal significance. If we live long, financially successful lives that means we are leaving behind a lot of stuff. We must leave properties, investments, money, vehicles, clothes, jewels, furniture, and every other physical thing we acquired during our lifetimes. Why? They're worthless anywhere outside of earth. That's why Jesus asked the question in Mark 8:36(NKJV); *"For what will it profit a man if he gains the whole world, and loses his own soul?"*

Really, what do you gain if your time on earth was spent focused on the things of the earth? What happens when you step out of time into eternity?

Life is short. Yes, that means you should live it to the fullest but that also means that you should think about what happens when it ends. According to Apostle Paul in 1 Timothy 6:7, that's the next step on the path to contentment. We brought nothing into the world and we're taking nothing out of it. Remember that and you'll be able to enjoy your portion in life.

> *For our light affliction, which is but for a moment, is working for us a far more exceeding and eternal weight of glory, while we do not look at the things which are seen, but at the things which are not seen. For the things which are seen are temporary, but the things which are not seen are eternal.* - **2 Corinthians 4:17-18(NKJV)**

If our focus is on eternity we will live completely different lives from those who are ordinary. Natural things that keep us up at night would pale in comparison to our thoughts about God. Whether or not we have our dream house, car, spouse, career, business, or ministry would take a backseat to our relationship with God and our fulfillment of His purpose. I may not have everything, but I have God in my life, and I am living my purpose. That's what keeps me going every day. It works for me and will work for you. Don't lose your soul over temporary things when the maker of all things has a plan for your life.

3) Be thankful for the basics!

> *But if we have food and clothing, with these we will be content.* - **1 Timothy 6:8(AMP)**

The third principle on the path to contentment is thankfulness for the basics. Do you have food to eat? Do you have clothes on your back? Do you have shelter? Then you have the basics. If your needs are met, you have something to be thankful for. You may not have everything, but you have what you need to live on this earth. That's a good starting point. The easiest way to look at it is to remember those who don't have the basics and reach out to help. When you think of them you should be thankful to God. However, that's not even necessary for true contentment. Even if everyone had their needs met, the fact that God has met yours is enough for you to be thankful. You don't need to compare yourself to someone who is less fortunate to give Him thanks.

> *I rejoiced greatly in the Lord, that now at last you have renewed your concern for me; indeed, you were concerned about me before, but you had no opportunity to show it. Not that I speak from [any personal] need, for I have learned to be content [and self-sufficient through Christ, satisfied to the point where I am not*

disturbed or uneasy] regardless of my circumstances. I know how to get along and live humbly [in difficult times], and I also know how to enjoy abundance and live in prosperity. In any and every circumstance I have learned the secret [of facing life], whether well-fed or going hungry, whether having an abundance or being in need. I can do all things [which He has called me to do] through Him who strengthens and empowers me [to fulfill His purpose—I am self-sufficient in Christ's sufficiency; I am ready for anything and equal to anything through Him who infuses me with inner strength and confident peace.] - **Philippians 4:10-13(AMP)**

I've learned to thank God for everything. I remember when money was tight at my house just after I finished graduate school. My sister spent the summer with me, and we didn't have much money to shop for groceries before my next paycheck. Fortunately, she found some frozen bacon deep in the freezer and transformed it into a huge pot of tasty soup that lasted us several glorious days.

Those were some of the happiest days of my life. Around that time I remember taking my CD collection to the music consignment shop to sell them. They were only interested in the most popular albums and since I only listened to Christian music, they handpicked the few that they wanted. I praised God all the way home with the cash in my hands.

I know what it's like to withhold tithes and offerings because I felt like I couldn't afford it. I sowed sporadically for almost a year before The Lord convicted me. He then showed me what to do to free 10% of my income so that I could tithe again. Once I gave Him what was due to Him, my finances improved. I had to learn that my sufficiency was in Christ and not my free cash flow. I understood then that if I have the Lord with me I have everything I could ever need.

Concluding Thoughts

But those who [are not financially ethical and] crave to get rich [with a compulsive, greedy longing for wealth] fall into temptation and a trap and into many foolish and harmful desires that plunge people into ruin and destruction [leading to personal misery]. For the love of money [that is, the greedy desire for it and the willingness to gain it unethically] is a root of all sorts of evil, and some by longing for it have wandered away from the faith and pierced themselves [through and through] with many sorrows. But as for you, O man of God, flee from these things; aim at and pursue righteousness [true goodness, moral conformity to the character of God], godliness [the fear of God], faith, love, steadfastness, and gentleness. Fight the good fight of the faith [in the conflict with evil]; take hold of the eternal life to which you were called, and [for which] you made the good confession [of faith] in the presence of many witnesses. - **1 Timothy 6:9-12(AMP)**

Greed is the opposite of contentment. It doesn't matter how much you get, if you are greedy you will want more. Greed cannot be satisfied. That's why certain greedy people will risk what they have and sometimes their own freedom to pursue greater riches. They love money and their focus is never on the money they have but on the money they don't have. As a result, they open the door of hell for evil to flow freely into their lives. Let that not be said of any of us in The Body of Christ. The scripture says that some have longed for money so much that they have wandered from the faith to be pierced with many sorrows. Don't be one of those people. It's definitely not worth it.

Whatever your hand finds to do, do it with your might; for there is no work or device or knowledge or wisdom in the grave where you are going. I returned and saw under the sun that— The race is not to the swift, Nor the battle to the strong, Nor bread to the wise, Nor riches to men of understanding, Nor favor to men of skill; But time and chance happen to them all. - **Ecclesiastes 9:10-11(NKJV)**

Stuff happens. Sometimes it's good, sometimes it's bad. We don't know why life must be like that, but it is. Regardless of what happens, do your best with the life you have been given. It's alright to be ambitious. It's alright to dream. It's alright to work hard. However, be content with what you have right now and whatever you get in the future. Maybe everything will work out exactly as you dreamed. Maybe it won't. That's not what matters in life. What matters is how you choose to live regardless of the situations you face.

Contentment doesn't mean settling for less than God's best. It's being satisfied with God's best for you in the current season of your life. God knows what you need and if you are walking in His Will, whatever you have is what He wants you to have. When He wants you to have more, you will have it. Make the decision today to be happy with the life that God has given you. Choose contentment, a master key to Godly success and satisfaction. It will transform your life. The time you have on earth is short so be content with your portion and enjoy it.

For what will it profit a man if he gains the whole world, and loses his own soul? - **Mark 8:36(NKJV)**

CONCLUSION

I thank my God upon every remembrance of you, always in every prayer of mine making request for you all with joy, for your fellowship in the gospel from the first day until now, being confident of this very thing, that He who has begun a good work in you will complete it until the day of Jesus Christ; just as it is right for me to think this of you all, because I have you in my heart, inasmuch as both in my chains and in the defense and confirmation of the gospel, you all are partakers with me of grace. - **Philippians 1:3-7(NKJV)**

At the end of a hard workout at my local gym, I often joke with some of the men in the locker room that the best part of the workout is the end of it. Once the hard work is over, we get to take a hot shower, freshen up and enjoy the onslaught of endorphins that are naturally released to aid our physical recovery. In some ways, that's how I feel at the end of writing this book. What started as a moment of inspiration at my wife's ministry school graduation ceremony has turned into a series of powerful messages and now this book. There's a certain joy that only comes from finishing what you started and that's the joy I feel as I write this conclusion.

Nevertheless, what matters the most is what you do with the information you received. Reading this book is the beginning of a good work that God is doing in you. Allowing the truth revealed within it to change your mindset and inspire better decisions is how you let The Lord finish it. In the end, you should never look at the time the same way again. It's more than what most people think it is and even if you were one of those people before reading this book, you shouldn't be anymore. You should value the time you have more than ever and choose to live your life to the fullest. Like the chronological clock that never stops, neither should you in your relentless pursuit of destiny.

He who keeps his command will experience nothing harmful; And a wise man's heart discerns both time and judgment, Because for every matter there is a time and judgment, Though the misery of man increases greatly. For he does not know what will happen; So who can tell him when it will occur? - **Ecclesiastes 8:5-7(NKJV)**

The heart of the wise discerns both time and judgment. It is my prayer that you are counted among the wise. May God grant you the ability to understand what decisions to make for every matter you face. May He also give you the wisdom to discern when it is the right time to make those decisions. In your natural ability, you may not know the future but if you are a born-again Christian, the Holy Spirit living inside of you does. This book was designed to stir up the gift of the Holy Spirit inside of you so much so that you would tap into His endless wisdom and understanding.

When I was much younger, I would live in the future. I believed in delayed gratification and personal sacrifice. The principle of seedtime and harvest continues to be one of the pillars of my existence. However, at some point, recently, I experienced an epiphany and realized that the future I was working toward had become my present. In other words, the future is now. This is the moment to do what God has called you to do. I have embraced it in my own life, and you should too.

This is the moment to transition from an individual with great potential to one with great accomplishments. This is no longer the time to simply dream but the time to act on those dreams and get them accomplished. When your perspective changes, your life changes. This book should have helped, even in some little way, to change your perspective on time. It is now your turn to do something about it. Take advantage of the possibilities that God presents to you.

Do not let time pass you by. Take hold of it and make the most of it. Though time itself is a mystery, it's one that God wants to reveal to you. Open your heart and hear His Voice. God bless you richly and if you received anything of value from this book, share it with a family member, friend, or co-worker.

THE MYSTERY OF TIME

BIBLIOGRAPHY

Cartwright, M. (2013, October 22). Roman Warfare. Retrieved 1 11, 2020, from https://www.ancient.eu/Roman_Warfare/

Chabad.org. (n.d.). Rabbi Yochanan ben Zakkai's Request and Starvation, The Destruction of the Second Holy Temple, A Historical Overview. Retrieved January 12, 2020, from https://www.chabad.org/library/article_cdo/aid/913023/jewish/The-Second-Temple.htm

Chabad.org. (n.d.). The Destruction of the Temple, The Destruction of the Second Holy Temple, A Historical Overview. Chabad.org, a division of the Chabad-Lubavitch Media Center. Retrieved January 12, 2020, from https://www.chabad.org/library/article_cdo/aid/913023/jewish/The-Second-Temple.htm

Chabad-Lubavitch Media Center. (n.d.). Chabad.org. Retrieved 12 30, 2019, from https://www.chabad.org/library/article_cdo/aid/953566/jewish/Battle.htm

Charry, E. (2011). Supersessionism. In L. J. Green JB, *Dictionary of Scripture and Ethics*. Grand Rapids: Baker Academic.

Fox, J. (n.d.). The First Persecution, Under Nero, A.D. 67. *Fox's Book of Martyrs*. (W. B. Forbush, Ed.) Retrieved from https://www.biblestudytools.com/history/foxs-book-of-martyrs/

Fry, E. B. (2000). *The Reading Teacher's Book of Lists* (Vol. 4th Edition). Paramus, NJ: Prentice Hall.

Great, K. A. (AD 890). The Anglo-Saxon Chronicle. (R. J. Dr. J. A. Giles, Trans.) London, England: Everyman Press. Retrieved January 2020, 2020, from http://mcllibrary.org/Anglo/part1.html

Josephus, F. (1895). Antiquities of the Jews. *The Works of Flavius Josephus*. (A. A. William Whiston, Trans., & J. E. Beardsley, Compiler) Tufts

University. Retrieved January 12, 2020, from
http://data.perseus.org/citations/urn:cts:greekLit:tlg0526.tlg001.pe
rseus-eng1:20.2.5

Josephus, F. (n.d.). Antiquities of the Jews. *The Works of Flavius Josephus*.
Retrieved January 12, 2020, from
https://www.biblestudytools.com/history/flavius-
josephus/antiquities-jews/book-20/chapter-5.html

Merriam-Webster, Incorporated. (n.d.). time. *Merriam-Webster.com*. Retrieved
January 2, 2020, from https://www.merriam-
webster.com/dictionary/time

Merriam-Webster, Incorporated. (n.d.). window of opportunity. *Merriam-
Webster.com*. Retrieved 12 30, 2019, from https://www.merriam-
webster.com/dictionary/window%20of%20opportunity

NOAA: National Oceanic and Atmospheric Administration. (n.d.). The
Significant Earthquake Database. Retrieved January 11, 2020, from
https://ngdc.noaa.gov/nndc/struts/form?t=101650&s=1&d=1

Pierce, L. (n.d.). The Outline of Biblical Usage. Retrieved 12 31, 2019, from
https://www.blueletterbible.org/lang/lexicon/lexicon.cfm?Strongs
=H6256&t=KJV

Strong, J. (2003). *The New Strong's Exhaustive Concordance of the Bible*. Thomas
Nelson.

Strong, J. (2003). *The New Strong's Exhaustive Concordance of the Bible*. Thomas
Nelson.

ABOUT THE AUTHOR

Donnell Duncan is the pastor of The Body Church in Metro Atlanta, GA alongside his wife, Angel. He is the son of Apostles Jemma and Emanuel Vivian Duncan, founders of Aetos ministries and pastors of Divine Destiny Worship Centre, headquartered in Diego Martin, Trinidad. He is also the grandson of Dr. Levi Duncan, one of the most powerful ministers in the history of Trinidad and Tobago. Professionally, Pastor Duncan is an Associate Vice President of a multinational engineering consulting firm. He holds Professional Engineer (P.E.) and Structural Engineer (S.E.) licenses in over 25 US states including California. He obtained a BS in applied physics from Morehouse College, along with a BS and an MS in civil engineering (structural emphasis) from Georgia Institute of Technology. This is Pastor Duncan's 7th published book.

THE BODY CHURCH

One Body... Many Parts

The Body Church
Website: www.TheBodyChurchInc.org
Email: thebodychurchinc@gmail.com
Phone: 404-969-6485

OTHER BOOKS BY AUTHOR

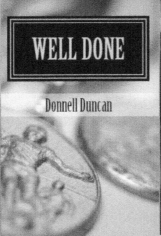

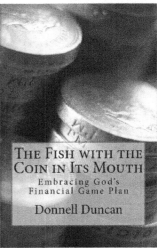

Made in the USA
Monee, IL
15 April 2021